"If you are going to try and make a show abou̶ have to have Seka. She is the real deal. A smaı the one and only 'Platinum Princess of Porn.' Seka Rocks, now and forever. Thanks again Miss S for making me laugh and hard at the same time… xoxox"

– Dave Attell, comedian and television host of
Showtime's *Dave's Old Porn*

"If you're reading this, you've probably surfed for porn on the big old World Wide InnerTube. There is some debate over who invented the Internet, but it's pretty clear that one of the people who invented modern porn, who set the table (or bed, or pool table, or back seat) for Internet porn was Seka. I, for one, want to read the whole story."

– Penn Jillette, of Penn & Teller

"As a girl, Seka was one of the prettiest, sexiest porn stars in history. As a woman, she is one hundred times more important to the world than she ever was as a porn star. With her big heart and personality, she brings joy and humor with her wherever she goes. Although we only worked together twice when we were both porn stars, her friendship since we've been retired from the business is overwhelmingly more important to me than any more sex we could have possibly had. I wish you tremendous success with the book Seka, and with your life experiences and artistic skills, I'm sure it will be a hit."

– Randy West, AVN Hall of Fame porn star

"As long as I have a face, Seka has a place to sit."

– Veronica Hart, AVN Hall of Fame adult actress

"My all time idol, from way back, is Seka. She is the most amazing looking, beautiful, classy woman that I personally have met in the industry."

– Amber Lynn, AVN Hall of Fame adult actress

"An insightful insider's book into an industry about which most of us know little. Dottie (Seka) opens the doors to the business and, most importantly, her life. Dottie's (Seka's) memoir is unforgettable."

– Michael J. Pollard, Academy Award nominated actor

"Seka is one beautiful lady. She make Iron Sheik happy when I see her. She is the legend just like the Sheiky baby. Anyone fuck with the Seka I fuck them in the ass and make them humble. Seka paid for her dues just like Iron Sheik. She is the legend who I only wish I could have the sex with. God bless the Seka on her book and I wish her best. If you don't like the Seka you can go fuck yourself and take a fucking walk. Have a good day."

– The Iron Sheik, former WWE Champion

"For me, Seka was the first porn star. I spent endless hours fantasizing about her and pleasuring myself to her as a young teenager. It was her insatiable lust that opened my eyes to the world of pornography and maybe indirectly landed me in the adult industry. I always thought it would be cool to shoot a scene with her now for old time's sake!"

> – Evan Seinfeld, rock star/porn star, lead singer/bassist for
> Biohazard and Attika7, actor in HBO's *Oz*

"Seka is not just beautiful in body and soul, but she has a great sense of humor and is smart as a whip. Before you finish your sentence, she knows the punch line and tells it in a way that always gets a big laugh. Seka always your back if she likes you, so when I am with her I feel so fucking safe. She is so generous, I love her to pieces."

> – Kitten Natividad, actress, exotic dancer,
> muse to writer/director Russ Meyer

"During the years I worked in Chicago, the city had two great cultural ambassadors to the outside world. One was Michael Jordan, the other was Seka. But as we were learning plenty about Jordan over the years, Seka remained the mysterious unobtainable goddess about whose world we could only speculate. Until now. With this book, which is by turns funny, raucous, titillating and terrifying, we are truly brought 'Inside Seka' for the first time. And as she tells us the story of how a girl from a small town in Virginia became the fantasy of millions, Seka also provides a crash course into the Machiavellian underworld that dominates the world's adult entertainment industry. As she has throughout her career, Seka spares nothing in this book, least of all herself. Read it and weep, and laugh, and learn."

> – Ron Rapoport, sportswriter, author, and sports commentator for
> National Public Radio's *Weekend Edition Saturday*

"A walking whirlpool of wit, wicked, and wild. Seka is a maven of the magnificent."

> – Justice Howard, erotic actress and photographer

"An interviewer once asked me what it was like to make love to Seka. I told him, 'It was like riding the winning horse in the Kentucky Derby.'"

> – Richard Pacheco, AVN Hall of Fame porn star and director

"In this business, you usually start out as hamburger and then work your way up to filet mignon. But the moment Seka walked into my office, I knew I was dealing with filet mignon. Seka was born hot. There have only been a few who have that ingredient."

> – Bill Margold, famed adult film actor, agent, producer, director, and activist

"This book has the feel of a classic Marilyn Monroe movie drama! The legendary platinum princess of porn bares her heart and soul, and paints an explicit picture of porn's golden era. Legions of her male porn fans will be thrilled to bits to get Inside Seka. However, women will enjoy it even more. It's absolutely wonderful that Seka has so generously documented her porn herstory in such a sincere, as well as sexy way. Buy this book! "

– Annie Sprinkle, Ph.D., porn star turned Sexologist,
Author of Post Porn Modernist

"The mark of a true friend? When you are in a restaurant and are told they don't have blue cheese stuffed olives for your martini, only a true friend would ask the waitress, 'Do you have olives?' 'Yes,' said the waitress. 'Do you serve a Cobb Salad with crumbled blue cheese?' 'Yes.' 'Could you bring me a cup of crumbled blue cheese and a cup of olives… and a martini for my friend, Larry here?' 'Yes.' And my friend, Seka, proceeded to pull out pimentos and stuff olives with blue cheese for my drink. You can search all you want but it doesn't get much better than that.

– Larry Thomas, Actor (Seinfeld's The Soup Nazi)

"As a teen, I had a framed photo of Seka (clothed!) on my desk. She was the woman I wanted to be."

– Nica Noelle, adult film actress, writer and director

"Seka is a Goddess!"

– Mistress D Severe, Filmmaker, dominatrix

"Seka is a LEGEND!"

– Veronica Avluv, adult actress, XBiz 2011 nominee for
MILF of the Year

"While a lot of ivory tower feminists were busy burning their bras and philosophizing, Seka was doing what they kept talking about—being independent from men who would take advantage of them, working at a job, making their own decisions, being sexually liberated, fending for themselves, overcoming a neglected background, being an entrepreneur—but because of the stigma, people still assumed they could use and abuse her. Yet she survived, and her tale has a happy ending. And she isn't guilty or regretful. Hell yes! I think a lot of women will relate to her stories because she did survive and she learned to stand her ground. Seka is honest about how the industry was—and in her day, it was 1000% better than it is now. She is one of a handful of true icons."

– Joanne Cachapero, Free Speech Coalition (FSC)

"1983 was my first year making adult films. Honestly, I was not a sexual person. I had never watched porn. I felt I was not very good. A friend brought over what was the first porn I ever saw: Inside Seka. This was a turning point. Her beauty, her presence, her strength—I wanted that. I wanted to feel that sexual power. The shy inexperienced girl I was bloomed into what I am today. Seka led the way. She made it okay to be aggressive and in charge, and believe me, I am so grateful for all she does and continues to do in the adult industry. A true legend. Love ya, Seka!

– Debi Diamond, adult actress, member AVN and XRCO Halls of Fame

"Seka's story will fire, inspire and maybe even spark your desire! An informative, titillating and hearty read to warm your bedroom on a cold night!"
– Sugar Blue, Grammy Award-winning blues musician and Rolling Stones' session man

"I was shocked and intrigued with the book. I found myself pitching my own tent while reading it. I strongly recommend this book, and also recommend for people to be reintroduced to her films, and truly understand why this incredible woman is an Adult Legend. To sum it up, Seka is a fan favorite and an industry icon. I'm privileged to call her my friend."
– Thomas J. Churchill, writer/producer/director of *Cold Plastic*

"Seka is a fun, lively, professional, knowledgeable and cool human being. Her book is real, revealing, open, informative, engaging, candid, and wonderfully playful. In short, I really like it… and her! Congratulations to you, Seka, and kudos on your unparalleled career and all your hard work, determination, and skill."
– Dr. Jimmy Star, celebrity Renaissance man, fashion, entertainment, and media mogul

"While doing an impromptu interview at a gig in Scotland I was asked, 'Who do you think are the three most beautiful women in the world?' I don't know why, but Seka suddenly popped into my mind. I explained how I used to sneak into my father's dresser and watch her movies when I was growing up.

A friend of mine thought it was a hilarious answer and tracked down Seka to send her the interview. What was most unexpected was that Seka personally answered the email. What was also unexpected was that it was the beginning of a wonderful friendship. Seka is just as charming, witty, funny, and generous in real life as she was in her movies.

We are now living in an age of content oversaturation. There are so many new songs, new movies, and new artists and personalities every day, and consequently it has resulted in the public developing a short attention span. Seka was from an era where stars had longevity and we were able to become encapsulated with their personality and character. The true proof of her legacy is that she is still loved and adored by so many people to this day. The sheer mention of her name not only brings a smile to people's faces but also brings back many feelings of a time when the adult industry had glamour, beauty, and sexiness. She was and still is the queen."
– Markus Schulz, international DJ and dance music producer

INSIDE
SEKA

by SEKA
with Kerry Zukus

**Foreword by
Jim Norton**

**Afterword by
Bobby Slayton**

BearManor Media

2013

Inside Seka

© 2013 Seka and Kerry Zukus

For information, address:

BearManor Media
P. O. Box 71426
Albany, GA 31708

bearmanormedia.com

Typesetting and layout by John Teehan
Cover design by Jacqueline Yorke

Published in the USA by BearManor Media

ISBN— 1-59393-272-3
978-1-59393-272-5

Table of Contents

Acknowledgements

I HAVE HAD A LOT OF TIME to think about whom to thank for their part in helping me get my book to the point of being published. There are so many people to thank I really don't know where to start, and I know I will leave some people out, so don't take it personally, please. The list is so very long it would turn into a chapter, so I will leave it at that. You know who you are, and that I love you all very much.

First and foremost, I wish to thank Mr. Evan Ginzberg. Evan is one of the best people I have ever known. He is kind, sweet, and hardworking, and the most supportive person I have ever known. Evan embodies what a true friend really is. Evan, THANK YOU!

To some of my friends who have been with me along this journey:

Debbie Ippilotto, for always being my friend no matter what, and for making me start my Web site http://www.seka.com. Without her, I would not have a web page.

I would like to say thank you to my family and friends in Virginia who have always stood by me. Thanks to Negro Webb, Harvey and Mary Scott, and Sara and Meredith. All of my Chicago friends who were and still are a big part of my life and always will be. To my Kansas City friends Belenda Harrison, and Morgan and Jackie Fleming. They have been a wonderful support system for me.

To Michael Gross: what a friend. Words will never be able to express the thanks he deserves; so Michael, thank you from the bottom of my heart. I love you so very much.

A well-deserved shout-out to my literary agent, Linda Konner, as well as to Utherverse, Video-X-Pix, Alan Thicke, Bill Kinison, Bucky Barrett, Richard Jezewski, Laurie Holmes, Jill C. Nelson, Dave Attell, Jim Norton, Bobby Slayton, Bill Margold, Al Goldstein, Bryce Wagoner, VCX, Alana Evans, Jessica Bangkok, Christy Canyon, Dr. Susan Block, Kylie Ireland,

Johnny Dare, George Marron, Ginger Lynn Allen, Jacqueline Yorke, Jeannine Smith, and all the people at BearManor Media: Ben Ohmart, Wes Britton, Sarah De Simone, John Teehan, Michelle Morgan and Sandy Grabman.

Kerry Zukus, what can I say? Thank you, my friend, for your understanding and hard work. You are one in a million, baby. Love ya, doll!

To all of my fans that span some thirty-odd years, the biggest thanks go to you. Without you I would not be who I am today. I care for and love you all. Thank you for your support.

Though this may sound silly, it isn't to me. I must thank my pets (cats). First of all Miss Jake, who was with me for eighteen years. I love and miss her every day. Also to Maxwell Cooter G and Miss Tippy, who helped pull me through the last part of this journey.

Last but not least to my husband, Carl. I love you. Without you pushing, nagging, and bitching at me, I don't think I would have gotten this book done. You are a pain in my ass that I always want to have around. Without you I am not complete. Love you, Puss.

Foreword
by Jim Norton

IF YOU SUGGESTED I READ the autobiography of a woman who was from a small town, went to church, and was a virgin until her wedding night, I'd probably tell you to go fuck yourself because I have no interest in reading about Marie Osmond. It would never occur to me you might be referring to the woman who would become the most recognizable porn star on earth.

Long before Jenna Jameson, Sasha Grey, and Belladonna came on the scene (so to speak), it was Seka who motivated men to abandon the comforts of home for a seat in the back of a dark movie theater. Even the overwhelming smell of ammonia and the fear of being recognized didn't stop guys from giving themselves Carpal Tunnel watching her do all the things their wives wouldn't (or couldn't) do. As you may remember, back in the seventies you really did have to leave the house to watch porn, which is a testament to how amazingly impressive it was to become a household name from being in adult films. Modern technology has caused us to forget that there was a time men had to stop for gas and look for parking before they could relax and jerk off.

Even the eighties required some work despite the availability of VCRs. I'll never forget the first time I saw an adult film. I was eleven or twelve years old, at my best friend's house across the street. His parents had a top-loading VCR in their bedroom, which is the equivalent today of having bell bottoms and a Korvettes credit card, but back then it was quite an impressive status symbol. We raided his father's porn collection, which was hidden in a brown paper bag in the closet (arguably, the only worse hiding space would have been in the VCR itself). As we rifled through his dad's fairly extensive collection, I was immediately drawn to a box cover featuring a platinum blonde with the most beautiful face and perfect, teardrop breasts I'd seen in my admittedly young, naïve suburban life. It read *Swedish Erotica* across the front and then I saw the name: Seka. If I'd have known the obsession that was about to be awakened, I'd have thrown that fucking tape back in the bag, ran back to my house and done Colorforms until my unimpressive boyish hard-on went away. But I didn't throw it back in the bag. I opened the top of that glossy box and handed my friend the tape. The only sound was the clicking and whirring of the cassette settling in.

The first thing that struck me was the video quality of the scene. It felt much more like real life than anything I had seen on television or in the movies before. It was early morning, and Seka and her husband have just woken up. He, of course, has the morning erection which needs tending to, but Seka, who already looks perfect two seconds after waking, insists on taking a bath first (at the time I didn't realize what a good egg she was for bathing before sex. I've slept with over thirty women whom I wish had seen this movie before I fucked them). I can't accurately describe the emotions I had watching her unclasp her bra, then slide down her semi-transparent blue panties, but I imagine it's the same feeling a person gets when they're suddenly driven to give away all of their possessions and serve God. I was, in that moment changed forever. The bath quickly turned into a Seka masturbation scene, which quickly turned into me running into the bathroom in my friend's parents' bedroom, laying on the floor with my head by the toilet and tugging my dick like a rhesus monkey.

Because my parents had none of the needed equipment to facilitate my new hobby/ love affair/ obsession, I had to walk a mile to the nearest Rite Aid to rent not only porn but also a VCR. Yes, Rite Aid rented porn in the eighties, and yes, I did write, "I had to walk a mile. . ." like I'm Abraham Lincoln. And, in a way, I was. He walked to go to school; I walked to pick up masturbation fodder—which of these is nobler is for you to decide. One disadvantage to renting from Rite Aid was the odds were good one of my grandmother's friends would limp up to the counter just as I was handing *Ultra Flesh* to the cashier.

As the epitome of beauty and sexuality, Seka became the image against which all other women were measured. And they always fell short. Even if they were beautiful, you knew there was just no way they could fuck like her. The point is that Seka became the face of sexuality not only for me but also for an entire generation. It's been almost thirty years and she is still the first name that comes to mind when I think of adult films. Reading about her life outside the business felt almost surreal. She's just one of those iconic, larger-than-life performers who I forget had a viable existence before and after her career in movies. She played basketball, sold hot dogs, and missed being killed once because she said, "*No, thank you*" instead of "*Yes.*" Actually, that's what I found most amazing: the real person behind the name. I loved the complete honesty and candor in every story. Seka doesn't try and make herself look any better or worse than she really is. She tells the truth—the good, the bad and the ugly. And most importantly, *none* of it is predictable.

Now pull up your pants and put away your dick—it's not that kind of book.

– Jim Norton, comedian, radio personality
(Opie & Anthony), author of two
New York Times bestselling books

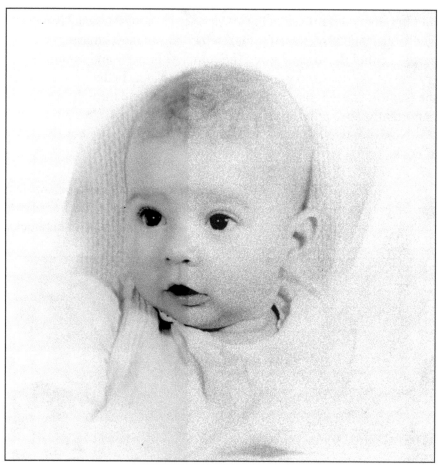

Hello, world!

1

Gone

THE OLD JOKE GOES, "I came home from school one day, and my family had moved." Well, it's not that funny because it happened to me.

I lived in a little white house in the very small town of Christiansburg, Virginia, with my mother, stepfather, brother, and sister. I was eight years old in 1961 and my mom and dad had gotten divorced because she was cheating on him. While they were married, they both worked at Radford Arsenal, the biggest manufacturer of propellant powder for space ships in the United States, and nicknamed "The Powder Plant." People would commute up to two hours to work there because the pay and benefits were good. It was the largest employer in the area and it's still there. If you ever wanted to blow up a good part of the United States, that would be the place to hit.

Dad was small and thin, around five-six or five-seven and one hundred forty pounds soaking wet. He had bright red hair and big doe-like brown eyes with very pale skin. He couldn't be out in the sun at all. I remember one time we went to the beach and within about ten minutes he became one big blister.

My mother reminded me of Jane Russell—a va-va-va-voom body and the most beautiful wavy dark black hair, olive complexion, dark brown eyes, and the straightest, whitest teeth I've ever seen. She was gorgeous with naturally arched eyebrows and long fingernails. And the woman knew how to walk in a pair of pumps.

My parents just couldn't get along and decided to split up. Mom married a guy named Terry who seemed okay, but what did I know? I was a kid and I was supposed to trust my parents. He was very tall and skinny, with dark curly hair and dark eyes. He laughed a lot and was nice to us. Terry liked country music and would take my mom out dancing. Everything seemed good between them as far as I knew. He never scolded me and was never off-color, nor did he curse. He liked his cigarettes, cock-tails, and cabareting, but he was a good man. He didn't seem to hold a job very long though, as we were always moving.

My name was Dorothiea but everyone called me Dot. I was named af-ter an old girlfriend of my father's, some girl he dallied around with when he was in Germany in the service. Mom had no say in it and once she found out where he came up with it she was none too happy. Back then, women were knocked out during childbirth and the father came in and signed the birth certificate and settled up the bill. I wondered for years if that damn name wasn't the cause of a lot of misery my mother sent my way.

I was a tomboy. I never, ever wore a shirt until the age of six. We'd go fishing, throw tomatoes, and play hide-and-seek and kick-the-can at night. We lived on the "other side of the tracks" because that's where my grandfather's job was. The railroad ran just in front of their house. I loved my grandparents dearly. My grandfather was secretary of the Norfolk and Western Railroad and my grandmother was a housewife. They were very kind people. My grandfather was of Viking descent. He was very short and bald, which probably doesn't sound very Viking at all, but he had big blue eyes like robin's eggs. He was round, very round, but didn't seem heavy to me at the time because it was just so comfortable to sit on his lap. And he always wore a suit. I don't think I ever saw him without a suit and hat. He was constantly smoking either a pipe with cherry tobacco or a cigar. I loved the smell of his pipe. Grandpa used a straight razor and kept a strap in the bathroom. It hung by the sink and us kids were deathly afraid of it because we knew he meant business if he ever pulled it out in anger. But he never, ever used it on us.

My grandmother was part Cherokee. She had soft brown eyes like clouds. She was very heavy and always smiling. Grandma had the biggest boobs of anyone I have ever known. As a little girl there was nothing more comforting than to put your head between her boobs and sleep. She was a great cook, which is how I learned how to cook. I was always sitting on the kitchen counter watching her at work. She made fresh biscuits at least twice a day. She'd have a cigarette in her mouth and the ash would be al-most as long as the cigarette itself, but I never saw her drop the ash in the biscuit ever. Hell, maybe she did and that's what gave it the taste.

I'd go down to my grandma and grandpa's house on weekends be-cause my mother was no cook. There were two bedrooms upstairs. My grandfather would put a piece of tin on the windowsill so the sound of the rain would be amplified. On clear nights we could hear the train in the distance. To this day, I can sleep so well when I hear rain or a train coming down the tracks, because it reminds me of my childhood.

My father's side of the family was Irish and lived in a little place called Poplar Camp, way up in the Appalachians. I never knew my father's father as he had passed away before I was born, but his mother was a very tall, thin, willowy woman. She had a very stern demeanor but she wasn't really stern at all. She never cut her hair in her life. It hung all the way down to her knees and was snow white. From the time I was a little kid her hair was very white. She was blind and dipped snuff and was always laughing. They had only three rooms: a kitchen, a bedroom and the living room. She had a wood burning stove and no inside bathroom, just an outhouse. She'd be sitting in her chair across from the stove and there were four eyes where you put the wood in to heat it. She'd leave the lid off one eye so she wouldn't have to get up to spit and would hit it from across the room.

My mother would do weird things to get attention. She would pretend she had taken all these sleeping pills and lay down on the floor and make believe she was about to die. She'd be groaning and you'd try to wake her up. Later we'd find out she flushed the pills down the toilet. I have no idea why the woman did the things she did but it was very scary. It wasn't like she didn't get attention, because when she walked in the room every head snapped around because she was so stunning. The woman could talk to a post and make it drool. In general, though, she was pretty even-tempered. Didn't yell, didn't get mad, didn't scream. But every so often she'd just go off into another land—The Twilight Zone.

I was in second grade and went to school one morning like it was any other day. My brother, sister, and I went to the same school because my sister was only a year and a half older than I, and my brother was only a year and a half older than she. Everything was fine when we left. But lunchtime came and I didn't see my brother or sister anywhere. I wasn't concerned because we were all in different grades. When 3 p.m. came around I still didn't see them, but we didn't always walk home together since they might be doing something with their friends. We all had keys anyway. The school was only about three blocks away and in those days parents didn't worry about kids walking to school. I got home and there was nobody there. I still had no sense anything was wrong because sometimes neither parent was home at that time.

The living room was messy and average-sized, with old, plain furniture. I sat down to do my homework. It started to get dark and I finally began to feel concerned. But I was fine; I was home. I made a sandwich because I was hungry. I watched TV and even though I was getting more anxious, I was also feeling sleepy and knew there was school the next day. I fell asleep on the couch.

I woke up quite early the next morning. Still nobody there. I took a bath, got dressed, and went to school. I don't know why, but I didn't call anybody. I just went to school every day, came home, did my homework, and went to sleep. This went on for almost two weeks. I never went to sleep in my bed because I was scared. I felt safer in the living room because there was noise from the TV. There was enough food in the house and I didn't need money for lunch since I packed it every day. The dishes started to pile up, though, and the water started to overflow when I ran it. At that age, I didn't do dishes. That was when I finally realized something had to be done. I called a cab and had them take me to my grandparents' house.

When I got there I told the driver to wait, that I'd be right back, and I went in and told my grandfather he needed to pay the man. It was like $54, which was exorbitant back then. Knowing my grandfather, he probably gave him a dime for a tip. It wasn't because he was cheap; it was just his way.

He said, "Why do I need to pay a cabby?"

"Because I don't have any money, Grandpa."

I proceeded to tell him I'd been home alone and he said, "What are you talking about?" He turned every shade of purple, blue, and red a man could turn. You didn't want to make my grandfather angry.

Evidently I hadn't bathed myself well because they threw me in the tub and scrubbed me. I loved that bathtub because it was one of those big old ones with the claw feet and was scooped down in the back. My grandmother would fill it up with warm water and I'd feel very safe with all the wonderful smells wafting in from the kitchen. At that point, I felt everything was going to be okay because I was in a safe, loving place. There was good hot food on the stove after more than a week of cold cereal and sandwiches.

I stayed with my grandparents, but they also had no idea where my family was. We were all confused and concerned. For all I knew, they were dead. My grandparents went back to the house and it was a lot more disgusting than I'd remembered. My mother wasn't a very neat person so I was used to it. They went to my school and discovered that my mother and stepfather had picked up my brother and sister there—but not me— and said, "We're going on a little vacation. We'll have them back in a week or two." My grandparents asked if they mentioned where they were going and they said Florida. I was so pissed off they went to Florida and I didn't get to go. I wasn't pissed off that they had left me and put me in harm's way. My brother wasn't much of a water person, and my sister had carrot orange hair, alabaster skin, and really pale brown eyes, almost gold. She looked like a little porcelain doll. Why the hell did she get to go to Florida and I didn't? I was the tomboy. I was tan and loved the water.

Eventually my parents returned. My grandfather was standing beside the car while I remained inside. My grandfather wouldn't let me out of the car or inside the house even though I said I needed to get some clothes. "Don't worry about clothes," he said. "We'll buy you some new clothes." Meanwhile, Mom looked at me, but it was pretty much like I wasn't there. She didn't seem to have the least bit of concern for me. I don't remember her asking if I was okay, or if my grandfather just didn't give her the opportunity. My grandfather wasn't a mean guy or a rough guy, but he was old school. He treated everyone the way he wanted to be treated: fairly and honestly. You always knew what was on his mind.

They began yelling at one another. I don't remember what they were saying, although my grandfather was really pissed off. He said something along the lines of, "You won't have those two other babies, either, in a few days."

And they didn't.

My dad in the army.   My mother in high school—quite a looker.

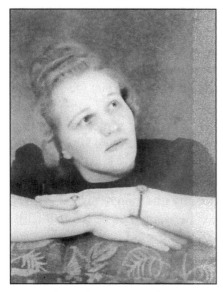

The original Dorothiea, my daddy's German girlfriend after whom I am named.

My sister Deborah and my brother Ray.

My brother Ray and my father, when he was still around.

Grandpa Hundley, my father's father, who I never met.

Grandma Hundley, my father's mother, when she was younger.

Grandpa Hartsock, my mother's father, workin' on the railroad.

Grandma and Grandpa Hartsock.

Me in first grade.

My brother Ray.

"To the sweetest mom in the world (and the prettiest, too). From your loving daughter, Dottie". Must have been before she abandoned me. Not my handwriting, either.

2

Given Away

GRANDPA NEEDED A QUICK-FIX situation to get us kids out of my mother's hands. It was decided that my brother and sister would go to live with my Uncle Hardy, while I moved in with Aunt Shirley and Uncle George. They had three children: Gary, Becky and Robin. They lived in the very small town of Christiansburg, Virginia, in a nice brick house behind the grade school. Becky was the same age as me, and I got along well with all of the kids. I absolutely felt like part of the family. They treated me as their own; they didn't favor any of us. They enrolled me in school and made sure I had everything I needed—new clothes, books, and school supplies. And thank God, I finally had a woman around who could cook. She made the best grilled-cheese sandwiches in the world, in a cast iron skillet with real butter. She always put a big slice of tomato on mine because I loved tomatoes. That was my thing, kind of like Elvis with his fried bacon, peanut butter, and banana sandwiches.

The rejection from my mother didn't really affect me at the time. I didn't see her after that for a long time and I honestly didn't miss her. There wasn't a whole lot to miss. Where I was now, the food was better and the house was clean. I was a kid; what did I know? I just proceeded on like normal. I wasn't angry or hurt about the whole situation until I was in my thirties. For whatever reason, that was when it finally hit me.

Financially, it was hard for everybody. Although they both had jobs, Aunt Shirley and Uncle George had a house, three other kids, and a couple of cars to pay for. I was a burden to them. There was a family meeting with the powers that be to decide what to do with my brother, my sister, and me. There is a town nearby called Wytheville, Virginia, and they had a children's home there. It was a place for kids who had parents who couldn't take care of them. One day my aunt and uncle suddenly told me we needed to talk. They sat me down and said, "We don't want to upset you, but we had to make other living arrangements because we can't afford to put you through school and raise you." It hurt because I loved that family. But I understood.

It was not a happy day when I had to leave. My sister was already there, while my brother had been placed in a similar facility in Tennessee. There were four brick buildings with a kitchen, a boys' dormitory, and two dorms for girls. I was put in the one for very young girls. There were two girls to a room, each with a twin-sized bed, a shared closet, and three drawers of a single dresser. We were never abused like in those horrible orphanages in the movies, but life was pretty dull. We had to go to church on Sunday. It was a Presbyterian service. We were required to do some chores like helping with the grounds and gardening and such. We were told, "Idle hands are the devil's workshop." Frankly, I wanted to see the devil's workshop to understand what they were doing in there.

We got a small allowance every week for our efforts. It was about a quarter. They had a little cantina on Saturdays where we'd get sodas and candy. Other than that we didn't get any of that kind of stuff. The home was pretty restrictive because we did have some problem children. There was always someone running away. The only reason they put us together was because they didn't have juvenile halls at the time in that area. In hindsight, that probably wasn't a good idea, because if you had a kid who was stealing and drinking, it wasn't a positive influence on children like me who were there because of unfortunate circumstances.

What struck me as odd was no matter where you were on the grounds, there were no odors at all. I had come from a family that cooked all the time, but you didn't have that at Wytheville because we were nowhere near the kitchen. In an odd way, this made it very lonely because without the smell of food there was no sense of family. It was like floating in an emotional vacuum. Even when they'd cut the grass it wasn't the same because it wasn't your uncle or cousin or neighbor doing it. There was no history to it. At home, you'd sit and do your homework and you'd smell the cooking and know you would have supper soon. But here you'd get up and leave one building to go to another to eat. It was very disorienting.

There was a little playground in the back, and games and toys and bicycles. The staff had a background in social work and each dorm had a master or mistress running it. The woman who ran our dorm was very nice, very grandmotherly. Although she was a caring lady, it still never felt like a real home. The girls stayed in that dormitory until we hit eleven or twelve, basically until you started developing. Once they had to throw a bra on you or you had your period, they tossed you into the big dorm. I don't know what they thought that would do to the little girls, but once you started to get some hair under your arms, you were out of there.

I remember sitting by the hearth of a fireplace watching TV when President Kennedy was shot. In the big girls' dorm we had to watch the news every day, sweep the floors, make our bed, get showered, and go to school. School was off-premises and we had a bus that picked us up. The kids in the regular school treated us like lepers. We were teased, bullied, and pointed at. It wasn't bad enough your family had deserted you. And of course our clothes weren't as nice as the other kids'. Each year we'd get clothes donated and the staff would see what fit you. But I'd recognize clothes from the school kids who wore them the previous year.

I was not a very happy person.

Sometimes we were given long weekends with family, or had two-week sponsored vacations. Strangers would take a kid to Myrtle Beach or some place as their "community service." It really made the kids feel like charity cases. I'd refuse to go with anyone but my own family.

The only time I felt really happy was when my dad came to visit. We'd have visitors every second Sunday. He couldn't take me to live with him though, because back in those days they wouldn't give fathers parental rights. No matter how irresponsible and eccentric my mother was, I wasn't allowed to live with my real father.

When I was with my dad, he was always apologizing for my situation. He constantly sent money so I'd have extra cash for snacks. I also got lots of postcards because he traveled so much. They came from places like Iceland, Greenland, and Canada. He was an excellent mechanic and one of the airlines hired him. He could take something apart in no time and make it better than it was before. He had a bit of a drinking problem, though. When Dad was younger he'd make home brew—moonshine— which was the nastiest smelling stuff I'd ever seen in my life. Even he'd make the most awful face when he tasted it. I think he just enjoyed making it. He even used 'shine as gas when he raced cars.

Dad never remarried. He was dating a woman in Canada and thinking of marrying her. I never met the woman, but felt like I had known her from all the stories he'd told about her. But one day she suddenly was killed. Lightning struck a tree and it was about to fall. She ran and pushed a kid out of the way and the tree crushed her. After it happened, Dad was never the same. He carried her picture with him to the day he died.

My aunts and uncles and grandparents would visit, too. My grandfather didn't care what the rules were regarding what they could and could not bring us as gifts. He'd bring a big watermelon or fruit—apples, peaches, grapes. They had all that stuff in their backyard. He'd always bring enough for everybody.

The mistress of the dorm would tell each kid if he or she was going to get a visitor. I remember out of nowhere her informing me my mother and stepfather were coming. I was in absolute shock. My sister wasn't there anymore because she wanted to be with my brother in Tennessee. I have a picture of that day with me in a dress at a picnic table—and I hated being in a dress. I was sitting at one end of the picnic table. My stepfather was standing with one foot on the bench smoking a cigarette and grinning about something—I can't imagine what. And my mother wore a suit and high heels and she was sitting all the way across from me. I had no desire to be near her. My smile was upside down. I was not happy. It had been probably a year since I had seen them. When she first saw me, she held her arms out like I'd be running through a field of daisies to hug her. Instead, I just slowly walked up to her and gave her a little peck on the cheek. That was about it. They didn't bring a present, didn't apologize about anything, and didn't have the guts to talk about any of it. All I thought was, "When are they leaving?" I was angry and wanted to go back and play and I didn't appreciate any of it. I didn't want her to visit me again. I felt the same way about Terry. He could have said, "What about Dot?" He abandoned me, too. With the three kids out of their hair, they had moved to Florida.

The home would have outings and field trips. They would take us swimming in a man-made lake because we didn't have a pool. That was where I got really sick. I contracted spinal meningitis from contaminated water. When I went to bed, I was fine. I was tired because I had been in the sun and swimming all day. But when I tried to get out of bed the next morning, the only thing that could move were my eyes and mouth. Everybody was up getting dressed for school. The lady who was head of the house, Ms. Booker, stuck her head in the door and said, "Get up; you're going to be late."

I said, "I can't move. Really, I can't move." I was scared to death. I was wondering what the hell was going on. She grabbed one of the other girls and they tried to help me up. I was rushed to a local hospital.

They put me in isolation and it frightened the hell out of me. Everybody wore hats, masks, gowns, and goggles. Even their shoes were covered. There was a door they would go through and a sanitary area where they'd put on their gowns. When my grandparents visited there was a chute and they actually had to throw their clothes down it to incinerate them. I felt like I was going to die.

As I lay in bed, I kept thinking of my dad, who always loved to travel. He was always on a plane or a Greyhound bus. I dreamed of going to some of the places he told me about: France, England, the Nordic countries. He had a thing for blonde women. Maybe subconsciously, that's why I became a blonde.

One day a team of doctors came into the room and told me what I had. They actually said, "Four out of five people usually die from this." Pretty blunt. Then they threw in that if someone survives, they're usually brain-damaged, which could explain certain things about me. Ha! They told me they had to tap my spine to make me better. I had to lie on my stomach. They swabbed me down with alcohol and a horrible-smelling orange substance, and they brought in a huge tray. The needle on the tray looked ninety feet long. It was almost cartoonish. They said I could not move. I had to remain on my stomach for a really long time. I don't remember it hurting, though. Maybe they gave me a painkiller, or maybe the fear squelched the pain. If things weren't bad enough, the fluid kept re-contaminating itself and they had to do it two more times.

My father would visit and stay all day in a mask and gown. He'd sleep in the chair next to my bed and it would be a comfort to me when I'd wake up in the morning and he'd still be there.

When I finally got better, they told me I could never give blood because the virus remains dormant and can wake back up and be passed onto someone else. It's a shame because I like to help people if I can, but I've never been able to donate.

I was terrified the whole three weeks I was hospitalized. Yet, it wasn't like I had a home to look forward to returning to.

My Aunt Shirley, who took me in. I love her so much. That's me on the right, photobombing her.

My Uncle Hardy, who took in my sister and brother, standing next to my mother.

Me, my sister, and my brother in 1966 in the orphan's facility in Wytheville.

3

Free

HAVING MY SPINE TAPPED repeatedly was like seeing the Grim Reaper three times. My reward for surviving was being sent back to Wytheville for several more numbing years. My only reprieve from the monotony was when family members would take me away for a bit of a vacation.

My mother's sister Anita, who we called Aunt Sis, was one of my favorite relatives. She was a spunky old broad, a hard-working grocery clerk. She had dark black hair with brown eyes and always had a cigarette hanging from her mouth. When she hummed, she just hummed; it was never an actual song. It was kind of weird because she never realized she was doing it. My Uncle John was also wonderful. He was a tollbooth attendant for the Virginia Department of Highways. Tall with broad shoulders, he had big blue eyes. He was bald and what little hair he had left was white. He had been a flaming redhead in his days of glory. John was just a very jovial, gregarious kind of guy. Very handy. He also loved to cook and was really good at it, making the best corn bread and scalded lettuce on earth. He used to sit at the end of the kitchen table with a cigarette and a Ballantine. My uncle gave me the nickname Peanut, because I was shaped like one.

It was the mid-sixties and they had three children of their own, but they were grown and out of the house. Wytheville allowed us a two-week summer vacation each year, so when I was middle-school age I wrote them, asking to visit. They lived in Hopewell, Virginia, which was about four and a half hours away. In spite of the distance, I'd seen them more than most of my other relatives and I loved them dearly for it.

We drove back to their house and my vacation with them was the most fun I had in a real long time. Their granddaughter Diane and I were about the same age—thirteen—so we'd do things together. There was a lake we would go to. Needless to say, after contracting spinal meningitis I wasn't that big on swimming in it. Hanging out with all the neighborhood kids, I stood by the lake and watched as Diane and her friends from school had a grand old time. Even though I was too scared to swim, it sure was nice to be around new people and away from Wytheville. Since I didn't know anybody, she introduced me around.

Uncle John worked the midnight shift and was free during the day. He would tinker on his old Rambler, working on the spark plugs and such. He always had his beer while fixing his car. He said, "You're going to be a young woman soon, so if you're ever stuck in a car in an emergency you'll need to learn this stuff." Uncle John would put me on his lap and I'd steer the car so I could learn to drive. He made me promise not to tell Aunt Sis because she would have killed us both.

My aunt would give me a list of chores to do and John would look at me and raise his eyebrows like, "Here we go again." Sis was a neat freak. When I was younger, I'd actually see her lug everything out of the house, and I mean *everything*. The curtains, the furniture, everything. Outside in the street, she'd furiously scrub it all down, and then bring it back in the house. It was a pain. Between my mom and her, I'd gone from one extreme to the other.

There weren't any special events those two weeks, like going to Disneyland or anything like that. But it was special to me because I was spending time with my family and away from that home.

Nobody but I knew at the time that I had no plans of going back to Wytheville. I'd had enough of the children's home. I was done. And I had a plan. I didn't care if I ever got my belongings back. I didn't care if they gave away everything I owned. I was planning my escape.

As the two weeks were coming to a close, I was getting pretty nervous. We were in my bedroom one evening after Sis had gotten out of work. Just as I intended, my tears started pouring. They were real, though, and came from deep inside of me. They were the only weapon in my arsenal as I begged her to let me stay with her for good. But she said, "You can't stay. You have to go back. I'm sorry. I don't have the authority to keep you."

So much for my plan.

I knew in her heart of hearts Aunt Sis loved and wanted me. She just didn't know how to make it happen. She figured they'd come after her if I didn't go back, and she had no idea how to get state funding to support me.

I got desperate. And defiant.

I told her if she didn't keep me I was going to run away and be one of those children they never found again. They would never know if I was dead or alive. Uncle John was walking by and overheard the commotion.

He stepped into the room and said, "Let her stay, Nita. Just call them and say she's not coming back. We'll figure out how to take care of it." After several years of living in a place that never once felt like my own, my "escape" had been that simple. I caught my uncle out of the corner of my eye and he gave me a wink, like he was saying, "Don't worry, Peanut; we got it covered."

The next thing I knew they were unpacking my clothes. It may have been the happiest moment of my life. It was hard for it to sink in, but this young girl finally had a home.

4

Blonde

I KNEW MY AUNT AND UNCLE would be good to me. What a wonderful feeling to be in a loving environment! There were even the familiar smells of food throughout the house. The next thing I knew I was being enrolled in school, so it all started to feel real. For the first time in a long time, I felt a sense of belonging. I knew I was going to be okay. My uncle let me do anything I wanted, but my aunt made sure my grades were good or I'd be threatened with losing certain privileges. Making it through eighth grade unscathed, I was just happy to be a normal kid. I had a new life and it was a happy time for me—even when I had to go to church on Wednesday nights and Sunday mornings. But I figured, what the heck? It was a small price to pay. Actually, it gave me some sense of structure. To this day, I'm not an atheist. I don't think, "*Boom*, we're here." I think there's a supreme being of some sort. There has to be some rhyme or reason to everything. The world's a pretty spectacular place.

Then came high school.

I went to Hopewell High. A lot of the students' parents worked in the factories. There was a Firestone plant in the area, the Reynolds Aluminum Company, and a factory called Hercules. It wasn't a rich town by any stretch. There may have been a ritzy part of town, but it certainly wasn't Beverly Hills. The kids were pretty normal. As the new kid on the block, I started to make friends.

I did well academically—usually a B average, which for somebody who didn't work that hard was pretty good. I was actually having too much fun to study because I had this whole new life. We had elective classes and I was told I had to take Home Economics, which was kind of boring to me. I really wanted to take Shop. I loved tools. To this day, I get excited when I go to a Lowes or Home Depot. When I walk in, I don't go

19

to the curtains or anything like that. The first place I go is the tool department. That probably comes from my dad and Uncle John.

I was still a tomboy. I wasn't interested in being a cheerleader. Instead of discovering boys, I found sports. My cousin Diane was on the basketball and softball teams, so I tried out for both. I made first string on both teams. I was a softball pitcher and the center on the basketball team. I ended up getting my cousin demoted to second string, but there was no friction between us. She still played, but she was much more involved with church and choir anyway. We were junior varsity in both sports in the ninth grade, ending up top five in the district. I also played field hockey. I loved those contact sports.

That year was probably one of the happiest in my life. I had a new home, a safe place to live. And although I didn't really hang out with my teammates, we had camaraderie. My aunt expected me home to do my chores and homework. She didn't allow me to date. At the time, I wasn't interested in boys anyway. Sports were more important to me. I hadn't had any urges yet. When she kept bringing up dating, I was like, "What is this about? Whatever."

At the end of ninth grade, I found out I could skip tenth grade if I went to summer school. I had enough credits to be classified as a junior. So I did. Summer was pretty uneventful except for my passing with flying colors.

I was suddenly a junior, a true high schooler with dances and parties and a real social life. The sports were still there, but I had to try out again because it was a different grade. I made all the teams. We were division champs in basketball, which was very exciting because we traveled to different schools throughout the region.

And then came the beauty pageant.

There was a girl on the basketball team named Debbie, a very pretty Greek girl. Mind you, there weren't a lot of "ethnic types" where I went to school. Just black kids and white kids. She had green eyes and beautiful long, thick, straight blonde hair down to her waist. She looked at me one day and said, "What do you think of this beauty pageant?"

I didn't know a thing about it. Once she filled me in, I said, "I think it sounds stupid."

She kept after me, saying, "We should do this, just for shits and grins. If we don't win, we can't shave our legs or armpits for a month. If we win or place, we can shave."

That was a real threatening bet.

Neither of us wanted to admit that we really wanted to do it. But being contestants wouldn't be in keeping with the fact we were jockettes.

We both tried out and made it. The day of the event, there were three judges and the whole school came. There were fifty of us on the large auditorium stage. There was no talent contest involved, which was good because I can't sing or dance. I was contestant #32, which I still remember to this day.

I was nervous as hell. The lady who lived across the street was a hairdresser. Before the pageant, I went to her to get frosted blonde streaks in my hair. But the whole thing turned blonde. That was the first time I'd gone blonde. Ironically, I said to myself, "Oh shit, this screws up my chance of winning." I wasn't used to it. As I walked up on stage, I thought it was the dumbest thing I had done in my life. I was an athlete with what I thought was a bad dye job. I just felt stupid. But my teammates and the boys' football team started screaming and applauding when I walked out, which kind of surprised me because I was still pretty unaware and uninterested in boys. It felt good but it also felt weird. I wasn't crazy about wearing a dress, either. And it was hard to walk in high heels because it was something I'd never done before.

The judges started eliminating contestants. They went down to twenty. Then to ten. Debbie and I looked at each other incredulously. I never thought for a minute I'd win. I never thought of myself as a pretty girl. Just average. And if you told me boys were looking at me, I'd have said you were crazy. I had male friends because of sports but that was about it.

Suddenly, we were down to the final five. The whole thing seemed unreal to me. I'm thinking, "Holy crap, I may actually pull this off." Debbie and I were looking at each other and laughing, "Are these people blind? Don't they know what they're doing?"

They eliminated number five.

If you won, you led the Junior/Senior prom and were crowned "Miss Hopewell High School." Not that there were a lot of duties. You were in parades for Christmas, Easter, Thanksgiving, those kinds of things. I looked at Debbie and whispered, "How is this going to affect our basketball games if we win?" She just laughed.

The final four were standing there and I started shaking like a leaf; I was so nervous. They called out the second place runner-up, which was Debbie. She just looked at me and gave me a thumbs-up.

Then they called the first place runner-up, which was the girl everyone thought was going to win.

There I was, standing next to the last remaining girl and the first thing that went through my head was that maybe being blonde wasn't so bad. Debbie was blonde, too. But I was getting ready to walk off the stage.

And then they called my name. Yes, my name.

It was like something out of a dream. Everybody's jumping on me and kissing me and putting a crown on my head and I actually said, "Debbie, what's going on?" I just didn't absorb it.

"You won, you crazy person."

It didn't sink in for two or three days, but it felt pretty damn good. I was starting to accomplish things. My time served had started to pay off.

5

Beauty Queen

I WAS INSTANTLY POPULAR. My picture was all over the school and local newspapers and suddenly everyone knew who I was. People acted like they liked me because I was the beauty queen. Ironically, this made me feel awkward because I felt I was on display all the time. I wasn't a feminine, prissy girl. I was still a tomboy and I liked it that way. But whenever I walked by I would hear, "There's Ms. Hopewell High School."

People would point and whisper and I had no idea what they were saying, but I assumed it wasn't good. I was suspicious and not at all used to being treated like a beauty. I never had any positive reinforcement that I was pretty. Being abandoned doesn't exactly make you secure.

To me, all this fuss was over nothing. I just walked out on stage and people stared at me. They weren't judging me on my abilities or anything like that. Going out for basketball, you were picked because you were good. But being picked on your looks, you didn't have much to do with that except for genes, personal hygiene, and maintenance. I guess I cleaned myself up pretty good for that pageant.

I'd have lunch with a group of students, but except for Debbie and some of my teammates, I didn't have a lot of people I considered friends. And I certainly didn't have a best friend.

Looking back, I probably chose not to get close with anyone because it seemed that everyone who was close had abandoned me. I wasn't going to let that happen again. There was always a simmering anger over what my family had done to me. Sometimes I was aware of it, other times it was subconscious. Teammates and opponents saw this and knew not to get in my way on the field because I'd kick their ass. And at five-eight and one hundred fifty-five pounds with big legs from running all the time, those little girls didn't know what hit them. But mostly I directed it towards my mother, and even my brother and sister for not standing up for me. Why didn't anyone ever say, "Where's Dottie? How come she's not with us?"

My aunt went to get her hair done every week and she found out about the Miss Southside Virginia Pageant. This event didn't involve just girls in our high school but also from neighboring towns. The beauticians put it together to showcase their hairdos and such. My aunt had her heart set on my entering it. Reluctantly I agreed, especially since there was a bathing suit competition I wasn't happy about. If I could have worn one of those big, long bathing suits from the twenties I would have. I knew I wasn't ugly, but I didn't instantly think I was pretty because I won Ms. Hopewell High. I picked a one-piece turtleneck bathing suit. I accepted that I had good legs. The rest of me, I didn't want anyone to see.

It was in a small meeting hall. There was no stage. Chairs were lined up on either side of the runway. There were maybe fifty to seventy-five people in the audience. Nothing too glamorous—far from it. I was scared and I still wasn't used to walking in high heels, but I was told they should to be very high because it made your legs look even better.

There were around twenty to twenty-five contestants and most of them were not very attractive. I kind of felt bad for them, and then I felt worse because I thought I was being egotistical.

I won.

I thought to myself, "I'm just glad it's over. I want to go home." I'd fulfilled my duties.

Now even more people knew me, but it didn't change me in the least because it was more about making my aunt happy.

In the fall of 1971, I was still a junior, and as Ms. Hopewell High School I was expected to be in the Thanksgiving homecoming parade. My aunt had an old Cutlass convertible so she volunteered to drive me in the parade. As we were all getting lined up, out of the corner of my eye I saw a group of men in white outfits and hoods. I tapped my aunt on the shoulder and said, "Hey, what's that?"

She said, "Don't look. You don't need to bother with that."

She didn't really look around, which I thought was pretty odd. They were all men and I looked again in spite of my aunt. When I did, one of them took off his hood and it was my aunt's boss. He looked directly at me and it was the coldest, blankest stare I had ever seen. He had always been so nice to me. I turned back around, did not wave, and stared straight ahead.

I didn't have a clue who they were or what they did. I was very naive. We didn't study them in school or see a lot about them on TV back then. I knew the Klan existed, but I didn't quite know what they looked like and never imagined they were in my town.

Although a lot of the townspeople and students were prejudiced, I never was. I may not have had much exposure to people of different races, but I would talk to anyone. I like everybody unless they prove to me they're a blazing jackass. But I knew this wasn't good. Deadness had come across the air. Somehow I knew they weren't supposed to be part of the parade, but it was eerie with them standing there waiting. They seemed ready to march. Suddenly, I didn't want to be part of this.

We got the signal to start and I went with the flow. As people clapped and shouted for the teams and bands and cheerleaders, in my youthful excitement I pretty much forgot about the Klansmen. When it was over and we ended up on the other end of town, I saw that they hadn't been in it at all. I had no idea why.

When I went into the store afterwards, my aunt's boss was never rude or mean to me, but he looked at me differently. The Klan didn't want people to know who they were. That was the day I realized there was evil everywhere, even in small town America.

6

Boys

LIVING WITH MY AUNT wasn't exactly carefree. The oldest of four girls and four boys, she was sort of the matriarch of the family after my grandmother passed away. She was "Big Mama."

There were certain obligations. I had to get good grades. Be a good girl. Not have sex. Not even *think* about sex. Be a nun, a vanilla wafer.

I think this was important to her because her reputation was so good. She could prove to everyone in the family that she was able to raise a decent kid—that I wouldn't turn out like her sister, my mother.

My second cousin Diane introduced me to a nice young man at church. He was everything my aunt thought a boy should be. He came from a good God-fearing, law-abiding family. His name was Woody. She was comfortable with him because she felt he was "safe." And he was. I still have the first piece of jewelry he ever gave me, a little pinky insignia ring. I really liked him. He had a great sense of humor and was a nice young man. I was even allowed to date him. Of course, I had to stand on the bottom step for him to kiss me good night because I was a head taller than he was. But I wasn't looking for a future with him. Getting married to your childhood sweetheart and having kids and a white picket fence just never entered my thought process. I cared about him, but at that age I didn't know what love was. I don't think anyone my age did.

Even then I didn't want to have children. My childhood had been hard enough. I wanted to live a little, and probably somewhere in the back of my mind I didn't want to risk doing the same damage to my kids my mother did to me. I probably would have been a good mother, but I just wasn't willing to find out.

I joined the school work program. It helped you build credits toward graduating. There were certain merchants in town who would volunteer to give students jobs, so I started working in a shoe store. The store was more for ladies and men than it was for children. One quiet afternoon, I was chatting with the other saleswoman who worked there. At the time, I thought she was "old" but she was probably only in her forties. Suddenly, this huge guy walked in and she said nervously, "You wait on him; you wait on him."

He was very imposing. Wearing dark sunglasses, he had shaggy, disheveled, curly blonde hair and had to be six-foot seven. I was immediately attracted to him because he was like the classic rebel bad boy. He was what every parent would tell a girl to avoid. And being a red-blooded All-American girl, I wanted what I was not supposed to have.

I walked up to him and said, "Can I help you?" Looking down at his huge feet I said to myself, "Holy shit, we don't have shoes to fit this man."

Measuring him, I discovered he was a size fourteen and found just one pair of shoes in the entire store that fit him. His own steel-toed safety boots were ragged and we were able to replace those, but we didn't have a pair of dress shoes for him.

Being a man of few words, he just grinned this sinister grin and nodded his head when I told him we could order a pair of dress shoes. I never thought at the time to even ask him what kind he wanted; I just decided I was going to get him what I liked. I didn't realize it at the time, but maybe he agreed so he'd have an excuse to come back. He paid for the shoes and picked himself up and left. I didn't even ask his name.

The store owner asked why I hadn't taken down his name, but the lady I worked with said, "Don't worry, he'll be back." She must have seen something between us I didn't.

I later discovered he played pool every day across the street at the pool hall, and he did come back a few days later to see if his order had arrived. That's when he first introduced himself.

"My name is Frank. You were supposed to order me shoes."

Being a smartass even at an early age, I said, "Frank what?" I wanted to know his last name.

"Patton. Frank Patton."

I went in the back and scribbled his name on the package. He paid and stayed there for a few minutes. He asked me my name and said, "I'll be back later," which I thought was funny as he had no reason to come back except to see me. My heart began beating out of my chest, I was so excited.

Frank would come in the store every now and again and finally asked, "Would you like to go out?"

"Sure. Why not?"

I was scared to ask my aunt's permission, because even though she was only five-three, she could be tough. She was the type who even when she was scared of something she wouldn't show it. But I knew she was a marshmallow inside and she saw I'd always been a good kid, so when I asked she said, "Sure." That was until she opened the door and saw this giant of a man standing there.

She took one look at him, slammed the door in Frank's face, and said simply, "Hell, no!"

I just stood there open-mouthed, absolutely humiliated.

"How old is he?" she shrieked.

"Around twenty-five."

Every time I mentioned his name after that my aunt had him ten years older. "You're not going out with some thirty-five year old guy!"

The next time he was forty-five. And later fifty-five. It got absurd.

His parents lived on the same street as us. They owned their own home. Nice yard. Clean. Honest, hard-working people. My aunt just thought he was way too old for me.

So I started sneaking around with him.

I told Woody I didn't want to see him anymore. I really had no good reason to break up with him other than I just wanted to see this long, lean, lanky hunk of a guy. It wouldn't be fair to Woody, even though lying to him wasn't fair either. Not wanting to hurt him, I said I had to concentrate on school and sports. He started crying and all I could think to say was "Don't cry." I felt just horrible.

Frank would come into the store and the other salesgirls would cover for me during my lunch breaks. It wasn't like a real date, as my aunt had forbidden it. Since we couldn't hide in such a small town, we just drove around in his car. I was always scared someone would spot us, since I knew what my aunt would do if she found out.

The funny thing was that we really didn't talk a whole lot. He was such a quiet person. I was scared to death being alone in a car with a rebel boy and nobody knowing where I was. The only boy I'd ever kissed was Woody, and that wasn't even a *kiss* kiss.

It all came to a head one afternoon. I still didn't have any real close girlfriends, but a group of "bad girls" had a sorority and I hung out with them a bit. They said, "Come on, we're going to skip school today." I said I couldn't do that, but they convinced me. When we got to a vacant house there were guys and girls there. Whoever's house it was, the parents were gone. The boys and girls were pairing up. It was clear they were about to sneak off to other rooms to have sex. That was something I wasn't at all interested in. I had never had sex. I hadn't even come close to having sex. I figured I needed to go home and tell my aunt I had skipped school and take my punishment. I knew I was going to catch hell.

I started walking home and Frank happened to drive by and he said, "Get in the car, I'll drive you."

Being a pretty good distance away, I took him up on the offer and he left me two blocks from my house. I told him I was going to be in trouble and didn't even know if I'd be allowed to go to work for a while. He just grinned. Here was this little schoolgirl with this big grown up guy.

My aunt wasn't home, but the school had called to tell her I'd played hooky. Evidently in the interim someone had told her I had been in the car with Frank. I was doomed any which way.

When she finally walked in, it got real ugly real fast. She called me a little slut and said, "You're just like your mother, sleeping with every man in town." Although she loved her sister, she never approved of her, and suddenly I had disappointed her, too.

Devastated, I told her I hadn't slept with anyone. But there was no convincing my aunt. With the mere act of skipping school and being in mixed company, she immediately assumed I had committed the "ultimate sin" of having sex.

I was monitored pretty closely after that. I was allowed to go to school. From school, I went to my job. Then home. The Gestapo would have loved her.

She never knew that Frank would come to the shoe store to see me. The strain of it all was wearing on me. One day when Frank paid a visit he asked, "What's going on?" and my tears just started to pour. I told him about my situation at home and he said, "You don't need to put up with that."

"I don't have much choice."

Just as casually, he said, "Well, we could get married."

And just like that I said, "Okay."

It wasn't exactly the most thought out decision I'd ever made, but it was a way out. I didn't want to be away from my uncle, but it would be a way for my aunt not to look at me in disappointment. A way for her not to be reminded of my mother.

I told him I was only seventeen and he said when I turned eighteen we would run away. It sounded exciting, but I didn't even know what romance was.

I told my cousin Diane I was going to get married and she gasped, "What!?" She, of course, told her mother, who was my aunt's daughter.

Mary Jo came to me and said, "You can't do this." But I had made up my mind.

"I'm going to get married no matter what." In turn, Mary Jo told my aunt and that was when all hell broke loose. There was a lot of screaming, yelling, and accusing.

"You have to be pregnant or you wouldn't be doing this," my aunt repeated again and again.

I was still a virgin.

I made the great escape and ran two blocks away to Mary Jo's. I talked to Frank and told him, "Look, I turn eighteen on the fifteenth of April." He said we'd get married a few days later. My cousin was a religious person and wanted it in a church. We planned for a small ceremony. Mary Jo invited my aunt, and I could hear her screaming over the phone, "Hell, no!" She forbade my uncle to show up, and he didn't. She may have been small, but she was mighty. He still had to live in that house. I was very sad they weren't there, and in spite of it all I loved them dearly. Even today with them gone, I miss them terribly. She meant well; she just didn't know how to handle it. Although she never said, "I'm sorry," she did tell me once, "Look, I know you're a good kid. I just didn't want you to be like your mother."

Dad gave me away that day. He wanted me to be happy.

As we began to say our vows, I kept looking at Frank. I was very excited. I didn't know what the hell was going to happen, but it was a new beginning. To me, it was like I had arrived. I was an adult.

Freshman year of high school. Still a brunette.

Junior year of high school.
Suddenly blonde.

My cousin Diane, the closest
I ever had to a real sister.

Miss Hopewell
High School,
1971-72.

The beauty queen in her junior year of high school, waving to the Klansmen.

Me, my mother, and my sister just after my birthday in 1971.
See how comfortable I look with them?

1972 senior class photo.

High school graduation, 1972.

With my first husband,
Frank Patton, two months
after our wedding.
Told you he was tall.

7

Wedding Night

AFTER SAYING "I DO," it kind of hit me that the honeymoon was on the horizon.

I knew that Frank and his dad had a little cabin down on Lake Gaston in North Carolina. It was a popular place for fishermen. Although it occurred to me we were going bass fishing for our honeymoon, it really didn't bother me since I used to go fishing with my Dad. I didn't know much about it then and still don't, but it was soothing to be near the water.

After the cake and punch and a round of "See you laters," we jumped in the car. Hopewell, Virginia to Lake Gaston was about a four-hour trip. I remember feeling like I was kind of outside myself watching someone else. It was almost surreal. It was April 21, 1972, and it felt very warm. I still felt like I was sneaking around—I was actually ducking down in the car seat while leaving town. Frank noticed and thought it was quite peculiar.

When we stopped for dinner, the restaurant had an old rustic look outside. It was fun and exciting and even strange to me, since growing up we almost never went out to eat because we couldn't afford it. And the way my family cooked, it was better than most restaurants anyway.

I ordered a glass of milk—not exactly the most mature thing I could have done, but I like milk. Later, I had my first glass of wine. I'd never had alcohol before, although I had smoked cigarettes. But now I was suddenly an adult. It was a white German wine. Kind of sweet. Frank lit up a cigarette and offered it to me. All these bells and whistles and alerts went off in my head. "Don't do this. Aunt Sis is going to smell it on your breath." Suddenly remembering I was married, it was the first time I took a cigarette without having to worry. I don't think a cigarette ever tasted so sweet or wine ever had the same effect.

Being the "wine virgin" that I was, I didn't think about the wine and milk and cigarettes not making a real good match. It kind of made me nauseous.

It had been a whirlwind week. Moving out of my Aunt's house, having the wedding and reception, driving to North Carolina, and now being on my honeymoon. Also, I had never had sex and was about to be intimate with someone for the very first time in my life. I was scared shitless.

The sun was going down and nighttime was coming. I had visions of a nice little fishing cabin nestled in the woods, with a few other similar places not far away. But it was busier than hell. It was like its own little city and I realized it wasn't going to be as quiet as I thought. Still, I liked the idea of camping. I wasn't going to let anything interfere with my fantasy of how this experience was going to be.

We went down a dirt road and I could hear crickets and the wind flowing down the trees. It felt like a Harlequin Romance novel. All the right elements were there.

We pulled up in front of this place and stopped. Frank turned off the car and said, "Okay, we're here." I was stunned. It was a trailer. I looked at him and went, "What?!"

He said, "What do you mean? This is the place."

"Holy shit. A trailer." Not that there's anything wrong with a trailer. But it wasn't what I envisioned for my virginal honeymoon. I don't think I was misled; it just ran completely against the fantasy going on in my head. I thought, "Make the best of this. It's only four or five days. How bad can it be?"

The trailer had all the amenities you could possibly want other than a phone. It was very well maintained, not dirty. A comfortable feel to it. Frank didn't carry me over the threshold, which is what I dreamed about. But that was okay because I had to go to the bathroom really badly. He told me the bathroom was the second door on the left down the narrow hall. About four steps into the hallway I got really, really hot. I started sweating and my throat started closing up. I had never been in such a tight place before. I found the bathroom and it was even smaller and tighter than the hallway. I didn't know I was claustrophobic. The only thing I could think was "I hope there's a trashcan in here, because I really want to pee and I'm going to throw up."

The combination of wine, cigarettes, milk, stress, and exhaustion hit me and I started puking. Once I relieved myself of everything that was inside of me, I got really clammy and cold. I was sitting there with a cold washcloth on my face. I also felt like I was burning up and my hands were shaking. Frank gently knocked on the door and asked, "Are you okay?"

"I don't know," and I didn't.

"Honey, unlock the door."

"I can't." I couldn't move. I was paralyzed from being in this small, tight space. I was thinking, "What the fuck is wrong with me?" I was burning up inside like someone had put a fire in me and I couldn't put it out. Yet, I was clammy on the outside. I knew I wasn't sick at this point; it was psychological. I felt like I was in a cage. To this day I do not like enclosed spaces, even crowded elevators.

So I spent my honeymoon on the bathroom floor in a trailer in Lake Gaston, North Carolina. Frank was excellent about the whole thing. He stood by the door for a while and kept asking if he could get me anything. I kept saying, "I need to sit here for a while."

I heard the pop of cans as Frank was drinking beers and I heard the TV go on. I covered myself with towels because I was cold. When I finally woke up I was ravenous. What woke me was the smell of bacon, eggs, and coffee. I thought, "God, something smells good."

I finally came out of the bathroom and squinted from the morning sun. Frank just looked at me and laughed. It was an affectionate kind of laugh. I also realized, although I didn't realize it at the time, part of what I smelled was pot. I didn't know he smoked pot all the time, which made everything seem funny to him. I got a pass on a lot of crap because of it. I think he was just stoned and didn't give a shit. In either case, it was a win/win for me.

He asked, "Are you hungry?" When I told him just how hungry I was he said, "I figured you would be."

We had breakfast and he had the windows and doors and everything open and I remember it being very noisy. It was the kind of noise I had never heard before. He said, "Come here, I'll show you something." There was a little porch and it was like being at an amusement park. There were all these little worker bee people doing things. There was a special buzz about the place. They were mowing and cleaning their yards. Boats were everywhere you looked. And there were "Bubbas" all over the place. Bubba shrimp, Bubba fish, and guys named "Bubba" or looking like they should be. It was sort of a civilized *Deliverance*. For me to think that it was "bubba-ish" is something because I was a country bumpkin myself.

As for all the activity, there was a fishing tournament that weekend and guess who was entered? Frank. Get married and have a fishing tournament and honeymoon all at the same time. But I didn't care. I was still feeling woozy and the idea of being on my honeymoon with a man I didn't know all that well made me anxious. I figured I could sleep some more and I didn't have to sleep with someone else. I understood at some point I had to get naked and have sex with this man. But at least with him fishing, I could familiarize myself with the trailer and try to be more comfortable.

It was really odd not having to hide or worry about what anyone thought. I kept thinking, "I'm going to catch hell when I get home." And then it would hit me. "That's not going to happen because you're married." It took quite a long time, a good six months, before I didn't feel like that, before I realized I was my own person.

Frank came back and was very excited because he caught some big fish that day. Not knowing what he wanted to do, I hadn't fixed dinner. We ended up making steak and potatoes, watched a little bit of TV, and he said he had to get up early because they left around 4:30 in the morning for the tournament. He asked, "Do you want to go to bed now?"

I said, "I guess." I didn't feel the panic I thought I would. But I had always worn long-sleeved pajamas with long pants, and at that moment I felt like there weren't enough pajamas in the world to cover me up and keep me protected.

I washed my face, brushed my teeth, and put on my pajamas. When I came out, Frank laughed at me because I was wearing them. My face got beet red and hotter than hell. I was embarrassed.

He came over and started unbuttoning me. Kissing me. I was five-eight and he was six-seven, so it wasn't that comfortable for him to be bent over. We were standing and then he picked me up and brought me into the bedroom. It was romantic. He made love to me. It was very slow and gentle. And passionate.

Considering I'd been sick on the bathroom floor the previous night, I thought it was a good experience. I had never been around anyone who told me about sex or anything like that. God, no. To say the word "sex" back then around my family was taboo. You were a nasty person if you talked about it. So I didn't know what to expect. But I enjoyed it. I felt very close to him. In my head, a husband was supposed to be understanding, and that's just what he was the night before. A real gentleman. I thought everyone was wrong about this guy. He was soft-spoken, gentle, and kind. I think I learned more about him the night I was in the bathroom than the whole time I was sneaking around with him.

It was the first time I knew this relationship was real and not just some teenage game. But right after he made love to me I thought, "I am going to go straight to hell." Then I realized again I was married. It still didn't seem real to me.

In general, my feeling about the lovemaking was, "Hmm, so this is what it's all about. It's good stuff." I thought I would be very freaked out about it, since I was still bashful and shy. I can remember somebody asking me after we got back how I liked losing my virginity. I was embarrassed about it because it was really nobody's business. But deep down, I felt funny admitting to myself I enjoyed it.

I finally made it through my first sexual experience without any broken bones or bloody noses and all was right with the world.

8

Wife

I WAS A HOUSEWIFE, BUT I WAS STILL IN HIGH SCHOOL.
The students thought I was kind of weird because they wondered why I would get married and still be in school. Most of the kids were okay, except the "frou-frous" or upper echelon, and I wasn't close with them anyway. I don't think anyone had ever gotten married before while still in school, or if they did they hadn't told anyone. I was in the heart of the Bible Belt in the early seventies. But I was Ms. Hopewell High and they didn't take too kindly to my marital status. They wanted to suspend me from school because I was married.

I said to the principal, "It's okay for the preacher's daughter (*who was pregnant and unmarried, not knowing who the father of the child was and with no intention of getting married*) to be in school. But you want to suspend me from school because I got married and made it legal?!"

They decided not to suspend me from school, but I couldn't open the Junior/Senior Prom because I was married, and they told me they would let me know if I would be allowed to even go to the prom.

I was pissed off about the whole thing. The girls at school were running around with their legs wide open, having sex with anything that moved, and I was being punished.

I decided not to even go to the prom. I just said screw it—I don't want to be around that anyway. I was plenty busy with a new life and a house to set up.

On the way back from the honeymoon I asked, "Where are we going to live?" We hadn't looked for a house or apartment or anything like that.

Frank said, "Don't worry about it. Everything's fixed."

43

He took me to a part of town I had never seen before. A nice part of town. He said, "Okay, we're home."

It was a second floor apartment with hardwood floors, a small kitchen, a large dining room, one bedroom, and one bathroom. It was nice except there wasn't much furniture except for a dining room table and bedroom furniture. There were curtains in the bedroom but nowhere else. It was nice enough. I'd been in a double bed back at home and when I walked in this bedroom, I saw a king-sized bed for the first time in my life. It was sort of like Ellie Mae comes to Beverly Hills. It was the largest bed I'd ever seen in my life.

Hey, at least it wasn't a trailer park.

I think Frank was a little anxious because he'd never shared an apartment with a woman. He'd fished in a tournament earlier that morning, we had a long drive home, and he had work the next day. So we just went to sleep and that was my first night in my new home.

The next morning I headed out to school. It was weird because Frank dropped me off. It was strange because I still felt like I needed to hide.

Things were all so new between me and Frank. He arranged his schedule so he could take me to and from school. He got off at 3:00 and I got off at 3:30. Since it was such a small town, we were never very far apart.

Frank also made it clear to me he wanted kids—lots of kids. My own feelings about children were still developing and quite honestly, I might have been open to suggestion either way. But this was an area where Frank was insistent and I opposed him very strongly for one important reason: I was still in high school! Here I was, trying to finish out my senior year as conventionally as possible, and he wanted me barefoot and pregnant. Like being "the married kid" wasn't weird enough. I didn't want to walk the halls with a big ol' belly out to here, nor did I want to drop out. Soon after we got married, I went to the doctor and got on the Pill. Frank threw them out—that's how much he wanted his way. So I just went back to the doctor, explained the situation, and got another supply and hid them from Frank. Frank was willful; I was willful. Kids would be a discussion for another day.

I didn't really know any of his friends. When we got home, I knew how to fix some dinner. I was going to make spaghetti, but there was a knock on the door and Frank was in the shower. There was some guy about my height—really skinny with long, long hair down to his rear end, a tied-dyed tee-shirt, with sandals and jeans and a cloth pack on his back, with a flute sticking out of the back. Who was this? A homeless person?

He looked like a member of the Manson family. I told him, "Wait here." I didn't want to let him in.

I described him and Frank laughed and said, "Let him in."

He introduced himself as Lee. He said, "Oh, you're cooking."

With Frank still in the shower, he took something out of his bag and threw it down on the table. I thought to myself, "Oh, nice of him to bring some herbs." I thought it was oregano. I grabbed the pack and figured I'd use it. I took some of it and crumbled it up between my fingers, rubbed it between my palms, and started throwing it into the spaghetti sauce. By the time Frank came out to watch they both looked at me like I was crazy and burst out laughing. They were literally on the floor. I was still clueless. Lee was suddenly sitting at the table rolling the stuff up with some papers. I still wasn't making the connection, even when they started smoking. I said, "What the hell is this?"

Lee said, "Pot," matter-of-factly.

"You're smoking pot?!" It was inconceivable to me. I couldn't fathom anyone doing drugs. It just blew my mind. I went into the bedroom and started crying. I thought I'd married a drug addict. I figured I would have to leave him and go back to my aunt.

They thought it was funny because they were stoned. They figured I was a crazy little broad who didn't have a clue. And they were right.

I locked myself in the bedroom and hours later I heard Frank's friend leave. I wasn't about to unlock the door with him there. Eventually, Frank started knocking on the door. I let him in and he said, "What's wrong with you?"

"I had no idea you were a drug addict."

He laughed and said, "It's just pot."

I was the perfect virgin. All of a sudden I was thrown into sex, booze, and drugs and didn't know what to do.

I let everything slide for a few days. The weekend came and between dealing with the bureaucrats at school, I was relieved to just calm down. I asked Frank, "What is it with this marijuana shit?"

"It makes you happy and you want to eat."

Now it hit me why he was laughing all the time. I figured if it made him happy and he just ate and went to sleep, how bad could it be? Still, I wasn't in the mindset to try it.

He wanted to teach me how to drive. He had a Volkswagen van with a stick shift. He took me to a huge mall parking lot where I wouldn't crash into anything. It took a weekend until I could drive the thing. I studied the Driver's Ed book and right out of the box I got my driver's license. Talk about freedom. Getting married and getting a driver's license—it was like the biggest jailbreak of all time.

June was approaching very quickly, which meant graduation. Frank said, "We need to talk about a couple of things."

I thought, "Uh-oh." The red flag went up.

"You need to think about getting a job. A real job, to contribute to the household."

It used to be I'd get out of school and have the summer off and get to play, but this wasn't going to happen anymore. I graduated, got my diploma, and I was suddenly an adult.

I called my Uncle John, who worked for the Virginia Department of Highways. I figured he might know somebody who could get me a job. I went to this office and got a mail clerk position, distributing all the mail and running all the reports. This was before computers. We had steno machines and I'd have to ink up these big drums and put the reports in there. We used masters to print out hundreds of copies. I even had my own office. I thought, "Wow, this is really cool."

I liked the people and was finally treated like an adult. They judged me on my own merits, which was really a cool feeling. They were all very helpful and got me oriented to the position.

As time went on, I got to know Frank's mom and dad, as we ate over their house frequently. They were really nice people. His mother couldn't hear very well at all and his father pretty much sat in his La-Z-Boy recliner and watched sports and drank beer. She reminded me of Edith Bunker and even looked a bit like her. The whole scene was all very Archie Bunker-ish. His dad was racist, but didn't know it. It was because of where he was born and raised. But I got along with them okay.

Meanwhile, Frank kept smoking his pot. He was on swing shift—eight to three one week, four to twelve the next, and then twelve to eight. I had never been alone except when my mom had left me. Now I was quite frequently. When he worked the graveyard shift, it was really scary for me. I was just afraid to be in the house alone. I don't know why. I stayed awake and watched a lot of TV. Somehow, I functioned at work. There were so many new things happening in my life I guess I was just on overload. But as the months went by, I kind of got used to that, too. We would have our weekends together and we'd even go back to the lake to go fishing.

One day while driving to the lake Frank said, "Try this," and he handed me a joint.

I said, "No," but eventually relented. The first time I tried it I didn't feel anything. No sensation. No hunger. No giggles. Nothing.

The speed limit was seventy-five. He started laughing and asked, "How fast are you going?"

"Seventy-five."

He laughed even harder. I looked down at the speedometer and it said thirty-five. Then I started laughing. I felt like I was going seventy-five, but I was stoned. It felt calm and peaceful. But I knew it would be best to pull over.

Frank introduced me to sex and alcohol, and now drugs. The party was just beginning.

9

Massage Girl

AS MUCH AS I ENJOYED the idea of being an adult and working, I realized I wasn't going to go any further where I was. My salary and benefits weren't very good so I decided to look for another job.

I put in an application with Reynolds Aluminum Company and ended up working on their production line. I sort of felt like the character in the movie *Norma Rae*. It was hot and sweaty factory work—a huge building with a metal roof. There was no air conditioning and their gigantic fans did little to cool off our massive production line.

After their Prell Shampoo boxes were labeled, fifteen or so would come at you. There would be one little box that would stick out, which they called the "kicker." You'd pick that box and stack the last group in it while waiting for the next bunch. That's all I did for eight straight hours. Pull and stack. Pull and stack. It made me hate Prell Shampoo.

It was the dog days of summer in Virginia. It was hot, humid, miserable, extremely noisy, and I was doing swing shifts. Right in the middle of the section I worked was this little room where the foremen would sit and watch everyone doing their jobs. They had a nice air-conditioned set-up. They were assholes who didn't particularly treat the women well. We did most of the hard stuff while the men did all the other work that wasn't as physical. And the guys got more money. After all, it was the seventies.

I took home economics class, so I knew how to sew. I made a pair of shorts and a top to go over the shorts. It was a jumper. The shorts were down to maybe an inch above my knee. I made it because it was something to wear to work that was cool, comfortable, and that I could stand to wear in this sauna.

One day, I was busy on the line when one of the other ladies tapped me on the shoulder and told me they wanted to see me in the office. The foreman said. "You're going to have to go home and change your clothes. And we're going to dock you. Your pants are too short."

I angrily said, "No, they're not."

He informed me he was going to measure my shorts and actually went to get a ruler.

"You're not going to touch me," I announced.

"If you don't change your clothes, you're not coming back."

Grabbing my time card, I threw it in the air. I watched the foreman's mouth grow wide in surprise as the card seemed to hover in the sky. "I quit!"

Storming out of the building, I got in my old Volkswagen Beetle and headed towards home when I spotted Frank driving the other way. He turned around, got behind me, and we pulled over.

"What are you doing?"

When I told him, he asked "What do you mean, you quit?!"

"I quit. I'm not working in that sweatbox. And I won't be talked to like that."

We needed both incomes, but he finally said, "Well, okay."

About a week later, he asked, "Are you going to look for another job?"

"After I get some rest." Hell, I was exhausted. That job had beaten me down.

One afternoon he got home from work and told me Bob, a guy he worked with, had a side business I might be interested in. He said it wasn't difficult work and if anybody could do it, I could. That was very intriguing considering I didn't have a formal education besides a high school diploma. I wasn't really trained in anything.

"What is it?" I asked excitedly.

The guy owned a massage parlor. I figured I could learn a trade and have a job for life.

The office was in Petersburg, Virginia, which is the next town over and is famous for being the home of Moses Malone. Right next to an Army base was a strip that had a few restaurants, quite a few adult bookstores, and two or three massage parlors.

When I entered the office for my interview I heard a little bell go off. There was a waiting room with maybe eight or ten chairs and some magazines on a coffee table. It reminded me of a doctor's office—very neat and clean, nicely done. It was actually kind of upscale. There were a couple of guys sitting there looking at me in a way that I hadn't been looked at before. I didn't understand why. It made me feel very uncomfortable.

The other door opened into a hallway of small rooms like when you go into a doctor's office. There was a slender, older lady in her forties with a nice build. She wore white go-go boots and a one-piece body suit that snapped in the front. I thought, "That's odd. Why would a receptionist not be wearing a skirt or a pair of pants?"

"You must be the new girl. Come on in."

Still, nothing was hitting me as odd.

I went into a regular-looking office that had a desk and lots of papers and some sort of machine sitting there. The room smelled heavily of cigarettes. Bob was heavyset and sort of disheveled looking. He chained cigarette after cigarette, lighting a new one with the last spark of the old. There were a couple of other girls in the room dressed just like the lady who answered the door. I wondered, "Why do all the girls dress like this?" I figured when you gave a massage you get warm, so maybe they just wanted to be comfortable until they got ready for the next client.

He asked the two girls to leave and he introduced the older woman as his wife. "So, you're Frank's wife. He was telling me about you. I understand you're looking for a job."

"What does this entail? Does someone here teach me how to give a massage?"

He got this quirky grin on his face. "Oh yeah. We'll teach you."

He asked me what my size was for the boots and the little jump suit. His wife went to the closet and pulled a set out. I tried them and he said, "That looks really good on you. You can start today. To begin with, you'll stick with my wife and she'll show you where everything is. If you have any questions, you'll ask her." I called Frank to tell him the good news.

It was much like any health spa with shelves, towels, creams, a small sink with soap, and a little radio for soft music. There was a men's shower room and four stalls. She walked me through the routine. I was told that when a client comes in I should tell him to put his clothes on the hook on the back of the door and shower. When he was done he'd come back to the room and leave the door cracked just a little bit so you'd know he'd returned.

Although I had never had a massage myself, I saw them being done on TV and figured, "I can handle this. No big deal."

We greeted the first guy sitting in the waiting room. After he showered, he was lying on his stomach with his butt covered by one of the towels. She proceeded to show me how to give a massage. They could buy a half hour or an hour massage. A half was $25 and an hour $50. There was a menu in the lobby. It said tips were accepted.

Everything was going along smoothly. "Not bad," I thought. I didn't have to sit in a sauna with those macho foremen telling me my clothes were too short. It was nice, cool, and clean. And the boss was friendly, as were the other girls those first four or five days.

After that, Bob said, "Today you're going to start working one-on-one with the clients. You don't need to have someone supervise you anymore."

Already confident in what I was doing, I said, "Well, okay."

The first two or three guys came in and it went just fine. It was just like all the massages I had done with the other lady. No big deal. Business as usual. The first guy gave me a twenty-dollar tip, which was excellent. But after I massaged the fourth client's back, he turned over with the hugest boner I'd ever seen in my life, and I'm thinking, "Whoa ... hold on Skippy."

"Sir, I think you need to calm down."

He started laughing.

"You need to calm down," I repeated.

"I don't think you get it."

"No, that's not something I take care of."

He said, "No, you really don't get it, do you? This is a massage parlor. The least you can do is give me a local."

"A local what?"

"A local is a hand job."

"A what?"

"I give you extra money to jerk me off."

"Are you out of your mind?"

"No. Why do you think this place is so busy all the time?'"

Naively, I replied, "I figured they just needed a massage."

It started to dawn on me that they needed their tension relieved, but not in the shoulders. "Oh my God," I thought to myself. And then it hit me that my husband was pimping me out. I recognized this client as one of the guys in the waiting room when I walked in the first day. Frank and Bob had set me up; they had planned all of this.

I was beyond angry. "You can jerk yourself off. I'm not doing that to you."

Finishing out my shift, I told Bob and his wife, "I understand the whole deal with this place now. And if you want me to stay here I will. But all I'll be doing is giving massages."

They said, "Well, we'll see how it goes. That's fine."

They probably figured I was shell-shocked and I'd come around and give hand jobs and blow jobs or do it "all" like the other girls. But I did give a good massage and had regular clients who just wanted that, so I figured I could continue there.

When I got home I was really hurt and just looked at Frank and said, "What in God's name did you get me into? Do you know what kind of place that is?"

"Yeah, I know what it is."

"Why would you want your wife to work in a place like that?"

"I didn't figure you would mind. It's just a hand job."

"You think I wouldn't mind?! Most men don't even want their wives looking at another man, much less touching their private parts."

He looked at me blankly and repeated, "I didn't think you would mind."

"Well I do. You must not think very much of me if you're willing to peddle me out like that."

I went and slept on the couch. I didn't know which way to turn or what to do. I had no family; I had no friends. All I had was a husband, and he was trying to pimp me out for a quick buck.

10

Alone Again

THAT WAS THE BEGINNING OF THE END between me and Frank. He never really apologized. Hell, he never said a whole lot about anything. I was pretty hurt, but was also pissed off. We didn't speak a lot after that. I didn't want to even look at him. I just went to work on the day shift and did my job. I wasn't about to work the night shift there, because God only knows what went on then. Guys would ask for me, but the owners told them, "No, you don't want her." But I didn't have many office skills per se and sure didn't want to go back to a factory job. It wasn't like I had a lot of employment opportunities to choose from.

I tried to save some money because I knew in the back of my head I was going to make an exit. I was trying to figure how to run away from home again. I didn't want Frank to know my finances before I had all my ducks in a row. If I was going to move I was going to need one month's rent, one month's security, furniture, and I still had to find a place. Even worse, I'd never really been on my own before. It was all pretty depressing. I felt like I'd been abandoned once more. I didn't trust anyone to begin with, and now I'd put 100 percent of my trust in someone to make my life okay and I was just wrong.

Meanwhile Ken, one of my customers who came in quite often, owned two adult bookstores on the strip where the massage parlor was. I let him know I was looking for a different job. He offered me a position as a clerk. It didn't take much for me to walk into Bob's office and say, "I quit."

I started to work behind the counter in Ken's bookstore the next day. At least at the bookstore customers were going in to watch other people having sex and I didn't feel like I was being pressured to prostitute myself. They weren't asking me for it or trying to fondle me or grope me.

I was there a week before my husband found out. Bob asked Frank how I was doing and that's when my husband discovered I wasn't working there anymore. It really took him by surprise as it was my first independent act. He demanded to know what was going on and was not happy I was employed at an adult bookstore. I didn't understand how he could be against me working at a bookstore, but it was okay to work in a whorehouse and be encouraged to give guys hand jobs.

My responsibilities included working the cash register, stocking the shelves, and splicing the 8mm movies together for the peep shows. I couldn't help watching them and I had never seen anything like it before. I thought they were pretty interesting. My initial reaction, though, was that the women looked really bad. It seemed like they hadn't bathed. Their hair looked dirty. The soles of their feet were dirty. They had pimples on their butts. It was appalling to me that women would allow themselves to look that way or have others present them that way.

The whole thing was strange and yet not so strange. Basically, I was working as a clerk in a store, period. It could have been 7-11 or Piggly Wiggly. It just so happened that it sold dirty magazines instead of hotdog buns and Mountain Dew.

Besides Frank's, I hadn't seen any other penises before. But when I saw the size of some of these guys in the movies, I said to myself, "Holy crap." It didn't scare me, though. In fact, it all interested me. Even though I was sheltered, none of it offended me at all. I figured they were consenting adults, whereas I wasn't given a choice when it came to working at the massage parlor. I guess you could say it was arousing to me, the same way it is when guys see big boobs for the first time. Ask them what's so great about them, they probably can't give you a really intelligent answer. It's just something hormonal, I suppose. At the time, I wouldn't have had any idea what to do with some big huge porn cock—what it would feel like or whether I'd even like it. But hanging around the store was making me feel more comfortable with my own sexuality.

The people who walked in the store were amusing. There were a lot of soldiers, but also a lot of dirty old men. They were the lecherous kind you saw in *Playboy* and *Hustler* cartoons. My counter was the farthest away from the door and it sat up about three to four feet higher than the rest of the store so the customers couldn't grab at me or reach into the register. I could see down the aisle in the back and notice if any of the films broke in the twenty-five cent booths. We changed the movies once a week and everybody knew what day the movies changed. On that day the customers were always primed. "Did you change them yet? Did you change them yet?" Surprisingly, a lot of them were good-looking guys who, nonetheless, came into the store to beat off.

None of this action bothered me because it had nothing to do with me; I was merely the clerk—a voyeur. Also, I was making good money, I didn't work particularly hard, and it wasn't boring. I heard everybody else talking about how dull their jobs were, but I never knew from one minute to the next who would walk in the door and what stupid crap they would do.

There was a guy around ninety who came in one day with a raincoat on. He suddenly opened the coat and flashed me. I said, "Oh, you ridiculous jackass!" He immediately got a boner—exactly the reaction he wanted. He came in the same exact time the next week and exposed himself again. Ditto week three. By the fourth time, I was ready for him.

When he came in that day, I looked at my watch and nonchalantly said, "You're late; come on in." He looked like he was going to cry because he didn't get the same shocked reaction from me. He never came back again.

Occasionally, women came in with their husbands or partners, but most seemed pretty timid. On the day the films changed, there were fifteen or twenty people in the back cruising each other and I'd say, "Okay boys, down with the quarters and up with the pants." I knew what was going on, but I wasn't in the mood to get that close to it for fear of being pulled into it. Gang rape was not on my bucket list.

In the beginning it seemed surreal to me, like a Salvador Dali painting. There was an older guy who cleaned the place up. Part of his job was to mop up the cum in the booths, which was where most of the action—solo or otherwise—was going on. It was the seventies, a liberal time, and I didn't care what anyone else did as long as it didn't involve me against my wishes.

Some of the customers did hit on me, but all in all they were respectful. Feeling burned by my marriage, the last thing on my mind was dating one of those guys or being intimate with anyone. I just wanted to keep to myself and get a paycheck.

Meanwhile, Frank and I continued to argue over my job for a couple of weeks. We had been married maybe eight or nine months and I was already looking for a place of my own. I found a little farm house outside of town in the country. It was away from everyone and I liked it, especially the garden. The owner said the rent was around $250 a month for three bedrooms and one bath. At eighteen, it seemed like a mansion to me, but it was just a little old farmhouse and nothing more.

I knew I had one foot out the door, although Frank was clueless and in denial. Since the massage parlor incident, I'd totally withdrawn from him and he hardly even noticed. I suppose he expected we'd just go on like that forever, which might have been fine with him, but not with me. I didn't love him anymore and I didn't believe he loved me in the way I felt I deserved to be loved. We had yet another argument over my job. I finally had enough and told him about the place I found and that I was going to move out. We were in the kitchen standing next to the refrigerator and there was a long window. The fight grew more heated and he grabbed me by my arms and was shaking me pretty good. My back hit the window and it shattered. That scared the shit out of me. I guess it jolted him, too, because he immediately released me.

"I'm done. I'll be leaving tomorrow."

He just turned and walked away. I don't think he realized how upset I was. The look on his face told me he felt bad it had come down to him getting physical.

I left the next day while he was at work. I felt sad on so many levels. Even though I was the one doing the leaving, it brought back all the feelings I'd held inside me when I was abandoned at age eight.

I went to the landlord of the new house and told him I needed to move in earlier and why. He understood and accommodated me. Unhappy as I was, it seemed kind of fresh because I was doing it on my own. It was a new beginning.

11

Daddy's Home

MY DAD CAME BY the first two weeks to help me paint. He was a professional house painter. I hadn't seen him since the wedding about a year before. The whole marriage was only about a year and a half from the time I said "I do" to the time the divorce papers were finalized.

I was very excited to see my dad, as we had always gotten along very well. I had no resentment at all towards him, even though he wasn't really in my life. I was still the baby in the family and Daddy's little girl. He really didn't say anything to me about the marriage. He didn't ask me any questions. More than anything, he just wanted me to be happy.

I told Dad what I was doing. I even told him about the flasher, which he thought was hilarious. But I didn't tell him about the massage parlor job because I thought it would hurt him. It would have bothered him that his baby was in that environment, touching people. The bookstore was more sterile—no touching allowed. The only concern he ever had with my job was working night shifts. "I know how those soldiers are," he said. But I was working the day shift, so he was appeased.

In addition to painting, he started fixing my screen doors, fixtures, plumbing, and anything else he could. He was extremely handy. I was happier than a pig in poop. I really enjoyed being around him. We had similar interests. We both liked baseball. He pitched in the Army and for a team from Austinville, Virginia. The New York Giants offered him a contract at one point, but my Mom vetoed it because she wasn't willing to leave. He always regretted not seizing that opportunity. He loved baseball. Maybe that's why I love baseball so much today.

It was almost like a vacation with my dad, as I had never spent much time with him before except when I was a little kid. And I was finally of legal age to drink. He was an alcoholic and I had seen him drunk a couple of times. He was a mean drunk, not a happy drunk. But during this time

I never saw him out of control. I just wouldn't bring a lot of alcohol into the house.

He absolutely adored traveling and wanted me to do the same thing. He was a big Greyhound bus rider. It was a way for him to travel, because he really couldn't afford to travel outside the U.S. Whenever he wanted to go somewhere, he just got on a bus. To this day I have a bug for traveling. It can be as little as three hours away, but it's fun for me.

"You're your own person. Take some time for yourself. Enjoy yourself. And then figure out what you want."

What I wanted at that point was some peace. I was happy being on my own for the first time in my life, without being in a children's home or married or having to live with family. Leaving Frank, I wasn't as upset as I thought I'd be. I thought I would feel like a failure, but I didn't. It was actually nice waking up in the morning alone, not having to answer to anybody. I made a living for myself. Paid my bills. I could eat and have a roof over my head. It felt like an accomplishment.

Frank didn't even call. He was out of my life completely. I didn't want to date. I didn't want to get that close to having a relationship. I lived out in the country so there weren't even a lot of people around. I got to know a few of my neighbors and some of them had house parties and hung out at home, but all in all I didn't do a lot of socializing. I didn't drink much. If I went to a bar it was a stretch for me to figure out what to order. I would drink a beer and a little wine once in a while, but that was it.

When I went back to work and did my nine-to-five, Ken was in and out of the store as always. He went to Baltimore to buy inventory and he'd bring the merchandise back to stock the shelves. The one thing I did see in the store that was a little odd, to me at least, was bondage stuff. Clamps and masks and things. I thought, "Was there a prison somewhere I didn't know about?" I just thought it was really weird. I came to learn bondage was different than S&M. You were bound and disciplined, as opposed to S&M, which involved physical pain. Being a clerk in a store like mine, you had to know stuff like this, believe it or not. I figured if that's what floats your boat, fine. But it wasn't something I wanted to do. I had no desire to inflict pain on someone or have it done to me.

Some guys would go to the magazine racks and, because of the way the store was set up, you'd just see the top of their head down to their nose. They'd stand in one place but shift around like they had to pee real bad or something. I'd come down from the counter, walk around the corner, and see a guy standing there beating off.

"Oh, man, don't do that in the middle of the store. Buy the magazine or take it in the booth. You know I have to touch that stuff… ."

Some would drop the magazine, turn beet red, lose their hard-on, and put it back in their pants—the hard-on, not the magazine. Some would go in the back and some would leave. The ones who would leave you wouldn't see for a week or so and then they'd come in, buy their quarters, and go straight to the back. I thought, "I turned that guy into a paying customer."

I tried to find an amusing take on everything that happened in the store. Women masturbate, but by and large they do it at home. I adore men, I really do, but they are such strange beasts.

Ken paid me in rolls of quarters and I paid for a car in cash with all that change. I told the salesman to bring a wheelbarrow to the trunk of what I was driving because it was filled with silver. He looked at me and said, "You must be in the dirty book business."

"As a matter of fact, I am."

All in all, this was a happy period in my life. Ken told me he was going to take me on some of his buying trips. We'd start in Baltimore, where I'd never been before. I'd hardly ever been out of the state of Virginia, so it sounded like Paris to me. I was excited about the travel, but also because I was getting established at a job. Maybe it didn't sound like much of a career to most people, but to me, it felt like I was going places. At least I wasn't the guy with the cummy mop.

At my mother's house in St. Petersburg, FL, 1973.

At Virginia Beach in 1974.

With the first boy who ever kissed me,
Larry Webb.

Mike Ackers, a boy I dated one summer.

With my Cousin Pop.

12

Ken

KEN LOOKED LIKE ELVIS PRESLEY. Especially his hair. And he had the attitude that he was a real cool cat to go with it. With stores in Newport News, Norfolk, Petersburg, and pretty much wherever there were Army bases or naval bases, I thought he was rich. Although he spent his money pretty well, anybody who made more than $10,000 a year seemed rich to me.

As time went on, I became very attracted to him. Maybe it was because he was my boss, an authority figure, combined with all the other things he seemed to have going for him. I was so excited to go with him to Baltimore. I had never seen a distributorship for adult material before. It was a gigantic warehouse—just enormous. They had 8mm movies, magazines, bondage material, all kinds of rubber goods; anything that you could possibly think of in the adult line. I was overwhelmed there was actually that much stuff available. That's when it hit me just how big this industry was.

We ordered what we needed and I thought to myself, "Maybe I should be hooking up with this guy, because there's a lot of money in this." I wasn't a goldigger, but the idea of being with a man who could actually take me out to a nice dinner once in a while seemed like a fairy tale to me.

Ken was very nice to me. He treated me well and spoke to me as an equal. Back in those days, women weren't always treated with dignity. Ken spoke to me in a more respectful manner than most men had in the past, especially employers. He was also a lot more sophisticated than Frank. He didn't work for some big company. He had his own businesses and did as he pleased.

He had a home in Baltimore, but reserved a hotel room for us. I was so excited by everything I didn't really think about the sleeping arrangements. He said we weren't going to be in town long, so why get two rooms? God, I was so naïve.

It was great being in a hotel—it was my very first time! Ken told me to get dressed, as we'd be going out to dinner after he ran a few errands. I was thrilled to death. It was like being a kid in a candy store.

We went out for a nice dinner and he didn't really drink. Ken was pretty straight-laced as far as drinking or doing drugs. He drove a red and white Cadillac with white leather interior, which also impressed me. You had to be rich to have a Cadillac, I thought. He always had Elvis's music playing as we drove.

I thought he dressed really sharp with the big collars on the shirts, and white belt and white Bailey shoes. Ken also always wore a Pulsar watch. It was digital, which I'd never seen before. And there was a lot of polyester. A whole lot of polyester. You have to understand, though—polyester was the poor man's silk and satin. Roughnecks didn't wear it, only "rich" guys like Ken. As tacky as it all seems today, in that place and time, this guy seemed like a movie star.

We went to dinner and had a good time. He loved live music, which was really cool to me. There was a lounge next door where we went dancing for a while before heading back to the hotel.

As we approached the hotel, it was kind of weird because I was working with him and it suddenly hit me that we were sharing the room and what his intentions were. It was okay, though, because I was into him. I appreciated how he had treated me up to this point. He didn't make it seem like I owed him a lay or anything like that. He wasn't all hands and there were no threats of losing my job if I didn't put out. I figured what the heck; I hadn't slept with anyone since Frank. I didn't see any downside to it. I figured, "I'm sleeping with the boss. Now I'll be treated even better."

The sex was good, but I don't remember having romantic thoughts like, "Where is this going to lead?" I wasn't in love with the guy, but I liked him well enough and he turned me on. I figured I was free, single, and on my own. I didn't have to feel bad about it.

We got up the next morning and I didn't feel any different. I had a good time and was treated like a lady. My impression was we would probably do it again and it might lead to something or it might not. But I wasn't really looking for a committed relationship with anyone. It was just nice knowing I could do what I wanted.

We got back to the store, I worked my shift, and when it was over I went home. When I went into work the next day, he asked me what I thought about Baltimore and the warehouse and I said, "Look, I had a really nice time. It was an interesting scene."

"Maybe when I go back, you can go with me," he said, simply enough.

"That would be nice."

"Meanwhile, I want to teach you a few things about the store so if I go somewhere, you can run things."

He showed me how to price the merchandise, where the new items went, and how to rotate the old and new stuff around the store. He was very good at placing things in the right area to get the best sales. Another responsibility was taking the money out of the machines, because each one had its own individual lock. You'd know which movie was doing the best and those would stay up longer.

I was left in charge and it felt wonderful. Somebody finally thought I was capable enough to handle something on my own. And I did a good job.

When Ken left my store, I never asked him where he went. I still thought of him as a boss as opposed to a boyfriend. I'd go out with him occasionally. It was very comfortable. We didn't see each other on any set schedule. When he was in town, I'd go out with him if he asked me. And if he didn't ask, I wasn't hurt.

When he got back from his trips, it was payday and I got my check in an envelope. The first one even had a bonus. I said, "What's this for?" For a second I was worried—like it was one of those tips I was offered at the massage parlor and he was paying me extra to sleep with me.

He said, "You took on more responsibility, so you get more money."

Relieved, I thought, "Could this get any better?"

13

Pin-Up Girl

I DON'T THINK I WAS EVER IN LOVE with Ken, but we started going out more often. He needed a place to crash near the store I worked; I had a place, so we both figured it would be cheaper if he moved in and we shared the rent. He said it wouldn't be like roommates, but rather boyfriend and girlfriend. I said, "I'm not sure how well that would go." I hadn't lived with anyone but Frank, and that was only after we were married. Other than that, I never even spent the night with a man, let alone shared a drawer or a closet with one.

When he told me he wouldn't be around much because of his other stores, I figured, "What the hell? Why not? I could save more money." But something inside me said this wasn't a great setup.

At first everything was pretty good. After a short time we moved out of my little place in the country and into a nice house in Newport News, but it was kind of unsettling because I didn't know anyone there. When Ken left for his trips, it was weird. I don't get lonely easy. I've been a loner most of my life. But I get a little scared at night, afraid something bad might happen, like someone breaking into the house.

I worked in a different store he owned in Newport News. The other store was by an Army base, but this one was by a naval dry dock. The Navy guys didn't have a whole lot to do since their ships were there to be repaired. They'd come to the store in droves.

The funniest time was when a ship came in from Indonesia. All the sailors were Indonesian and they couldn't find anything to do in town. Right down from the adult store was a game room that Ken owned. The guys were always hanging out there, but they complained there were no ping pong tables, only pool tables. So we put in ping pong tables and they loved it. I learned to play, too. What more could a shipload of Indonesians like better than a big-titted blonde to play ping-pong with? They would come in to see me, so I was reassigned to the game room. They'd spend more money that way. Besides, I thought it was a lot more fun.

I started organizing ping pong tournaments to keep them in the building. They were very competitive, but the guys who came in to shoot pool got pissed because they didn't have tournaments. So we started one for them, too. It was an awful lot of fun, much better than getting flashed by old pervs or stopping guys from jerking off in the aisles.

There was a transient hotel above the bookstore and an old man lived there. Everyone on the street called him Pops. Pops would clean up the peep show booths for me. I sure as hell wasn't going back there to clean that stuff up! Technically, he was a street person who made enough money for alcohol and a room by mopping up the booths. He smoked cigarettes and his mouth was kind of sunken in. He was never completely clean-shaven. He looked a little like Popeye and he got drunk and stayed drunk. But never so drunk he couldn't mop the booths. He needed the wherewithal to do the job or he wouldn't have enough money to buy his next bottle. He was a nice old man, wasn't lazy, but made just enough for booze, cigarettes, and a meal or two a day. In his own way, he got exactly what he wanted out of life.

The Indonesian ship wasn't in very long. Ships would come and go, but the crews always found their way to our businesses because they'd hear from their buddies where to have a good time. A lot of them weren't big drinkers, which made them gravitate to us since we didn't serve alcohol at the pool hall or the bookstore.

Everything seemed to be going okay, but Ken started traveling a lot and I wasn't crazy about being alone in that big store. I had to close up with four, five, six thousand dollars in my purse, which wasn't the safest thing for a woman alone. I didn't know anything about guns and didn't *want* to know anything about guns. I was very nervous at midnight, putting that money in my car and driving home so I could take it to the bank the next day. I also had it in my house overnight, which only made me more paranoid. This put a strain on the relationship. One night we had an argument about it.

"Well, this is what a manager does."

"Not this manager," I responded.

I left Ken and went back to the Hopewell area. Back there, I bumped into Frank, my ex, and was actually happy to see him. It was a familiar face. After some small talk, we ended up going home together. Shortly after, he asked me to go to Vegas. I thought he was proposing a vacation. I had no idea his intention was to stay there. But money was getting real tight because I wasn't working and he wasn't doing too well either. Frank thought Vegas was the land of opportunity.

I went to the Dunes to apply for a job. The guy who interviewed me said, "Why don't you be a poker shield?" I told him I had no idea how to play. He told me a poker shield was a pretty girl who sat at the table to lure the guys to stay and play. They gave me $200 a day to play with. I lasted three days. I was just supposed to place small bets and dawdle around; make the money last. It never worked. I simply had no damn idea what I was doing—I never played the game before. They fired me.

I thumbed through a newspaper and saw an ad that said MODELS WANTED. NUDE OR SEMI-NUDE. Frank wasn't having any better luck in the job hunting department, so I said, "What the hell?" I figured it wouldn't bother Frank since he'd already tried pimping me out once before.

Having worked in an adult bookstore, the idea of being nude or semi-nude didn't bother me. I'd begun to look at porno material with an educated eye. A lot of it was downright gross, and I'm not necessarily talking about the sex or the kink. The human body is beautiful. Some of these magazines were downright ugly. In real life, I wouldn't touch some of those people with a ten-foot pole. The idea of doing it right, of being naked, but beautiful and classy, appealed to me. I thought that was how it should be—Hollywood-style glamour. And the money sounded real good. It was like $300 a day, which was a helluva lot of money back then. I had no idea where the pictures would end up nor did I care. I didn't think about friends or family seeing them. People in my family didn't read men's magazines.

The shoot was in Vegas, which at that time wasn't built up like it is now. It was in the outskirts of town, outdoors in a wooded area. I had on a deerskin vest that just had a string tied in the back, with little feathers hanging down from it. It was a hippy-ish thing that was pretty much what girls were wearing at the time.

There was only one guy. Pleasant. He seemed old to me, but he was probably just in his late thirties. He never came onto me. Very professional. It didn't bother me to take my clothes off, as I knew what I was getting into. It wasn't like going in to give massages and finding out guys wanted hand jobs.

I was a little shy, but the guy made me feel comfortable. "It's okay; I'm not going to touch you."

"I know you're not, because if you do, I'll kill you." I was serious about that, at least in my own mind. I had more guts than brains, but if you can pull off a bluff convincingly enough, people buy it. Whether I knew it or not, I was establishing my reputation before I even knew I was going to have an adult career.

He told me which way to move; which way to look. Bend over and touch my ankles. Nothing distasteful. No inserting fingers into orifices or anything like that. It was like what would be in *Playboy* around that same era. It took about four hours.

All in all it was a good experience. With the 300 bucks, I'd eat another week. He handed me the cash and told me I did a really nice job and looked really good. But he told me he didn't usually use models more than once a month. Overexposure.

I thought it was a one-shot deal. I needed fast dough, the car needed gas, I needed food, and it was so easy I would hardly even call it work. I doubted I'd ever be naked in front of a camera again.

14

Murder

MY RELATIONSHIP WITH FRANK WASN'T GOING WELL. AGAIN.
He didn't seem very interested in trying to find a job. I had no idea why. It was always hard to read that man. He told me he was looking, but I didn't see any evidence of it. There was rent to be paid, food to be bought, everyday cost of living expenses to be met. And nobody was working.

My thought was to go back to Virginia because nothing was happening here. There wasn't a lot of fighting or anything. I was just disgusted. I told him he could probably find a job there and I had my family. In my mind, it was a safe place for both of us.

We drove back and it felt depressing, defeated. Inside, I felt nothing for him. I'm not even sure why I hooked up with him again in the first place. Maybe it was just convenient comfort combined with loneliness and horniness—the devil you knew was better than the devil you didn't. I dropped him off at his mother's house and went and got a hotel room. I was tired and wanted to be by myself. I didn't have a place to live and had very little money—basically nothing but the clothes on my back and a suitcase. But I was sure I was done with Frank for good this time. (The next time I saw him, years and years later, he was a Born Again Christian. After pushing me to give handjobs, and sponging off me in Vegas while he gambled, he finally turned to the Lord. Oh well, if it weren't for sinners, the church would be out of business.)

I had no clue as to what I was going to do and figured I'd stroll on back to Ken, if only to scratch that off my list of options. So much for swearing off second chances.

He was over at one of the stores and nothing was really discussed except he hired me back on the spot. Outside of all else, I was a damn good employee and he knew it. We just picked up where we left off, no questions asked. Although I did have feelings for him, it wasn't love—

71

even more so now. Yet next thing I knew, we were back living together in the same place we had. Again, I was opting for familiarity. Some new guy would have been like diving into a whole new thing, with all the good discoveries and bad, and all the butterfly feelings you get in your stomach. I guess that didn't set right with me at that point. I needed relationship comfort food.

There was a new guy working at the store. I would say he was fiftyish. His name was Woody—the second Woody in my life.

Woody was gay and had a little dog, a sheltie, a wonderful miniature collie that was always with him. Woody was kind of short with brownish grey hair that wasn't always combed. He had a pockmarked complexion with oily skin and usually wore jeans with a plaid shirt or polo. He had a little bit of a tummy and black horn rimmed glasses that were always sliding down his nose, so he had to keep pushing them up all the time. There was always the scent of cheap drug store cologne on him, but somehow he was able to carry it off. He always had a smile and something pleasant to say to everyone. He was a very loving man, a sweet soul. I always enjoyed having him in the store to keep me company. He just loved all the Navy guys who came in. Cruising a lot, old Woody scored a lot of dates out of there.

Around this time, the cops started coming down on all the bookstores in the area. They'd make us take certain things off the shelves. It was starting to be a hassle and drove business away. It was the politics of the day. Community standards and all that. They decided that instead of a blanket law that you couldn't have an adult bookstore, they'd instead leave it up to each community to set its own standards. We'd be forced to take down the bondage films and equipment. They really could have told us to remove everything, but they only objected to the most bizarre. It was the seventies and for as much freedom as women were getting, some of our feminist leaders like Gloria Steinem were raising a lot of ruckus against pornography.

I felt it was all very hypocritical. There were men's magazines on the newsstand like *Playboy* and *Penthouse* that they weren't bothering with. And they didn't do anything to the strip clubs in our area, what few were around. They were just targeting bookstores. As far as I was concerned, it gave the guys a place to go. Even if they were jacking off in the back, it was a release for them. And if two consenting adults are doing what they want to do, I don't think it's anybody's business.

We'd take stuff down and the next day they'd pick on some other item. It became a hassle getting staff to work the store and I had to work a lot of hours because of it. We hired a black gentleman and immediately noticed the sales were going down and merchandise disappearing. Despite the coincidence, I just didn't feel he was the kind of person to steal.

One night on the way home, I was in the car behind him at a red light. The light changed and he wasn't moving. I sat there trying to figure out what was going on and finally got out and knocked on his window.

He was dead asleep.

Turned out the guy had narcolepsy. He would fall asleep all the time in the store. The customers were taking stuff right off the shelves while he was snoozing. One day, I actually saw him asleep while standing. Yes, standing. I took a newspaper and winged it at his head. It scared the crap out of him. I told him, "I'm sorry, but I don't think this is going to work. You need to go home."

I felt bad, but it wasn't good for business. And it wasn't safe for him. They could have knocked him over the head and did whatever they wanted because he was falling asleep pretty regularly. But as soon as we got rid of him, sales went right back up.

So we had to give Woody more hours. I walked into the store one evening and there were two other guys there with Woody, who was behind the counter. I could feel a bad vibe in the air. Woody looked really nervous when I arrived.

I asked, "What's going on?' Nobody said anything. I announced, "If nobody's going to tell me anything, you two have to leave."

Later, Woody admitted it was a fight, a love triangle. One of the guys didn't know Woody was seeing the other. I said, "I don't know what to tell you, but if you're going to do this, you have to keep it away from the store. I don't want your boyfriends bringing drama in here. It's not good for business." I didn't see any of his boyfriends or tricks after that.

Ken and I were home one night and got a call from the police that we needed to come down to the store. Something had happened. I thought maybe Woody had another spat with a boyfriend, or the morality police threw a brick through our window or something. I didn't know what to expect and was nervous the entire ride down.

When we arrived there was a detective standing outside. He said, "You may not want to go in right now."

I said, "I do. What's going on?"

Someone had murdered Woody.

I changed my mind; I didn't want to go in.

It was a gunshot to the head at close range. The police said whoever it was just walked in, walked right up to him, and fired, execution-style.

No sign of a struggle. No robbery.

They told Ken to get Woody's beautiful dog out because he wouldn't let anyone near the body. Looking like he was in shock, Ken walked in zombie-like. I'd never seen him so visibly upset over anything before. He had been very friendly with Woody.

We went home after talking to the cops. It was a crime scene and there was blood everywhere.

The store was closed for days. While the store was closed, Ken had some guys do some carpentry work and move the counter to the other side of the store so it wouldn't be right by the door when you walk in. We were that scared.

I was freaked out. I had never been close to a crime, let alone a murder. About a week later, we reopened the store and I started shaking the minute I walked in. I refused to stay there alone.

After that, Pops usually stayed with me in the store and I went and got a Doberman. She was a great dog named Tammy. Very protective. She was enormous and when she'd put her paws on my shoulder she'd be taller than me, and I'm no little girl to begin with. Ken added guns to the store as well. A .38, a .44, and even a .357 Magnum. I visualized the headlines: FEMALE ADULT BOOK STORE CLERK CHARGED IN MURDER OF CUSTOMER. I was scared of guns. And after the murder, I was scared to death, period.

They never found out who murdered Woody. We were left to guess whether it was personal or against the store in general.

Business got even slower. The cops came even more often because not only were they taking stuff off the shelves, they were questioning customers about the murder. And dirty bookstores are not the sort of place in which guys want to give their names and be interviewed. The police were killing us.

15

Porn Star

THE VEGAS PHOTO SHOOT I DID APPEARED in some no-name, run-of-the-mill adult magazine and we were stocking it back in Virginia. Ken knew about it and didn't care. It was selling like ice cream on a hot summer day even though we were doing nothing to promote it by telling people it was their very own cashier on the cover.

We needed more product for the store and some more of that one magazine in particular, so I went back on the road with Ken to Baltimore.

The head guy at the warehouse had an air of sophistication. He had been in the business for a while and seemed very approachable yet savvy. He always wore nice clothing and smelled of quality cologne. He looked at me and said, "See, I always said you should do this. We can't keep that magazine of yours in the warehouse."

I kind of brushed it off. Not because I was embarrassed about it, but I didn't know what to say. More than anything else, I think he was feeling out the situation to see how Ken would react. When Ken didn't blow his stack, he followed with a nonchalant comment about a friend of his who was shooting loops that very day down the street. Suddenly he asked us both, "Would you be interested in doing one?"

I don't know why, but I wasn't stunned or offended. I looked at Ken and he looked at me and I said, "What do you think?"

"It doesn't bother me, but I'd like to know what they're paying." That should have tipped me off about Ken.

He said, "Two hundred," and Ken said that wasn't enough. The guy just kind of looked at him inquisitively and Ken said, "Four hundred."

"That's not a problem. I'll be right back." Walking off to make a phone call, we kept shopping. It was that blasé.

75

When he came back he said, "If you want to do this, they can shoot right now. They have a guy you can do it with. Here's the four hundred bucks"—and handed it to me, just like that.

This should have been one of those mega-moments in one's life, a turning point where a person has a major ethical dilemma to wrestle with. It wasn't. I'd posed nude on a whim because I needed the money, the experience had been pleasant enough, and now because I'd been so well received, some other people wanted me to appear in a movie—right that very minute, in fact. And I *still* could use the money, so what the hell?

I really wasn't nervous. I don't know why, I just wasn't. Maybe because it was moving so fast and had caught me off guard. I mean, I didn't wake up that morning figuring I'd be asked to star in a porno. Maybe being around it all the time in the bookstore made it seem less unusual to me. I saw the films and magazines constantly. Or maybe it was because I didn't have any emotional investment in Ken. Our relationship was convenient. I enjoyed his company and had a nice time with him. But I was emotionally unavailable because of what had happened with my mother and then with Frank. I didn't realize this consciously at the time, but that was the bottom line. Ken never "romanced" me. He wasn't cooing "I love you" in my ear, nor did I desire him to.

There's a thing they tell young girls who vacillate on whether or not to do porn: "Do it now; you'll never look better. Capture it on film." I figured this was a chance to make money while I could. Maybe I was just being selfish, but I didn't feel concerned about what anyone else would think. Also, I figured it was a one-time thing that nobody I knew was going to see, just like my magazine shoot. It would be hidden in little bookstores like ours. Of course, the light bulb didn't quite click that the magazine had been seen by plenty of people and the same would happen here. Hell, my family didn't look at adult material, so I didn't feel I had to worry about that.

Back in the 1970s, most people didn't make $400 in two weeks as opposed to two hours. If I liked it and Ken really didn't, I could always do magazines or films and make a good living on my own. At the time, it wasn't like I was fucking the boss in order to have a job in Ken's store, but to the rest of the world, it may have looked that way. But this, this would be *my* thing. The thoughts passing through my head were not, "I'm being exploited." They were, "I'm being liberated."

I was strangely curious about the whole process. Working at the bookstore, I'd become kind of jaded. Detached. The magazines, the toys, the loops, they no longer seemed weird to me. If I thought about it at all, I wondered about how it all came to be—who made this stuff, and how did they know what would sell and to whom? I got a kick out of the customers, many who were regulars. Sex was important to them. It was less important to me. I didn't sleep around. I was pretty damn monogamous and not very kinky or adventurous.

A lot of it had to do with sex being such a taboo subject when I grew up. I was never part of a family that discussed it. The only thing I heard about it was "NO!" That's not very informative. But at the store, I saw guys—and a few girls—who liked how it felt and did something about it. They weren't bad people. They didn't hurt anybody. I liked that.

He handed Ken the directions to the shoot and said, "They're ready when you are." It was about three or four blocks down the street. I was kind of shocked, though, when we walked into the building. I was born and raised in a small town, so to me, Baltimore was a big, glamorous city. But I thought this place was kind of run down and dirty. It was an apartment. We knocked on the door and my "co-star" answered. I don't remember his name or even what he looked like. I think it was because I just didn't care. All I remember is he was around my age and skinny as hell.

I was told this was the person I'd be working with. There was a bed with a flowered pattern that was God-awful 1970's yellow. Seeing this dump, and having viewed so many loops back in the store, I could just hear that horrible porn music in my head—they all had the same bad music.

This wasn't exactly going to be glamorous.

The guy working the camera was the whole ball of wax: director, cameraman, and lighting guy. Not that there was a whole lot of direction. And there was certainly no dialogue. He said, "You don't have to worry about talking or learning any lines. It's not that kind of movie." No shit.

It was a silent film. I was like Gloria Swanson all of a sudden. Oh God, it just brings back memories of *Sunset Boulevard*. The director spoke in a friendly yet no-bullshit tone. "I know this is the first time you're doing a movie, but we're here for the fucking." He had already done three films that day and had more to shoot after mine.

My co-star seemed friendly enough and was pleasant. One thing I did notice was he was freshly showered. He had also shot one or two films previously that day.

The director told me the first position. The guy was going to perform oral sex on me. Since he didn't know my name, he wasn't trying to be rude, but kept referring to me as "You." I said, "My name is Dottie."

He said, "Raise your leg. It may not feel good, but people need to see it." It was similar to the magazine shoot, with the photographer directing me.

I felt excited. I was enjoying the sex, believe it or not. The guy was clean, decent-looking, nice to me, and good at what he was doing. What was there not to like? Maybe it was because it was so taboo. Things that are forbidden are usually exciting.

There were several standard positions we had to do. I didn't know that at the time, but I was learning fast. Missionary. Girl on top. Doggie style. Oral. And you had to have all four of those in the loop or you didn't have a complete film. It was basically understood you had to have four positions in each sex scene.

Ken had totally left my head, but then I happened to glance over and he seemed to be extremely excited. For a second, I wondered if he would suddenly bolt in and deck the guy, but instead, he was really into watching me have sex with someone else. I didn't know what to make of that or how it made me feel. I turned back to look at the person I was working with because that's what I was being paid to do.

The guy ejaculated on my face. I wasn't real excited about that part, even though I had seen it before on loops and had been told beforehand what to expect. It never bothered me to watch it, but since this was the first time it happened to me—ever—it kind of flipped me out. Actually, I thought it was pretty disgusting.

Afterwards, there was small talk between me and my co-star. "Nice to meet you. Nice to work with you. Hope to see you again." Blah-blah-blah-blah-blah. No different than if I'd just worked a shift at McDonald's with a new fry cook.

I looked at the director and said, "Do you mind if I take a shower?" He gave me some clean towels. I took my shower all the while thinking, "Not bad. Four hundred bucks for an hour and a half. *And* I got laid. Got laid, got paid. Win-win." It didn't bother me, even with the cumshot.

Maybe it was because Ken was so into it. It also didn't hurt that the director and the actor were cool and treated me nicely. There was no one around to put a damper on things. If some church lady burst in and screamed, "Heathen!" I might have felt differently, but that wasn't the case.

We had no plans to remain in Baltimore, but we stayed later than we'd expected because of the shoot. I was ravenous after ninety minutes of steady sex, so we got a hotel room, went out to eat, and then went back to the room.

Ken was all over me like white on rice. He was hornier than hell. I thought, "This is fabulous. He's so into me sexually." But as we were having sex, he started talking dirty to me.

"Did you like that guy having his cock in your face? Did you like him fucking you from behind?"

I never had anyone talk dirty to me before. Since it was a silent loop, even the porn actor didn't do that. Ken kind of freaked me out. I'd had sex with a total stranger that day, while being filmed by another total stranger, while being watched by Ken, yet it was Ken talking dirty to me that made me uncomfortable. I'd been able to compartmentalize the sex on camera, but expected more from the guy I took to bed in private.

I lost my virginity to Frank. Ken was my next lover. The third man I had sex with was a total stranger and it was on camera. Each time, it had been my own sober decision. I was good with that.

16

The Morning After

I **DIDN'T EXPECT PORN** to be a long-term career move. Let's just say I'd crossed it off my bucket list. I thought it could be a way of making money if I ever left Ken again, but since I wasn't exactly racing out the door from him for any reason right then, I figured it was just a one shot and done deal.

I thought the movie might be popular for a few weeks and that was it, because there were always new movies coming out. I didn't give it that much thought at all. It wasn't even a full-length movie like *Deep Throat* or something like that. It was just a loop—it lasted about twenty minutes or so. Low budget, no plot, no dialogue, two actors, one set. Dime a dozen.

Ken called the store and there was trouble brewing again with the police department—the same old deal with the bondage and fetish films. We had to get back because none of the employees knew what to do since the cops were threatening to arrest them. The part-time help got scared and even locked up three of the stores.

Meanwhile, the 8mm film I shot had to be edited, packaged, mass-produced, sent out to distributors, and then to the stores. I knew it was going to be on the market, but it would take at least two months or more to actually be released. Unbeknownst to me, the distributors from California who owned the rights to the film got the footage and had it developed. They were flipping out and calling the warehouse in Baltimore asking who the blonde girl was. They wanted more film. The Baltimore dude was calling Ken, who was speaking on my behalf without my knowledge.

Things began to get a little strange with Ken. He started talking dirtier to me in bed and asking me what my fantasies were. It never occurred to me to *have* fantasies back then. Sexually, I was very conventional. Even what I did in the movie was pretty straightforward and not a lot different than what most couples did in their bedrooms every night. No ponies, clowns, or Shriners.

Seeing the bookstores were a sinking ship, Ken suddenly asked me, "How do you feel about moving to California?"

"Fine, I've never been to California before."

It sounded exciting so we just up and moved. He had a partner I didn't know about and I believe he sold the stores to him. We packed up our belongings, put them in a U-Haul truck, and traveled across country.

When we arrived in California, there were free newspapers all over the place in those stands on the street. They have those ads you always see for nude modeling. Ken picked up one of them and said, "Oh, look. How do you feel about checking it out?"

I'd already checked it out, in Vegas, so there was nothing new about this suggestion. I knew I could do it. It was more a question of how badly did we need the money and was I again in the mood.

He kept pressing. "I think you can make a big name for yourself."

We followed the ad to an agency headed by Bill Margold, who would one day become one of the major behind-the-scenes movers and shakers in the adult film biz and a member of every adult Hall of Fame ever to exist. I was so excited to see Hollywood and Vine until I saw it was a freak show, a conglomeration of strangeness. There were bizarre-looking street types walking around in the strangest outfits. Stepping into Bill's small, cluttered, ratty-looking office in an old building on Hollywood Boulevard, I said to myself, "Oh my God. This is supposed to be glamorous Hollywood?!"

Bill had reddish-brown hair and at the time was thin and very pale, which I found extremely odd for someone who lived in Southern California. He wore black horn-rimmed glasses with some sort of Hawaiian print shirt that he still wears today. He wasn't a particularly neat person, although he was pleasant enough.

After talking to him a few minutes, he said, "Okay, stand up and take your clothes off."

I said, "Excuse me, why should I?"

"You might as well get used to people telling you to get naked," he responded.

I thought there could have been a better way to treat a strange lady from out of town than "Okay, get naked." It wasn't the request that was shocking, but the presentation. I took my clothes off anyway and he told me to turn around. Bill exclaimed, "Wow, that's the best body I've seen in Hollywood since Monroe!" He immediately said I would be the next big thing in the adult business.

Imagine that.

Informing me he would send me on calls for some still photos, he advised that I shouldn't get burned out by doing every photo shoot and film that came my way. I had absolutely no idea this was a life-changing moment.

There was one person in particular he wanted to send me to. Bill believed he was "the best in the business." It was Ron Raffaelli. Ron, in fact, was already a legend, acting as Jimi Hendrix's personal photographer. He would eventually do tons of rock album covers, erotic art, and have his works displayed in major exhibitions.

Bill picked up the phone and said, "Ron, I have a girl you just have to shoot." And just like that I was whisked away.

Ron was really strange. He was very tall, thin, and even paler than Bill Margold. I went from one really pale Californian to another and thought, "Is there something I'm missing here?" They all had jailhouse complexions like they hadn't seen daylight in twenty years.

Ron was very much an egghead. Very intellectual. Smart and sweet, actually. He listened to the same type of music I liked at the time: Pink Floyd, Jethro Tull, and the Rolling Stones.

Living in a huge loft with a lot of photo equipment, it was like walking into a photo store. I was extremely impressed with his gear and figured he was really big time.

Showing me a bunch of his work, I loved it and realized he truly was a world-class talent. He told me he would take some test shots I could use in my composite book. I was trying to act all sophisticated, but had no idea what a composite book was. He said, "I like the way you're dressed." I had on a pair of chocolate brown silk pants that were slit down the side and tied in a knot around my ankle. It was like a pair of *I Dream of Jeanie* pants. My silk blouse was cream and beige. I figured this guy is a nude photographer, so I started to take my blouse off.

He said, "No, no…I want to shoot you with your clothes on."

Now I was really confused.

He wanted mostly head shots and I didn't know why other than I was going to have this "composite book," which I was still too embarrassed to ask about. When we were finished, he said he simply wanted to see how comfortable I was in front of a camera. And I was *extremely* comfortable in front of him. Ron was so easy to work with. When he got a good shot he was very excited and vocal. He gave good directions. "Look over your shoulder." He knew what he wanted and how to get the best out of a model.

All in all it was a wonderful day and I walked out very excited. Ron made me feel beautiful and I knew he'd create art with his shots. I was thinking, "Dang, this could be a lot of fun. And I get paid to do it."

I never considered I would be the next big adult star, or even a star at all. Although by now I knew I wasn't an ugly girl, I was still slow to come around to understanding how men really viewed me. Deep inside, I was still the tall, muscular girl who pulled down rebounds. The "pretty-pretty girls" were still somewhere else across the room. I wasn't one of them, at least in my own mind. It wasn't like I needed validation from people like Bill and Ron in order to pump up my self-esteem. I was secure in who I was as a person. I felt if you were clean and took pride in your appearance, even if you weren't born a genetic beauty you had every reason to hold your head with pride, which I did.

I figured this was still just something to do, a rest stop in life for a week, a month, a year maybe. I could make a decent living until Ken found something else to do. But I had no idea he had already technically become my manager.

17

Seka Is Born

RON WAS VERY PLEASED with the shoot and called me back wanting to do more for him. But now it was for pay. And the pay was real good.

He did a lot of photo shoots for *Puritan Magazine*, which also had a line of 8mm films, so Ron asked me to do both. I didn't realize it, but I was in the midst of the beginning of my career.

I was on the set of one of my earliest loops when I was handed a model release to fill out. Hungry and tired, I was anxious to get out of there and was zipping through it until I read the letters "AKA."

"What's this?"

"What name do you want to be known as?"

I knew in this business using my real name was out of the question. I thought for a few seconds. For some odd reason, I flashed back to when I had briefly moved to Vegas with Frank. Frank loved his gambling and was always "looking for work" but never managed to find any. Making matters even worse, he asked me to tell people I was his sister, because the big shots wouldn't find you as attractive and hire you at the hotels and casinos if they thought you were attached. I truly believed he wanted me to support him.

We were living in a one-room apartment near the Sands. It was back when the Sands was really the Sands. The person who owned our apartment complex was a casino pit boss. He took a fancy to me because I was young, pretty, blonde, and all that good stuff. He had a live-in girlfriend who became a friend of mine. Either Swedish or Yugoslavian, she was a stunningly beautiful girl with natural platinum blonde hair, big blue eyes, a great body, and a wonderful personality to match. She was all that and a bag of chips with salsa on the side. The landlord tried getting the three of us into a ménage a trois, which made me flip out because I hadn't done a movie yet and my real sex life was completely conventional. The idea of having sex with a girl or three people was just too much for me at the time. The vibe I got was he only cared about her looks and used her to lure people into his web.

Her name was Seka.

Being exposed to someone like her was so exotic; she made a great impression on me. I was a barefoot hick at the time. It was probably the first time I even met a girl born in another country.

The vision of this girl with the exotic name stuck in my head. As I sat on the set trying to think up a catchy stage name, for some reason I blurted out, "Seka."

The guy asked innocently enough, "How do you spell it?"

"S-E-K-A. It's short, simple, it's a four letter word, and considering the business I'm in, I think that's appropriate."

He just looked at me. "No last name?"

"No. Just Seka. Like I said, four letters and nothing more."

I watched him jot it down and I immediately knew I had something. I don't remember if I knew anyone else at the time using just a one-word name. Cher might have just started moving in that direction at the time; I don't recall. Madonna was still wearing a training bra. Ironically, the gestation period was about nine months from the time I met my inspiration to when I made my first movie.

I had given birth to "Seka."

And to this day I wonder whatever happened to my beautiful muse.

18

The Platinum Princess

I BEGAN LIFE AS A BRUNETTE and then went to the local beauty salon as a teenager with the intention of getting some frosting—highlights—and they pulled too much hair through the holes in the plastic net they place on your head and ended up as a total blonde. It was an accident, but because of it I won my high school beauty pageant and based on that decided to keep the same look. It was a sandy, beach girl kind of blonde—not very unique, but it looked nice and I adjusted to a life of people referring to me as "the blonde girl," which took some getting used to.

Sometimes cash was tight or I simply didn't make time to go to a salon to keep up with the natural darkening of my hair, so I'd buy a bottle of dye off the nearest grocery store shelf and do it myself in the sink. No big deal.

Once I began doing photo shoots as well as movies, I figured I should make sure the "carpet matched the drapes," as they say. I'd put some of the dye on my pubic region so I wouldn't have blond hair up top and a dark brown bush below. I'd seen enough of that on the loops I saw back in Ken's store and I thought it looked ridiculous.

While I was down there, I would give myself a nice bikini trim. Some of the photo work required me to be in bikini bottoms and I didn't want some big panty afro sticking out and looking gross. This was all part of how I felt about the material I sold in the store. There is a right way and a wrong way to do everything, and if you're going to do erotica, make it sexy, make it nice. Look good.

One day I was scheduled to do a loop. It was in this motel in L.A. that was commonly used to film pornos. Everyone knew about the place and if you watch enough films from the late seventies, you'll see the same damn furniture, carpet, drapes, and bedspread over and over again. The Sahara, I believe it was called, on Hollywood Boulevard. In fact, the motel was even featured in an A-list Hollywood movie called *Hardcore* with George C. Scott.

George C. Scott was a wonderfully talented actor, but the only other person I tip my hat to on that movie was the location manager, who found our motel. Other than that, *Hardcore* represented exactly what Middle America wanted to think about porn. Everyone in the business was lured away from their wonderful families, drugged, forced to perform heinous acts against their will, and then murdered by a guy in a black leather mask in a snuff film. I am living proof none of that ever happened. In every snuff film I ever made, the guy in the leather mask missed. Ha! But seriously, all that stuff is bullshit, yet it's the tale America wants to believe in order to sleep well at night, so Hollywood keeps accommodating them by making movie after movie spinning that same, tired yarn about how no one makes adult films willingly and we all get murdered.

Anyway, I got to the set early so I could get ready right there. I mean, it *was* a working motel, so they had a full bath and shower. My hair needed touching up, so I brought along the dye to do it.

I don't know if I got the wrong stuff in my haste, I left it in too long, whatever. All I know is when I rinsed it out, it wasn't normal blonde. It was white. Platinum. From the roots to the tips, without a hint of any other color anywhere.

I screamed! I looked in the mirror and didn't recognize the girl looking back. I thought for sure they'd fire me for looking like such a freak.

When the cast and crew got there, every jaw dropped. God, I knew I'd really blown it this time. No one made a sound. Finally, someone said, "Wow. Cool." I still didn't know what to make of it. Wow, cool, good? Wow, cool, bad?

We started to work. No one could take their eyes off me. As the female in the scene, that's not uncommon, but this was more than usual. It was freaking me out. I figured I'd never work again.

In addition to the platinum blond hair, I always shaved my eyebrows. Oddly enough, even though my natural hair color is almost black, my eyebrows are very light-colored and fine. I also don't have a lot of body hair, and what I do have is rather blond—again despite not being a blonde. I think some of it has to do with my being a sun worshipper, but even on my ass and other areas that rarely get sun, what little tiny hairs are there are extremely light.

I shaved my eyebrows because it was too hard to see them to pluck them properly. Then I'd fill it in with an eyebrow pencil. Shaving them off allowed me total freedom in shaping them any way I wanted, so I made them as perfect as I could—although I wasn't always successful, in my own humble opinion. I look at some of the pictures taken of me and I scream, "I look like Gloria Swanson or Joan Crawford!" It was such a severe look, like I was frightened or something. Again, I thought I'd blown it. I was simply trying to compensate for my natural flaws, as I saw them to be.

After I'd done a few movies, some director came up with the idea that I completely shave my pussy. With my girl-scaping and dyeing, I never looked like I had much bush down there as it was, certainly nowhere near as much as most of the other girls of the era. But this was a whole new thing for me and I think they even put it in the script. The shaving itself may have ended up on film. I can't say for sure because I hardly ever watched those things once I filmed them, but that's another story.

So part of my look, literally from the start, involved me being either closely shaved and then dyed, or completely shaven. For an era that was otherwise known for big, dark bushes on both men and women, I was different. I liked that part of the look. I still like it today. I don't think everyone has to be shaved and it's a pain in the ass to keep up with, but it beats having a monstrous chia pet down yonder.

Today, everybody in porn is shaved like a newborn baby. Some have credited me with starting the whole trend, but I can't say for sure I had much to do with it. I'll leave that argument for the film historians. But to me, being trimmed down there even feels better. More sensitive. And guys seem to like it, which is an opinion supported by all the movie girls today being totally waxed and shaven.

After that scene that day, I figured I was done for in the business. Little did I know the opposite was true. Industry people screened it and said, "Oh my god! Look at that hair, those brows, that pussy, that makeup (I always wore makeup, even during this hippy-era when lots of girls were going with the "natural" no-makeup look)!" And, of course, "Those tits!" I'm a naturally large-breasted girl. So were most of the women in my family. Today, any girl can go out and buy herself big bazoongas, but back then all the girls in erotica were natural. Some were big, some were small, and some were in-between, but we were what we were. I was one of the big-breasted ones, and deep down, most men never lose that infantile breast fixation.

After my dyeing accident, no girl in XXX looked like me—none. My look was dramatic, glamorous, and bold. While other girls looked like the girl next door, I looked like…I don't know *what* the hell I looked like, which scared the living crap out of me. But I quickly learned it sent shock-waves throughout the business. *Everyone* passed that film around and began asking about me. Ken's phone—not my phone, but Ken's—began ringing off the hook. This look, which was as much accident as on purpose, got me more bookings than I could handle. The "Platinum Princess of Porn" was born.

19

Swinging

KEN WAS ALWAYS THERE while I was filming and it was uncomfortable because he was always lurking. The photographers and movie guys didn't like to have the boyfriends on the set because the girls didn't like it, but he'd still sit through the entire shoot, clearly getting off on it. I didn't completely mind him being there because I really didn't trust anyone else. I thought he would protect me if anyone tried to do something to me that I didn't want done. They agreed to let him stay on the set to appease me.

Swinging was starting to be a big thing in mainstream society and Ken pressured me to try it. This had nothing to do with the movie business; it was just something that was going on between couples all over America.

Quite frankly, after having sex all day on the set, I didn't want to have it at night. I was also getting tired of Ken always talking about my on-set exploits while we were in bed the night after a shoot. He was all turned on, but I was not only tuckered out, I was skeeved out that he wanted to turn our bedroom into a live sex show.

For me, sex was one way on film, another way with a lover in private. They talk about that whole "life imitates art" thing. I had no desire to "make love like a porn star" at home. I like to cuddle. I like to be romantic, more than graphic. I like the lights off most times, which you can't do on a movie set unless you film with night-vision goggles.

Ken was different. Ken watched the porn, and then wanted to *be* the porn—with me, the real life porn star! When was I ever going to get a break?! I didn't want to be on stage all the time, performing all the time, talking dirty all the time. That stuff isn't love; it's lust. Lust is fine; lust is great. But what is life without love?

In the adult biz, we'd heard about swinging for quite a while. But then the dams burst open and it was being written about in almost every mainstream newspaper and magazine in America. It became all Ken would talk about.

After reading some stuff on this new lifestyle, I figured, "What the hell? I can meet some interesting people. I won't do anything I don't want to." And maybe it would get him off my back.

It was the days of Plato's Retreat. But in California they had swing parties in people's homes. The first time I went it was in a big, gorgeous house in the suburbs of Los Angeles. There were probably sixty to seventy people there. They were upper middle class and a mix of all races, creeds, and colors. My reaction was like, "Oh my God, don't these people have any modesty?" This, coming from me, the porn star! But I always had that separation between work and play. Furthermore, I wasn't an actual star yet. My first party was after only being in California a very short time.

There were fully clothed and naked people throughout the house from the second I walked in. There were skinny people, heavy people, well-built folk—it was a cornucopia of anything you could imagine. People were talking, swimming, eating, and oh yes, having sex.

It was at this private swing party that I saw two women together for the first time, and it didn't shock me. In fact, I was intrigued by watching them. Yes, I'd seen it on film, but with the little experience I had making movies at the time, I assumed the lesbian scenes were just actors doing their jobs. But these ladies were clearly having a helluva good time. To top it off, there was a circle of people around them watching, like a peanut gallery. And it sure didn't seem to bother them.

Being in the business, I had become far more comfortable around sex and nudity, but I still felt uneasy here and didn't know what to say or do. There was no script, no director! I didn't want to talk to anyone and chose to just sit, watch, and decide if I wanted to participate or not.

I had never been exposed to something like this before. I actually had a hard time looking people in the eye, because the first thing you want to do is look at their crotch when they're naked and it's hard to avoid that. It was a lot of information to take in all at once. Quite overwhelming.

Ken suggested we walk towards the back and see what was going on. There were bedrooms with nothing else in the room except mattresses with folks furiously going at it. I thought, "My God, this is a fuck fest." It was a real, live porn movie, except expanded and without cameras, spilling out all over a huge house, all at once. It made my head spin. The loops I was shooting were nothing like this.

Ken wanted to go into one of the rooms and I really was not comfortable doing that. He was quite excited, so I told him, "If you want to go, then go." I was tired. I didn't want to have sex. I'd just come off a film shoot two days earlier. I was exhausted. I figured if he got off with someone else, at least I wouldn't have to do it with him later that evening.

There was a little patio outside the dining room area leading to a pool and a Jacuzzi. People were hanging around in bathing suits. Decent music was playing. I was hitting the free buffet, more interested in eating and drinking than fucking and sucking.

A couple came up to me and started talking. They were probably in their mid to late thirties. Both were a little heavyset, he more than she. They just sat down and chatted with me. No pressure. No nothing. I was enjoying the conversation with these very nice people. His name was Jack and she was June. She was an executive at a bank and he owned his own business. I found it interesting that swingers seemed to come from every walk of life.

An hour or so passed. In the meantime, my boyfriend was in another room having sex with someone and it didn't bother me at all. In fact, I wasn't even enjoying sex with him that much anymore because it felt like it wasn't with me, but rather about what I had done on set. Ken no longer made love to Dottie; he just fucked Seka.

Ken suddenly came walking out. He was naked, which kind of surprised me. I said, "If you're done, put your clothes on."

He looked at me and asked, "Are you okay?"

"Everything's fine." I introduced him to Jack and June and soon after I said, "Do you mind if we go? I'm really tired."

We went back to the hotel where we were staying and he asked me what I thought about the whole thing. I said, "It was interesting. But I don't know if I'd feel comfortable having sex there." I told him I noticed the female couples were having so much fun and he brought up that they might ask me to do that in a film one day. I thought, "How bad could that be?"

He started to get in bed and it occurred to me he'd just been with someone else and God knows how many others so I said, "Go take a shower." When he came back to bed he started to try to play around with me and I responded, "Look, I'm really tired. I'm not in the mood for this," and I went to sleep.

In the morning we got up, took the dogs out, and over breakfast I looked at him and asked, "We've been out here a couple of weeks. Are we staying?" It wasn't easy living out of hotels with two dogs and all our crap.

He found us a place in Diamond Bar in Pomona County. We go to the house and it's in a great looking neighborhood. I thought it had to be really expensive. It had a circular driveway with iron gates and a pool. Two huge front doors opened at the same time leading into a large foyer and staircase. There were a couple of steps into the living room. Then there was a dining room area and sliding glass doors that led to a pool and Jacuzzi.

I was like a kid at Christmas. To me, it was a mansion. I'd never seen anything that was so elegant. But in my awe and immaturity, I never asked how the hell we could ever afford anything like this. I didn't quite have a handle on how much I was making doing loops and posing for stills. Ken wasn't really doing anything except "managing" me. Meanwhile, it was Bill Margold who was getting me the actual gigs, so I didn't really understand where Ken came in at all. I didn't know if he had savings from the stores back east or what, but I didn't ask enough questions and I should have. In the meantime, I wasn't about to look a gift horse in the mouth.

Every Sunday morning, I had mimosas and shrimp in the Jacuzzi and read the newspaper. That was heaven to me. What I would come to discover was not only was I paying for most of this, Ken chose it because he knew companies were paying location fees for photo shoots and movies, and he had planned from day one to pocket that money on shoots at our house. I had no idea whatsoever. I was looking at it as my home, while he was thinking of it as a business. Since I didn't have to travel to a set in the morning, I didn't mind doing some of my shoots there. Still, I didn't realize I was getting screwed in more ways than one.

I thought I had placated Ken by going to that one swing party. Boy, was I wrong. Once he'd gotten a taste of it, he wanted to go again and again and again. The thing is, single guys were rarely allowed in, so he needed me as his ticket, and that's exactly how I felt—I was nothing but a ticket. It also didn't hurt that I was attractive. Even if I wasn't participating, I made Ken look good by being his date. It's the same thing in everyday life. A guy walks into a bar with a mousy-looking woman and no one notices him. He walks in with a stunner and all the girls want to snatch him up, figuring he must be something special.

I tried to find ways of entertaining myself, but I was never really into it. It was Ken's thing, he was my guy—despite there being little real love between us—so I went along. It was like being a football widow. Even if you hate the game, you pull on his favorite team's jersey, go to a few games, and try to amuse yourself. I know, most women would not have done this for their man, but I was in the sex business, so it was less odd for me than most other women. But it wasn't for me, it was all for him.

Me and Ken in Vegas.

My first agent, Bill Margold.

Me and Ken.

Swinging with Ken at the original Plato's Retreat (his idea, not mine).

20

Miss Swedish Erotica

THERE WERE LOOPS AND THERE WERE FEATURES. Only the biggest stars got to do features. On the other hand, there were a lot more loops being done than features, so lots of A-List porn stars did loops as well, in between features. The whole thing was like baseball. You began in the rookie leagues, then moved up to the minor leagues, and finally the majors—except even those in the majors still played in the high minors now and then just to make ends meet.

Loops were often compiled together into a sort of feature, kind of like a mix tape. For that reason, the same scene might be used not only in one compilation, but in any number of compilations. That's why it's a joke when porn actors try to count how many movies they've been in. You do one scene and it ends up in twenty different compilations. Is that one film or twenty? Worse yet, we never got paid for the multiple times a scene was used. We'd get paid for a day's work and that was it. Sometimes we'd complain and get suckered into making a deal for "something on the back end," which was a total joke. We'd be promised some sort of percentage or something down the line, but none of us ever saw a dime. We got what we got paid for that one day's work and not a penny more, even if that scene was used a million times, forever and ever, amen.

The top name in loops was Swedish Erotica. They were the big time, the place where even the features actors continued to work even after they'd become big stars.

Soon Swedish Erotica came calling for me, and I completely flipped out. Unlike most new girls who came on the adult scene, my time spent working in Ken's stores taught me who was who in the business. When I went to meet with them I thought, "Damn, I can really make a living at this. If these guys are here, I've arrived."

97

We met, we hit it off, and I was the new Swedish Erotica Girl. Of course, there were a lot of Swedish Erotica girls, but now I was part of their stable of players. Their loops were probably the most popular in the adult book stores, and their compilations were spliced together and ran as if they were features in adult movie theaters—a thing of the past from back in the days before home video. And once home video came around, their compilation tapes were always top sellers—not that I saw any financial benefit.

I was doing scenes constantly. It all became more comfortable and natural for me. I began to see some of the same faces both in front of and behind the camera, which made me less apprehensive when I'd show up for a day at work. And it was work. For a twenty-minute scene, I'd be there all day long, doing this, doing that. Waiting, lots of waiting, just like in a mainstream movie.

Whenever I walked into a room, all eyes were on me. This crazy, accidental look of mine was turning heads. It made me very self-conscious, but I used that to my advantage. Do I shock you? Good. It puts you on your heels and me in a position of strength. I became less and less of a wallflower. I wouldn't call myself a diva, but if something was way out of line, I wasn't afraid to say so—politely and professionally—and it usually got fixed. The bedspread was dirty—get me a clean one. I needed a cigarette break—I asked and I got one. Pretty basic stuff that professional, polite parties should be able to work out without a big fuss, which was not always the case between filmmakers and actors. Some of the girls were treated like meat and it continued because they accepted it. I didn't. I liked the money I was making and the attention I was being given, but I wasn't really thinking long term. It was good for now, but if they fired me, I'd do something else tomorrow. It never occurred to me that if I pissed someone off I'd be lying in a gutter, begging for spare change. I always seemed able to bounce from one thing to another. I may not have been a career girl in the classic sense, but that actually worked to my advantage. Someone who wanted to be an accountant would be more worried that if they had a blow-out with a boss they'd not only lose their job, they might never work as an accountant again. Me, I had no problem changing what I wrote on an application when it asked for "occupation." I was whatever I was doing at that moment. Work of some kind was everywhere for a person willing to do it.

Swedish Erotica had a certain image. For whatever reason, they wanted the girls in their scenes to wear lacy scarves. It was weird, but as it was explained to me, they wanted customers to see that scarf in a scene and make an immediate association in their head, "Oh, a scarf. This is Swedish Erotica." It was like a hood ornament on a car: every car had its own design and it helped you know what kind of car it was.

Swedish Erotica thought that scarves were classy. I thought they were itchy and a pain in the ass to wear. I mean, in real life, who wears a scarf to bed? I can see keeping some article of clothing on—usually sweat socks. Ha! But even to be sexy, there are a lot cooler things to wear, like silky lingerie. But that was their signature and for as much as I asked for things here and there, removing the scarf was one thing on which they would not negotiate.

The more loops I did for Swedish Erotica, the more I became personally associated with scarves. People started to forget all the other girls in their loops who wore them, too. But I was doing so many scenes for them, I started being known in the industry and even among the fans as Miss Swedish Erotica. At one point, Swedish Erotica even gave me that title officially, like it was another beauty contest I had won. It was all good. They'd invite me to public appearances and things and introduce me as Miss Swedish Erotica, just like when I was Miss Hopewell Virginia. I don't know how they came up with it. I don't believe there was any official voting of any sort. It was a publicity stunt, which flattered me because they were saying, essentially, that I was now the face of their franchise. I was moving up in the world.

But the scarves—those damn scarves. I hated them. You'd go to a shoot and they'd have them lying around everywhere and would just throw one at me or the other girls. They'd been lying on the floor—dirty, dusty, covered in cum and whatever. They made me want to retch. As soon as I was handed one, I'd go to the bathroom and hand-wash it, then blow it dry before I'd let it touch my skin; otherwise I thought I was going to pick up some kind of disease. It was like being asked to wear someone else's skanky underwear that was just fished out of a dumpster. They never washed those things on their own. It wasn't like they were fancy or expensive or anything. For a buck or two they could have given us brand new ones for every scene; but no, they recycled them. Makeup, sweat, and cum, lots of dried cum. Maybe it was more noticeable when I wore one in a scene because mine were nice and clean and fluffy. I can be pretty anal sometimes. I may have been raised poor, but we were always big on cleanliness.

One time I was doing a phone-in radio appearance. I put my phone on speaker and started doing housework. When the station called, the first thing they asked me on the air was, "So, Seka, what are you doing right now," expecting some sort of sexy answer. I, being slow on the uptake, opted for honesty. "I'm steam-cleaning my toilet right now." They laughed hysterically and thought I was being funny. I wasn't. Steam-cleaning toilets and hand-washing scarves: that's how I roll.

People were recognizing the platinum blonde from all the scenes I was doing, but especially the Swedish Erotica ones wearing the scarf. Even once I moved up to features, I continued to do Swedish Erotica scenes, except now I was doing them with all the top stars. I became the franchise. And as for the scarves? As time went by, I started to get fan mail and stuff and realized how much the scarves stayed in people's minds, so I began packing mine away after I'd used one. Those things are worth a pretty penny to fans today, and I've still got some.

21

The A List

AROUND THIS TIME, Bill Margold called us to ask about doing a feature-length film. It was *Dracula Sucks* starring John Holmes, Serena, Jamie Gillis, John Leslie, and Annette Haven. I thought, "My God, I can't work with those people. They're movie stars!" And I was *certainly* intimidated to work with John Holmes and his thirteen inches. But the pay for full-length feature movies was a lot better than the loops I was doing and I was about to meet my idols.

The stars of the upcoming film *Dracula Sucks* were the A-List of adult actors of that era. I was so excited and nervous. Annette Haven was one of the most beautiful women of the day, and there was something awfully alluring about Serena, too. Jamie Gillis was dead sexy. I knew who John Leslie was but wasn't sure if I liked him or not. He was a nice looking guy but there was something cold about him. John Holmes looked to me like he would be really pleasant, but not only was he the biggest *name* in adult films, he was literally the <u>biggest</u> in the business. I actually felt shy about seeing his penis.

I was told I'd be working with Jamie and Holmes and Serena. I was going to play the part of the nurse and it followed the same plot any Dracula story would. But I was also terrified because I would have to speak lines for the first time, and figured these veterans would blow me out of the water. In the loops, I'd get to improv a few basic non-sexual lines like, "Come on in," and "Why don't we just remove those uncomfortable clothes." In a feature, I'd be expected to do much more, and to emote and get into a character I would have to sustain over numerous scenes. I just didn't see myself as an actress. And to this day I'll say I'm not an actress. I'm a performer, but no actress.

We were in Hollywood when we got the script and met a bunch of the crew and supporting cast in a parking lot. It was just a portion of the script actually, as they hadn't finished writing it. We were told what day and time to be back at the parking lot because we weren't informed of the location due to police busts at the time. Bill Margold said, "Pack for a week, because you're going to stay for a while."

The location was way, way out in the middle of the desert. It was like being nowhere. Just a small town with a Motel Six. And it was cold as hell. It was actually an old castle in Calabasas, California. I checked into the motel with Ken, had dinner, and went to bed. We had a 5:30 a.m. call for make-up and wardrobe.

The idea of waking up and having someone make me glamorous made me think I'd arrived in Hollywood. I was so excited I could hardly sleep. Getting up, I had some breakfast and went to the set. We sort of caravanned along a dirt road to a place that truly looked like Dracula's castle. The fog was starting to lift in the mountains and the castle was surrounded by it. The excitement of doing my first movie probably had something to do with my heightened sensations, and I felt a chill go down my spine.

When we walked into the castle there was this long, stone staircase leading up to two huge double wooden doors that opened out. The whole inside was stone. There were huge fireplaces. It was larger than life with twenty-foot ceilings. Damp and cold, it also smelled kind of old and musty. The set really was scary. I actually expected Dracula to walk out.

Serena, Annette, Jamie, John Leslie, and John Holmes were already staying there, as they were the stars. They got the comfortable place to stay and the good food, while Ken and I were at the Motel Six. Annette and Serena both wore long flowing robes when I met them and I thought, "Wow, movie stars."

Nobody knew me, but Serena said hello. Annette, however, threw her nose up in the air and walked off without saying anything. I figured she wasn't fully awake. Regardless, she seemed just as beautiful the first thing in the morning as on screen.

The guys were having breakfast and turned around and looked at me. All three of them were staring and I felt uncomfortable. "There's fresh meat in town," I imagined them thinking. Jamie got up, though, and introduced himself. He seemed the most interesting of the trio. He was very polite and always has been.

Seemingly out of nowhere, tons of people appeared. The castle was suddenly buzzing with movement. Quickly ushered into wardrobe and makeup, I felt a rush of anticipation and nervous energy. Since I was playing the nurse, I was handed a nurse's outfit that was supposedly worn in Dracula's day. I had brown and white saddle shoes which I thought were far from sexy.

They gave me the script, telling me to learn my lines. I was notified they'd be ready to shoot in "a little while," but a little while turned out to be three or four hours. I figured, "Fine. I'll learn my lines." I assumed wrongly we'd be shooting the story in order. In loops, there was only one scene, so this whole deal put me completely out of my comfort zone. In spite of being confused, I just rolled with it.

There's a scene where the nurse walks in on one of the doctors, played by John Leslie, while he's doing something with another female. I don't remember exactly what they were up to. The script did not say anything about me having sex with his character. But about an hour before shooting, John Leslie approached me and walked us through this whole scene he'd just come up with. He wanted to be very rough and concluded by stating, "Then you'll get down on your knees and give me head."

I said, "That isn't in the script. I'm not going to do you."

The filmmakers wanted to appease him but I told them, "He's not going to smack me and push me around and make me give him head."

He started screaming and said, "What do you know? You're just a dumb kid. You'll never work again."

My feelings were really hurt. I was standing around five or six feet away from him. Everybody was watching because they heard the raised voices. I felt really low, about two inches higher than dirt. I was scared, embarrassed, and angry at the same time. Here was someone I didn't know, screaming at me in front of strangers. And I was new.

I said, "I really don't care if I never work another day in this business. If I have to work with you, I'd rather flip burgers." I took off my shoe, which was heavy, and winged it at his head. I think it missed him by about an inch.

The whole place went dead silent. I just walked off. And I hadn't even done my first scene yet.

He had the most stunned look on his face. I doubt anyone had ever stood up to him before. He was a major star at the time and very demanding. If there was fresh meat, he wanted to be the first to work with her.

Ken just stood there and never said or did anything. I was so mad I didn't even think about him as all this was going on. But what use was he? He'd been on set for all my loops as my "protector." But now that I finally needed protecting, where was he? He was useless.

A lot of the other cast members were going, "Good for you. It's time somebody stood up to him."

The director said, "It'll be okay. We won't let him do anything to hurt you."

I responded angrily. "It doesn't matter. I'll do the scene as written. The scene does not call for it and you're letting him have his way. I'm not working with him. He's an asshole. I won't fuck him."

It took about an hour and a half for Leslie to calm down. He was still complaining about me. He wanted to fuck me. I reminded them, "If that's a requirement, I can leave now."

It was mentally draining to even be in the same room with John Leslie the rest of the day. And it was ever-present in my mind that I was going to have my big scene with big John Holmes. We ended up muddling through the scene with my three lines, which made me more nervous since I was still mad. Even for adult cinema, it wasn't the glamorous Hollywood moment I had envisioned.

Breaking for lunch, they took down the lights and everything. We had already been on the set five hours and it was ultimately going to be a sixteen-hour day with another 5:30 wake-up call the next. By the time I was scheduled to do my sex scene, I was tired, stressed, upset, and generally in a pissy mood.

There was a barn there and they told me we had to head that way. As I was walking over, John Holmes startled me. Putting his arm around my shoulders, he said, "Hi, I'm John. I hear you're the ballsy new broad on the set. Good for you. Somebody needs to smack Leslie in the head."

He was quite nice to me and seemed like a really decent guy. John said, "Let's sit down and talk a little."

He spoke like a teacher would to a student. "Whatever you do, stand your ground. Don't let anybody make you do anything you don't want to do. Above all, demand to be treated with respect."

John Holmes was always very decent to me and respectful. He was nice and polite to everyone. I heard stories he could be terrible as well, but I never saw that side of him. John said, "Why don't we see where we'll be working." He helped me off a tree stump and we walked down to the barn. It was buzzing with people doing light tests and meter readings. Checking for sounds. I had never seen this before in the loops.

He said, "We're going to be working over there." It was just a pile of hay with a wool army jacket on top—not what I would call a pleasing place to have your first sexual experience with John Holmes.

He must have seen the look on my face because he said, "This won't do. It's scratchy, it's smelly, and it's not fitting for a lady. Get something nice for her to lie on."

And they did. They did it very quickly in fact.

John took me to the side and asked, "Do you have any problem with anything in this scene? When you're ready, we'll make the lookie-lous who don't need to be here, leave." He was referring to those not on the crew, who just wanted to see my first scene with him. "If you want to see it, go to the theater and pay your admission," he announced to everyone.

John was very charming.

It was a delight to work with him, a very positive experience. It felt like someone was making love to me. And at that period in my life, it didn't seem like my boyfriend was. Yes, John was huge, but he was gentle and thank God he didn't get hard as a baseball bat. I don't know why that was, but he was certainly hard enough to perform his duties, so everyone was happy, including me.

And John was right. Pay their admission they did. *Dracula Sucks* did very, very well. I was about to become an adult movie star.

22

Inside Seka

I DID SEVERAL LOOPS AFTER THAT, nothing particularly memorable, but I hadn't hit big yet. *Dracula Sucks* had yet to be released, so it was just business as usual.

I still didn't think of adult films as a career, although the work did start pouring in. Meanwhile, things were starting to get tense with Ken because he wasn't really working. He was shooting stills of action on the set and peddling those to the producers of the film. That helped some, but he wasn't the principal photographer and they just used his material as back-up. The directors didn't really want him there and he was becoming an annoyance.

Finally, they decided to put him to work and made him a porno star. I was glad 'cause I figured if someone else was doing him, I didn't have to.

Arthur Morowitz of Video-X-Pix and Distribpix out of New York called to see if I wanted to star in a movie. Video-X was known as one of the biggest in the business and supposedly paid the most and was quite fair with the talent. He had done films like *Inside Jennifer Welles* and *Inside Gloria Leonard*. He specialized in creating star vehicles where a girl's name was right in the title. It was smart marketing, and as I got to know Arthur I came to expect nothing less. People didn't come to see a XXX movie based on the title or topic—they came to see the stars, so Arthur put them front and center.

He offered me a very generous sum of money. He knew my Swedish Erotica compilations were flying off the shelves, and *Dracula Sucks* was about to open as well. He was projecting ahead that I was going to be the next big star. I jumped at the offer.

His concept was a film to be entitled *Inside Seka*. *Inside Seka* became so successful it still sells like mad today.

107

He offered to fly Ken and me to New York, put us up for as long as it took, and shoot the movie there. I think I was more excited about going to New York than anything else.

The storyline was supposed to be about my life with Ken. Everybody thought we were married at the time, but we weren't. Ken told everyone we were married because it kept the hound dogs away from me. I went along with it like everything else this domineering man told me. In the movie, we were portrayed as married and it depicted our supposed swinging lifestyle. Honestly, the proper title should have been *All About Ken* because it depicted his dream life and his fantasies, not mine.

By now we had, in fact, started to go to more swing parties and I did participate. It had become fairly regular because Ken was practically addicted to it and he needed me to get in. A lot of these clubs had pools and Jacuzzis, a grill, steam rooms, and great music. The original Plato's Retreat in the Ansonia Hotel in New York was the most famous. Shortly before opening as a swing club, it was the Continental Baths, a gay cabaret where Bette Midler and her accompanist Barry Manilow got their start. These places were always packed. And it was pre-AIDS—the last relatively safe and unencumbered moment of the free-love era.

The first time I was at Plato's was during the time we were getting the script ready for *Inside Seka*. There had to be several hundred people in this club. There were lockers to put your things. They had a color scheme and every room was a different color. One particular room was very dark with blue lights. And there was nothing but wall-to-wall mattresses. And bodies everywhere. It was one big orgy.

Ken kept pushing me to go in. You didn't even have to introduce yourself. You'd just lie down and start playing with someone or something.

Ken couldn't wait to go off on his own to see how many scenes he could get into. Me, I just kind of closed my eyes and went with it. I wasn't really thinking of anything. Once, as I was nearly dozing, I looked up and there was a really good-looking guy on top of me. I said to myself, "Thank you." At least he was pleasant to look at. The guy was quite good, too, and he really seemed to care about what he was doing. My own boyfriend never really cared—he just wanted to get off and my pleasure was just an afterthought.

It was kind of ironic that this was a good experience. Meanwhile, Ken was in the corner with two women. This made me very happy because I figured he'd be satisfied and I wouldn't have to deal with him myself.

When my guy was done, I got up, took a shower, and got dressed. There was no conversation at all with him, which was okay by me. I figured it wasn't someone I was ever going to see again.

All in all, I wasn't opposed to swinging, but it wasn't something I wanted as a lifestyle. Deep down, I wanted to be with one person. In spite of being in the porn industry, I needed a loving, committed relationship.

Ken was still busy with his pair of ladies so I just got up and went to the main section of Plato's—the action-free area—where people were dressed, half-dressed, and undressed. To me, that was more interesting than the sex.

It was a fascinating group of people. You had doctors, lawyers, and judges—people from all walks of life and from all over the world. You often met nice folk at these events and I had even stayed in touch with June and Jack from my California swing party experience, and we ultimately swung with them.

As far as the sex in my movies, that was just a job. The movies, the swinging, it was all in the context of the era. Women were no longer embarrassed about sex. It was the seventies and everyone was on the Pill. I'd waited until my wedding night—actually *after* my wedding night—to lose my virginity. Now I was in this "open relationship" with a guy who wanted every piece of ass he could find, and encouraged me to do the same. As far as the movies, unlike all these people at Plato's, I was getting paid good money to get into scenes. And it wasn't prostitution either. I was getting paid, the guys were getting paid, and if I didn't like some guy, I didn't have to be with him. I did not feel morally inferior to anyone. I doubt there were many other jobs I could have worked at that point in my life and with my education where I could have made more money. Plus, there was an air of celebrity about it. I never dreamed that would mean anything to me or I would ever be a part of such an enterprise, but it was kinda neat.

It took several days to write the movie—days, not weeks, months, and years like a real movie. The movie wasn't a helluva lot different than my Swedish Erotica stuff. The only through-line was me and Ken in bed, talking about "my" fantasies, as well as our erotic memories, both together as a couple, as well as me without him. I'd talk about a scene and then they'd cut to it, kinda like a talk show host saying, "Do we have a clip? Oh, here it is." Each scene was like a separate loop. There was no other plot. Still, it was hot, and to this day people come up to me and quote certain scenes as being their all-time adult favorites.

There was one scene where I was giving oral sex to three or four guys at the same time. In the script we blurred the line between truth and fiction, as this certainly hadn't happened to me in real life, nor was it a real life fantasy of mine, but I had done similar things in my other movies. In the scene, Ron Jeremy came in and asked if he could do me, too, and I said he should go do himself.

Which he did.

Ron could blow himself. He said, "I'm the cheapest date I can ever have. I can do myself, take myself out to dinner, and not have to deal with anybody." That was Ronnie. Always funny—and formerly flexible.

As far as the movie goes, that was the highlight for me because it was hysterical. I had a guy in each hand and one staring me in the face, and I actually made the director stop filming because I had to see Ron in action. I was too distracted to continue.

One of the other scenes was actually filmed at the real Plato's Retreat. Don't ask me how they got permission to do that, but they did. So if you ever want to see what the real, original Plato's was really like, buy *Inside Seka,* the movie.

We shot the movie and it usually takes about three months to edit and get it ready for release. In the meantime, we went back to California and the guys from Swedish Erotica called again. There was a big summer show in Chicago called the Consumer Electronics Show and it was in June in Chicago and January in Vegas. It was the biggest convention of the year. They wanted me to go and be in their booth and sign autographs for them. It was a four-day show in Chicago. Wow, another big city I'd never been to. They had five hundred pictures for me to sign for four days. I figured I'd never go through that many pictures and they'll be disappointed.

I went through five hundred pictures the first day.

They had to get more pictures printed so I'd have something to sign. I was amazed all these people were fans, since my features were only beginning to dribble out. That was when the light bulb went off:

I'm not getting paid enough money.

For the first time, I realized why everyone put up with Ken being on the set. The adult industry needed me.

Inside Seka was finally released and I loved it and hated it. I loved being the star, the girl whose name was in the title. My ego is no different than anyone else's. Before the movie, no one really knew me or Ken. Now we were celebrities—the Sonny and Cher of porn. Where once we'd been able to attend swing parties and clubs with a bit of anonymity, now everyone knew us and for me, that part was uncomfortable. Everyone wanted a turn with the porn star. Ken was reveling in it. I kept trying to figure how to get the hell away from that scene. Whatever curiosity I'd once had about it was now gone.

What I also hated were the lies. Sure, most PR is lies or exaggerations, but certain things about *Inside Seka* particularly irked me. For one thing, Ken and I are credited as directing it. What?! Neither he nor I could have directed traffic at that point in our lives, let alone a film. Joe Sarno directed that film. But Sarno made a number of well-received soft-core and exploitation films in the sixties, and supposedly considered hard-core "slumming it," so he wouldn't allow his name to be on the film, or so I've been told. Joe had also done the Jennifer Welles film, the Gloria Leonard film, and would do the next film in the series, *Deep Inside Annie Sprinkle*.

Then there was the soundtrack. All porn soundtracks are laughably bad, but *Inside Seka* may have set a new low. I don't know who wrote all the music, but there was a title song that, I suppose, must have been called, "The Ballad of Seka and Ken," because it was one of those "story songs." The lyrics went, "Radford, Virginia. Selling books… ." It was pretty much a musical version of this book. "Seka tried on some sexy clothing. Took some pictures in the raw." Honest-to-God, these are some of the lyrics. They even threw Ken in there somewhere. Painful.

The title song was sung by a friend of Ken's named Kenny Dino, an Elvis impersonator (natch) who sang on a lot of The King's demos, as well as minor recording artist in his own right. Picture my life story, with all the specifics, sung by Elvis, on a bed of bad middle-of-the-road seventies country pop. Yeah, painful.

The rest of the score was all the standard porn clichés. Whenever Ken and I were in bed together, there'd be a kind of classical love theme, and when I got down in all the other scenes we'd have all the typical variations on "boom chicka-wow-wow."

I later discovered the soundtrack was released as a picture disc (this was back when music came on vinyl), with my mug all over it. Despite how I personally felt about the music, it apparently sold well and is now considered quite the collector's item. I may still have one or two copies myself.

Did I know they would be selling a soundtrack? No. Did I ever see a dime from it? No. But since Ken had something to do with Kenny Dino singing on it, I'm sure Ken collected a nice sum of money on the deal.

But worst of all was the postscript—the writing they put on the freeze at the end of the film. It read, "Ken and I have been married for over 6 years. We have spent every single day of our marriage together, never separating once. All the events in the motion picture you have just seen have been true or actual reenacted events of my special fantasies—Seka."

As I said, we were never married. But it was one thing to say it around the set in order to keep guys from hitting on me and to explain Ken hanging around all the time. Now it seemed more to service Ken's need to be a star, too, and glom onto me for as long as this ride was going.

The other thing was the unoriginality. In January of 1980, Paul McCartney was arrested in Japan for carrying pot. He and his wife Linda had a wonderful, storybook marriage, and it was stated in all the news reports that the nights Paul spent in jail in Japan were the only nights they ever were apart in their entire marriage. *Inside Seka* was being edited less than a year later. Coincidence? I think not. Ken thought he'd make us out to be the Paul and Linda McCartney of porn. As if.

In our case, the "never separating once," part was almost true, but in an insidious way. Ken wanted to answer every phone call. Ken always had to be the one to get the mail and open it first. If Ken was out, I might get to do those things and who knows what I'd find. So Ken never left my side because he was hiding things and didn't want me to know what was going on. If I got away from him, someone might clue me in on how he was screwing with my finances. I've heard some girls complain about "living like a prisoner." It wasn't quite like that. Ken never stopped me from going anywhere or doing anything. He just tagged after me like a fly that wouldn't leave me alone. He wasn't abusive; he just drove me batty.

When *Inside Seka* came out, I officially became a porn star—the top of the A-List, the girl whose name alone could open a film. It was the beginning of my career and soon to be the end of Ken.

"The Platinum Princess" look,
from "Inside Seka", 1981.

Me and Ken, the "Paul and
Linda McCartney of Porn".
As if.

At the height of my fame.

With 1980's idea of a hot, young, bad boy, Tony Mansfield.

I've got everything well in hand with Tony Mansfield and Richard Bolla.

A young Ron Jeremy about to fellate himself.

Filming inside the real, original Plato's Retreat.

Getting romantic with Ron Hudd.

A little girl/girl action with Merle Michaels.

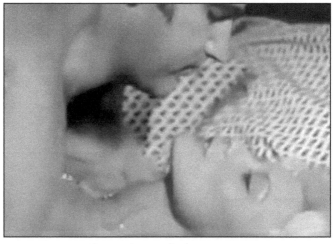

Ken and me in happier times.

23

The Gang

AT THE TIME there were several "regular players" in adult films whom I ended up working with time and time again. I didn't do a lot of socializing outside the set with my co-stars. Although I generally enjoyed the sex, it was still a job and at the end of my "work day" I left. But I did bond with some of them. It was more difficult with the female co-stars, as I was having a lot more sex with the guys. Women can be catty bitches sometimes, especially to the new kid on the block.

Annette Haven was a bitch. She thought she was all that and a bag of chips, and quite frankly I thought she was looney tunes. She was absolutely neurotic about everything. She had to have her private dressing room, she required certain kinds of foods, and everyone had to be quiet on the set. She was just very demanding—a princess without the royal blood. Once, we were doing a movie and she had a scab or something on her chin and she was just going absolutely nuts. She made the makeup artist put a big stone—a jewel—on her chin to cover it up, which made absolutely no sense as far as the plot. But they let it stay in because they didn't want to deal with her craziness. She happened to be very intelligent and well spoken, but needed a straitjacket most of the time. I never did a sex scene with her and didn't even like being around her on the set, so it was just as well.

The only person I knew who could calm Annette down was Kay Parker because she's just a very gentle soul. I love her. It was always wonderful to have Kay around because she put a peaceful ambiance in the air. She's beautiful inside and out and was never a prima donna or a princess. I consider Kay a friend and our sex scenes together were fabulous. We were always in tune with one another. The sex was a lot more personal. There were other women and men I had hot sex with, but no personal connection, so with Kay it was on a whole different level. It made it awesome.

Today Kay's a priestess, and deals with all matters spiritual and the power of forgiveness. I don't really understand some of this stuff, but she's very masterful with it.

Desiree Cousteau was an interesting character. Very pretty. She had a tight body to die for, with a pair of early implants. But she was another one who was absolutely wacko nuts. She could be hot and heavy in the middle of a scene with a dick in one hand and a mouth full of pussy, when all of a sudden there was a look on her face and a total change would come over her. "I can't do this anymore. God told me not to." She'd just stop what she was doing and walk off the set. A few minutes later she might come back and start the scene all over again, or sometimes she'd just disappear entirely. This happened several times. She was just crazy. Nobody knows where she is today.

Serena was interesting. She was a real hippie, a very pretty flower child from San Francisco. She was not threatening, nor was she threatened by others. She was just very down to earth, sweet, and always in a happy mood. We first met doing *Dracula Sucks*. I also remember working with her on a couple of Swedish Eroticas. She also did some mainstream work on that George C. Scott movie, *Hardcore*. One day on the set she was wearing this huge chain with a big padlock on it. It was the kind you would see on a Doberman Pinscher. She was dating Jamie Gillis and evidently they were into bondage. He had put it around her neck and was the only one with a key to unlock it. Like Annette Haven, she still lives in San Francisco, and is evidently a very fragile person today.

Another co-star I really liked was Jessie St. James. I didn't know her well on a personal level, but worked with her a couple of times. She was also very pretty—handsome, actually. She seemed very sweet the few times we worked together. Jessie was about my height and had a mystique of oozing sensuality about her. What was memorable about her scenes is you'd never know if she was going to be like an uncaged animal or go the reverse route and be very timid. She used that to her advantage. If she sensed the scene wasn't steamy enough, she'd turn it up a notch or two. And if the sex was too over the top, she'd instinctively know and tone it down. I always enjoyed the films we made together.

Lisa Deleeuw was a big, busty redhead who was quick witted and a lot of fun. She was an absolute hoot—a crack-up. I truly believe Lisa could have been one of the best stand-up comics of all-time as she had this incredible infectious laugh and was like the Lucille Ball of porn. But she had another side where you didn't want to piss her off. As funny as she was, she could be equally mean if pushed to that point. It took a lot to get her mad, but it was not a place where you'd want to send Lisa. If a guy did something to her on set like smacking her butt or doing something not called for in the script, she would just let loose on him. I worked in Swedish Erotica with her as well as in *Downstairs, Upstairs* and she was so upbeat, fun, and goofy that there was never a dull moment around her. I was very sad to find out she died a while back, although I'm not sure about the details.

Veronica Hart was very sweet and innocent when she first got into the business. She was extremely intelligent and actually a very good actress, but just didn't know what was going on at first. She's a really down to earth human being who I consider a friend. We still talk on occasion. We did a scene together in her first movie, *The Seduction of Cindy*. I was the star and Veronica had a supporting role. She was scared to death of not just her sex scenes, but the acting as well. Even though we had a script, the director knew he had a newbie on his hands and decided he was going to do whatever he wanted to "see her dance." He'd say something like, "We're going to have you do a scene with these four guys." And it was her first day on a set of an adult movie! It was like she was filet mignon and they were throwing her to the lions. She was actually crying, so I said to the filmmaker, "You need to stop it." I told him if he didn't, I'd walk out. She was trembling. Not only were they acting rudely, but in a cruel manner. I kind of rescued her.

I never worked with Samantha Fox, but I met her and remember she wore too much perfume. She seemed a little quirky, but I honestly didn't know her well at all.

I only worked in one movie with Vanessa del Rio. She was like a tigress in heat. It was called *Beyond Desire*. She was very exotic looking and just plain steamy. You could look at her and start to sweat. She had a way of making your panties wet like nobody else could. I liked her, but we never really hung out so I don't know Vanessa on a personal level. She's living in New York and will always be an icon in adult films.

To this day I think Gloria Leonard is an absolutely wonderful human being. She's smart, sweet, kind, fair, and has that New York swagger about her. She's an interesting, intelligent woman. I never appeared with her on-camera, but she was behind the scenes on a few of my projects and I would see her at various industry functions. She's called me several times to be on panel discussions about First Amendment rights.

Juliet Anderson was known as Aunt Peg. I never knew her age, but she was older than the rest of us. She was probably the original "MILF." I didn't know her off the set, so I can't say I had any real feelings towards her. Nor can I put my finger on just what made her tick, but it did seem like she was pretty much willing to do anything they asked her to do. And she was certainly fun to work with. I was sorry to hear she suddenly passed away in 2010.

I also liked Ginger Lynn a lot. She was cute, tiny, perky, and bubbly. She had this kind of sweetness and innocence to her. She was just a lot of fun. I never did movies with her, but we did *Club Magazine* shoots together.

I worked with Amber Lynn at *Club* as well. She was the polar opposite of Ginger. She was tall and statuesque with this animal magnetism about her. It was like she was more grown up than Ginger.

As far as "the boys," I did a lot of work with John Holmes. I heard many years later, in a book written about the terrible murders he'd somehow been involved with, he told everyone I was his favorite co-star. That's flattering.

Another frequent co-star was Paul Thomas, who was almost too pretty to be a man. He had done some legitimate acting, was always a gentleman, and kind of quiet. The first time I worked with him we were in a car. I remember feeling he could have been a descendant of a chinchilla because he had hair in places that people don't have hair. It was soft like fur. He had beautiful, sparkling blue eyes and wavy blonde hair—just a pretty boy. And he was very nice and sweet. It didn't feel like work when I did movies with him.

Jamie Gillis was also an absolute pleasure to do movies with. He also had a legit acting background, having done New York theatre. You never knew what Jamie was going to do, which made it interesting. He was dark, swarthy, and mysterious. He certainly had a mystique about him. Sometimes you'd glance at him and he looked like Satan himself. Other times he'd look angelic. One night I walked into the Show World Theatre in Times Square. There was a circle of mattresses lying around and when I walked in he was doing a live sex show there. So I did a show with him because it was Jamie and I felt like doing it. There we were with tons of guys in the peep booths watching us as we went at it. You could hear the quarter machines going crazy, because you had to keep pumping them in or it would close down on the viewer. It was fun and a great turn-on. From time to time I had sexual thoughts about Jamie because he's dead sexy. When we did have the opportunity to see each other or speak to each other after not being in touch for a while, it was an absolute delight. When I heard of Jamie's passing it was a sad, sad day. It was like losing a family member. I always adored Jamie and always will. He lives on in my heart.

Mike Ranger was my housemate at one time. He rented a room from me since I gave him cheap rent. We were always platonic off screen. He was like the All-American guy. Sandy brown hair, blue eyes, but he had one hell of a dick on him. He was a really nice guy, fun to work with, and could cum on cue. He was always prepared to do his lines, his penis came up when he wanted it to, and he was always sweet to the girls. I don't know where he is today; he totally fell off the grid.

Richard Pacheco had the All-American boy look as well. When he'd start to do a sex scene, Richard would have a difficult time if he didn't like the person or if there was a crowd of people on set making a lot of noise. He also had the tendency to ad-lib and throw these big long intellectual words into the scene and the director would stop him. "What are you talking about? It's porn. The people won't know what you're saying." They'd make him dumb down the dialogue. He was a very pleasant guy. It was always fun to have sex with him because invariably in the middle of a scene he'd make you laugh. Today he is very in tune with his family and lives in Berkeley, California.

John Seeman was bald with a big bushy moustache. He was a nice guy, but looked like an accountant. I have no idea how he got into the business. Working with him was interesting because I didn't find him sexually attractive. But I didn't mind him either, because he was just so pleasant. He's still in San Francisco, but I don't know what he is doing.

John Leslie became a director and his films reflect the John I knew back then. He was kind of violent towards the women. Very aggressive. And that's why I didn't like to work with him. He recently passed away.

Herschel Savage is tall, dark, handsome, sweet, and mischievously sexy. I never really hung out with him much but really like him. One thing for sure was you never had to worry about Herschel being able to perform.

Randy West was the All-American, blond-haired, blue-eyed boy next door—make that MAN next door, for Randy was all man, all the time. Personally, I was never really attracted to blond guys, but there was just something that drew me to him. I've never been able to put my finger on it because of the blond hair, but Randy West is even better looking today than he was in the seventies or eighties. Today, I would *definitely* like to put my finger on it.

Bobby Astyr was married to Samantha Fox. He was a little, tiny guy with curly hair. He was a nice Jewish boy from New York, as were so many of the guys from my era. What was it with Jewish guys and porn? He came across as a slapstick comedian. Even though he did the sex scenes, he was more of a character actor. He looked better with his clothes on. I've always liked comedians, but there was something kind of handsome about him because I just loved his personality and comedic style. He didn't blow my skirt up sexually, but he was so much fun to be around. He, too, passed away far too young, from lung cancer.

Richard Bolla wasn't a bad person, but there was nothing exciting about him as far as appearance or sexuality. He didn't do anything bad to me; he just plain didn't do anything for me, period.

Ron Jeremy is a really, really nice guy. He comes from a good family, an intelligent family. I admire him for the sheer fact he's remained this long in the business and stayed healthy. He's one of the true classic woodsmen left. Woodsmen are the actors who don't need Viagra to get or stay hard. Ronnie's been called the Clown Prince of Porn, but the Ronnie I know is a very sensitive guy. Back in the day, Ronnie had that whole Saturday Night Fever/John Travolta thing going on. He was sexy. But he let it go and now, I believe, he covers over a lot of his insecurity with humor, God bless him. Ronnie just needs to change his clothes once in a while. He wears the same pair of gym pants and black T-shirt all the time. I love Ron to death, but damn Ronnie, change your clothes!

I have a lot of respect and admiration for these people because they were in the industry at a time when it wasn't easy. It was a time when you had to hide what you were doing. It was taboo and not as readily accepted as today. You couldn't reveal where you were working. Cops, vice squads, and overzealous DAs loved to stir things up by busting in on us like they were breaking up a terrorist ring or something. One thing that has proven itself over time is once you've been in this business, it's hard to find a nine-to-five. It's okay for the vanilla world to watch, but they don't want you to be in their world.

A lot of the folks I mention have families and children. I know Veronica Hart does. Gloria Leonard has a daughter. John Leslie was married. Howie Gordon (Richard Pacheco) has kids out the yin-yang. Ginger has a child, as does Serena. But at times it's difficult for a husband because their friends or peers wonder, "How can you marry that person? She's done porn." But it doesn't mean we don't like to garden, travel, or go out to dinner. It's not like our whole lives are drenched in sex. It's quite the opposite, really. The people who watch us are more likely to be the obsessed sex addicts. For most of us, it was simply a paycheck and a place on the outskirts of movie stardom. A lot of us—not me, but others—really wanted to make it in acting but either weren't good enough or couldn't catch a break. It's like the people who spend their careers doing TV commercials—only with orgasms.

The camaraderie and the relatively small number of us working regularly in the business was also what helped differentiate us. There was a frat house feel to a lot of what we were doing—a private club only we knew and understood. We could laugh at ourselves; we could console one another if someone was having a rough time for some reason. I hear Broadway is a lot like that, too, much more than Hollywood.

A lot of that seems to have changed over time, though. Now girls seem to come and go in a year or less. Most don't stick around long enough to find a following or even get to know many of their contemporaries. When we did full-length features on film in the days before video, we had regular Hollywood-style premieres with red carpets and all. We had fans. Real celebrities—not just from the adult world, but from the mainstream world—would come out to see us. As I said, it was the last gasp of the free love era, and what we did played a role for a lot of people who grew up in the seventies and eighties. We were part of the culture of the era, just like rock and roll and bad hairstyles.

There was also a sort of theater-like "repertory company" feel to our industry back then. Our movies, even our loops, had plots, thin though they might be. That required casting. For example, you wouldn't have Juliet Anderson—Aunt Peg—playing the young girl next door. Yet we all worked, so how did they do it?

A lot of times it was like classic movie casting. They'd have a script (believe it or not) that called for a male lead who was a real son of a bitch. Calling John Leslie! Nearly every film he did, Leslie played a prick—and not the good kind. There was often a lot of improv going on, both from the actors as well as from the director as we began shooting. Some of us were rather limited as actors (me), so we'd change things around a bit so what we were filming was more believable and stayed within our range.

This provided us all with our own individual personas. People ask, "Are you the same person in real life as you are on screen?" In porn, the answer is more apt to be yes, whether you're asking me or any of the others from my era. I was the cool, detached, quiet one—the ice queen, the unattainable statuesque blonde—the girl you couldn't have. Never the innocent, even when I *was* rather innocent, because when I went on the set I usually put on a "don't fuck with me" front, which was my way of protecting myself. It all fit who I was at the time, at least to the people in the industry. As I said, I didn't hang; I didn't date my co-stars. I showed up on set, ready to work, then left at the end of the day and went to bed—with any luck, not having to put out again. Today, I'm more of a talkative broad, cracking wise and funny.

Jamie Gillis could play anything. He may have been the best actor of all, which meant he was never out of work. Randy West, though, played Randy West—the John Wayne of erotica. And like John Wayne, he did it so convincingly you'd be crazy to try to make him play the fool or the wimp. Maybe he could, but who would pay to see it? Richard Pacheco was a really, really nice guy, so that's what he always played on film.

I feel about the old gang the way most people feel about their high school graduating class. It's good when we have reunions every now and then. Some I've kept up with and some I haven't. Some I loved and some I didn't care for. Many have passed on, which is sad and makes the living among us feel all the more mortal. But I suspect as long as a few of us are still breathing, we'll still get together once in a while and reminisce about the good/bad old days.

24

Casting Couch Minus One

THERE WAS A BIG BUZZ AROUND HOLLYWOOD that a major director was going to put adult stars in a new film and there was going to be a casting call. At the time, Bill Margold was booking me and I got a call from him that John Frankenheimer wanted to see me. I was very nervous. I didn't know what to expect or what he wanted. Why me? There were quite a few good-looking women who had been around longer than I had, and others who were younger and fresher. I guess I was naïve and thought I was special or something.

Ken and I were given directions to his office. John was a tall, distinguished-looking man with full, wavy hair. He was built nicely and casually dressed with a presence about him. I imagined his Hollywood office would be more elaborate. The furnishings were nice but modest. It wasn't that large, maybe eleven by sixteen.

He had his secretary get us something to drink. He started telling us about *52 Pick-Up*, which eventually starred Ann-Margret and Roy Scheider, and I was so mesmerized I didn't hear a word he was saying except for him mentioning a pool scene orgy in which I would be prominently featured.

"What do you mean, 'There's an orgy?'" I asked.

He hesitatingly answered, "Or you could play the hostess of a swingers' party."

Well, was it an orgy or a swinger's party? I said, "Excuse me, what are you talking about?"

That's when he went in for the kill.

"You wouldn't have to do anything. I really just want to take pictures of me fucking you. We could do it right now. I have a camera here."

My ever-gallant boyfriend jumped right in and said, "Okay, we're ready."

"Ken, are you out of your mind?" I blurted out.

I turned back to Frankenheimer. "You want me on your casting couch so I can play a character in a *movie* having sex, when I already *have* sex on camera? I'm not doing this. I wouldn't fuck you even if you paid me. You're a rude, ignorant man."

I got out of my chair and glared at him. He looked pretty pissed off. Ken was still desperately trying to convince me to reconsider as I walked out.

I was proud of my sticking to my guns. A lot of my peers in the industry thought I was insane not to jump at the opportunity, and virtually all the chicks from the adult industry did end up in the film. He even got Ronnie, Herschel, Randy, and Jamie, although I doubt the boys had to fuck Frankenheimer to get their parts.

And it did absolutely nothing for any of their careers.

One of Frankenheimer's peers at the time was a major studio head known to be a womanizer. All I heard was he had a huge-budget blockbuster—not *52 Pick-Up*, but another film—and he wanted to see me. He was going to be in New York and offered to fly us there and put us up at the incredibly ritzy and exclusive Carlyle Hotel.

We got there and checked in and I was, of course, extremely impressed. I said to myself, "Damn, this little country girl just stepped out of the woods and into high society." Meanwhile, our famous host was conveniently situated in the suite next to ours and he invited us over.

I thought, "I hope this isn't another Frankenheimer moment." There was so much caviar and lobster and Cristal champagne I couldn't help but be impressed. I feasted my eyes on chandeliers, antiques, and gorgeous, gorgeous furniture. I just hoped my mouth wasn't wide open like Ellie Mae's.

I was handed a script. It was a period piece set in the thirties, which interested me because I like that time period. But he didn't ask me to read. Another fellow came in and started to play the piano to give me an idea of the music of that era. I said, "This is cool. I like the music."

"We're all going out to dinner this evening. Would you like to go?" he offered.

Believe it or not, I wasn't with Ken this trip, but with my gay makeup man, Fred, because after the Frankenheimer incident I didn't want to be alone with these "respectable movie" people. Fred, of course, said yes.

Everybody practically tripped over themselves to get us a table. We were out with a nice enough group of people and it was a mellow evening with good conversation. The mogul asked us to meet him the next morning around 10 a.m. for breakfast. Since it was fairly early, Fred and I decided to hit the town. We went to almost every gay bar in New York, like The Anvil, Hell's Kitchen, and The Eagle. We danced, we drank, and the boys treated me like a queen. I was a tall, big-titted blonde and back then there weren't as many gay porn films. They love boobs—I don't know why, but they love boobs. But nothing sexual happened, obviously. It was just a fun night out in the Big Apple. Back in those days I could roll into bed at 4 a.m. and still look cute in the morning.

The breakfast itself was uneventful and mundane. It dragged on into the early afternoon and I thought it was going on forever. Nothing had been said about the part, the pay, the shooting schedule, or anything else. I wasn't a total idiot. I knew some of this stuff had to be covered, so I was getting kind of leery.

We broke after lunch and I said, "I'm going to have a little nap."

Suddenly he said, "I'd like to have dinner with you alone."

Here it comes, I thought. I was scared. Not that he would hurt or rape me, but that I wouldn't know how to handle the situation with the decorum I thought this person deserved should something happen. Strange as it may sound, I just didn't want to be rude to him.

Fred said, "Don't worry, she'll be ready."

He tried to reassure me it would be okay, but something told me it wouldn't. I was really nervous.

There was a knock on the door as Fred was doing my make-up. A gentleman was at the door with a box. Inside was a man's tailored shirt that had been made for me. It was an absolutely gorgeous shirt with Mr. Mogul's name on the back and a note that said, "It's going to be a casual evening. Please wear jeans and this shirt."

It fit nicely, but I thought it was really strange. The hair on the back of my neck stood up and when I went to meet him, he couldn't stop complimenting me on the shirt.

Odd.

We went to a really nice steakhouse. There were linen tablecloths and napkins, and the service was quite good, but it wasn't over the top with guys with white gloves or anything like that. There was a lot of heavy Mahogany wood, which kind of reminded me of those private New York men's clubs you see in the movies. It was a place for real meat lovers. I was suitably impressed. God knows Ken didn't take me to places like this. My nerves settled a bit and he informed me he was expecting some guests to join us.

Woody Allen and Mia Farrow.

At first, I thought it was wonderful, but they were actually quite dull. Woody looked disheveled and unkempt. His hair was messed up and his clothes were wrinkled. I never suspected he actually walked around like that on his own time.

Mia was very quiet and had the most gorgeous alabaster skin. She was very proper and a bit mousy for my tastes. I never thought of her as an extremely pretty woman, but she was quite elegant.

My host introduced me as Seka. All I got was a "Nice to meet you." I think they were both oblivious to who I was. This has always been a double-edged sword for me. People generally watch my movies to get horny or get off. What does this say about them? What does it say about the people who *don't* watch my movies? I've never come up with an answer to either question.

I assumed we were having dinner together, but they just joined us for cocktails. They excused themselves and that was that. We had a nice enough meal with pleasant conversation, but something still struck me as odd about my host.

Stepping out of the restaurant, he motioned for a limousine to pick us up. He asked if I wanted to have a drink with him in his room. I said, "Okay," because so far everything had been all right. He hadn't been forward and hadn't made any advances. I also knew Fred was in the next room if anything got out of hand. If he got a little handsy, I'd just leave.

When we opened the room there was flowers everywhere. It smelled great. Suddenly, out walked a beautiful girl with olive complexion who looked like a runway model. She was wearing the same shirt I had on.

I asked, "Just what are you doing?"

He looked at me like I was nuts. "I thought you wanted a nightcap. Isn't she beautiful?"

She certainly was. And she was also clearly a "woman of the evening." I told him, "I'll sit on this chair. You sit over there. And you tell me what the hell is going on."

"I just want some pictures of you two together."

It was harmless enough. I'd been paid to pose for pictures before. But this was disingenuous. When I did modeling gigs, I knew I was there for modeling before I even woke up that morning. Furthermore, I was getting paid and I knew what the pay was. Tonight, I'd been wined and dined and it must have cost a pretty penny, but that made it barter, not a gig. I decided I wasn't going to do it.

Meanwhile, I spotted plenty of pictures lying around of the two of them in various states of undress. However, nothing sexual was going on.

He looked at me and said in a disappointed tone, "You mean you won't take any pictures with the two shirts?"

What the hell was with these fucking shirts?!

"No, I don't think so."

"Okay, let me come clean with you."

This is going to be good. "Thrill me, chill me, shock me, amaze me, but just tell me."

"Let me tell you what I want from you."

"And what would that be?"

I noticed him glancing at a lovely glass coffee table. It was huge. I mean, two to three inches of heavy glass. You could have a party on it or underneath it, it was so big.

"I loved your ass from the first time I saw you. I would love to see you sitting bare-bottomed on top of the coffee table while I'm underneath so it can be as if you're shitting on my face."

Lovely. And here I was, thinking it was going to be something weird.

Without blinking an eye, missing a beat, just very matter-of-factly, he made that statement sound like something you'd hear in everyday conversation. I didn't say anything for a couple of moments. The man had shocked me speechless.

We stared at each other for what felt like the longest time. He just asked a woman he didn't know the grossest request I had ever heard, and I'd heard a lot. For some reason, out of nowhere, I just started laughing. I could not contain myself. I was so stunned I was laughing my ass off, cackling like a hen.

He said, "Well, are you going to answer me or not?"

I managed to say, "Not," through the laughter.

Once I'd collected myself, I stood up and said, "With all due respect, you set a very nice stage." I looked at the girl who stood there silently throughout. I picked up two bottles of Cristal and said, "I'm going to bed," and left the room.

Clearly, I never got a part in that movie. But I did get to keep the shirt.

Another time I got word that Tommy Lasorda wanted to meet me. I love baseball so I figured "What the hell?" It was a casual restaurant on Sunset. Nice food in an open area with brick walls where you could see out onto the Boulevard and people-watch. Tommy was very flamboyant but it was just basic B.S. chatter with Tommy talking about himself, which is what most people do. In the middle of the conversation he told me about a friend of his named Sy Sussman, who worked for the William Morris Agency. I had no idea at the time what that was so it didn't mean a whole lot to me, but Fred seemed impressed by it. We took Sy's number and gave him a call.

It turned out he was the third agent from the top at the number-one entertainment agency in the world and he wanted to meet me.

I had no idea what Sy looked like, nor did I know much about him. But I figured after the other two Hollywood bigwigs, the third would be more of the same.

The Morris office complex was huge. It was like three city blocks with screening rooms and everything else. We went to the front desk and asked for Mr. Sussman. I don't know what I was expecting, but he wasn't it. He was rather short, gracious, older than I thought, and a nice Jewish boy from Brooklyn.

He took me around the office and introduced me to everyone. Sy would talk about different things—not just the agency or himself. He seemed sincerely interested in everything I had to say. But I caught myself. "Don't fall for this," I thought. "You're slipping."

He had to go back to work and invited us to dinner. I figured, "Here we go again… ."

The dinner was more of the same. I was practically ready to ask the guy what he *really* wanted from me, just to get it over with and save me time, but he remained a perfect gentleman. I went back to my room and was waiting for his heavy-breathing phone call. But nothing. No hits. No runs. No errors. Nothing.

The next day he did, in fact, call. He told me what a pleasure it was to meet us. But there was no come-on. No kink. Nothing except a genuinely nice, lovely human being. A salt of the earth person. Just a joy to know.

And twenty-five years later, he's never approached me in a rude or sexual fashion. We've seen plays and movies together and that's all it's ever been. It may be one of the best friendships I've ever had with anyone. I guess there truly are some nice guys left in the world. Even in Hollywood.

25

Behind the Scenes

RUNNING ADULT BOOKSTORES, I was used to seeing gigantic cocks on porn men. It was part of the whole enchilada. Did it excite me? Yes, in the same hormonal way men feel about big boobs. I can't explain it; they can't explain it, but big boobs make them hard and big cocks make me moist. I may have fantasized about what sex would be like with one of those one-eyed monsters, but it wasn't like I was holding out for one in real life and I wasn't obsessed with the thought.

Once I got into porn, of course, I actually did get to play with them right off the bat. How was it? Pretty cool overall, but it never jaded me or made me a "size queen." The first time I saw one live and in person I was still shocked. Seeing the magazines and loops at the store, I wasn't sure if there were camera tricks or something that made every guy look so huge, so seeing my first big one was surprising—a pleasant surprise, I might add. But it never stopped me from going back to normal-sized ones and enjoying myself. It's not all about the dick; it's about whether the person attached to it is a dick or not.

Something I got to see that the public never did was the transformation. Everyone knows there are "showers" and there are "growers." Some guys are well hung all the time and when they get excited they get just a little bit longer, but mostly just harder. Other guys may end up just as long when they're erect, but they start off pretty darn small. In real life, it's all good. I mean, who cares how it starts out; it's how it ends that matters. But in porn, you never see a small, limp penis. It is always either hard, or it is flaccid yet still enormous. Are all the porn guys "showers?"

No.

I got to see a lot of these famous woodsmen with tiny little limp dicks when they weren't filming. It brought a breath of realism to the experience, although this realism was never shared with the general public.

Perhaps it should have been. It may have made men in the audience feel less inadequate.

Of course, every "grower" does not sprout up to porn star size, so seeing the transformation of these guys from literally nothing to their version of "full bloom" blew my mind. Honestly, I might have paid to see that if I was never in the business. Actors would go off into the bathroom or into a corner and start jerking off so they'd have at least a semi by the time the cameras rolled. Or else they'd start off limp and the cameras wouldn't roll until they were almost there. Either way, the audience's illusion was maintained.

I had assumed the rigid size itself was an illusion, but it wasn't. These guys were all big once they were hard. The women at that time could get away with breasts of any size—although most all of them today are ridiculously stacked and full of silicon or saline. But the men all had to be very, very well hung, and that continues today.

Speaking of erections, I get asked a lot about "fluffers." Fluffers are these girls who are allegedly hired to blow guys to get them hard for a scene. They're supposedly girls who want to work in porn but aren't considered pretty enough, so they just use them off-camera to do their thing.

I never saw one. I'm not saying they don't exist, but I never needed one. Not to brag, but if a guy couldn't get hard when he saw me, there was something seriously wrong. Even if he needed a little encouragement, that's all it took—a *little* encouragement. Maybe that's why I became so popular with the fellas. Lots of guys from that era would say in interviews I was their favorite co-star. I was nice to them, I was professional, but lots of other girls were, too. But I got them hard and got them off, which was what we were paid to do, as I saw it. For me, that was where the illusion became the reality. Some girls, no matter how beautiful they looked, were really bad lays. They didn't care. Their minds were elsewhere. When I was in a scene, I meant it. The sex was true. It didn't mean I loved the guy; porn scenes are rarely about love. They were about lust and about cumming and that's what I was about. If a guy needed a fluffer, I tended to blame it on the girl.

Herschel Savage tells a great story about me when he's interviewed. Apparently one day, a director was busting my chops about dialogue. According to Herschel, I replied, "Look, I came here to get laid, so let's do it!" I don't remember it, but it sounds like something I'd say and do, so I'll second Herschel's motion. I knew what the people paid to see and I gave it to them, and if that meant the sex had to look real, I made it look real because for me, it *was* real. I got into it.

On the other hand, there *were* "stunt cocks." If a guy was having a hard day (no pun intended), people were fighting on set, or they wanted him to film too many scenes in too short a time and *no girl* could get him up, they would switch in some other guy who was the same basic body type and cut the shots. The main guy would still get into position and make "porn faces," like he was cumming or about to cum, but the actual "gynecological shots" were with some other guy. It's no different than when they use body doubles in mainstream movies for action scenes or dancing scenes. It's all done with camera tricks—cheap camera tricks, not CGI. Hell, we had no budgets to speak of, but we could afford to shoot from a few angles and edit things together. Anybody could.

Something about the low budgets: it made our movies downright funny at times. They sometimes remind me of that Johnny Depp film *Ed Wood*, about the world's worst filmmaker. He'd use body doubles that looked nothing like the original actor, or he'd have boom mics or shadows of crew members in shots and wouldn't fix it. We were often the same way and it put us up for the same level of ridicule. Comedian Dave Attell created a TV series on Showtime called *Dave's Old Porn* exactly about this. Dave could run that show forever if he wanted to; there's so much of that crazy stuff to see if you look for it.

I'd have some skinny guy with hardly any body hair on top of me. Suddenly we're doing it and there's this husky, swarthy guy inside me. Audiences would think it was a threesome and wonder how and when a second guy came into the room, but it was all supposed to be the one guy. Crazy.

Speaking of stunt cocks, I would be remiss in not mentioning the biggest stunt cock of all: Long Dong Silver. Yes, the guy made famous from the Anita Hill/Clarence Thomas hearings. To the best of my knowledge, I am the only woman to co-star with the real Long Dong Silver in a feature length movie, entitled *Beauty and the Beast*.

So what does this have to do with stunt cocks?

Long Dong was a black British guy who allegedly made John Holmes look like a teeny weeny peeny. And he did. But it was all fake.

I've kept my trap shut about this for years now because I don't like to hurt people's feelings and I certainly don't like to hurt their careers, but since he's no longer making films and since other sources have already publicized this, I'll concur that Long Dong was just a normal guy wearing a plastic penis—a prosthetic. It was just like the thing they slapped on Mark Wahlberg at the end of *Boogie Nights*, only longer.

Long Dong had been making loops for years, but someone came up with the bright idea of pairing us in a feature. I guess since I'd done so much work with John Holmes, I was being positioned in the marketplace as "the girl who could handle anything," or something like that. Again, not that I was a size queen in real life, but yes, I did work well with John and I believe it showed on screen. So since this guy dwarfed John… hoo boy! I mean, that plastic thing hung down to his knees!

The film itself was softcore. Not only was his dick trick, but almost all the sex was simulated. He was a really quiet guy; hardly spoke at all. But in the end, I never really had sex with him—none of us did—if the definition of sex is having penetration or oral with a real live penis. So John Holmes remains the largest man I ever had sex with. You're still The King, buddy!

Long Dong was also black, as I mentioned. Today, black guys with white women is almost mandatory in porn. Apparently there's this whole fantasy about BBC: Big Black Cocks. It's a spin-off of that mainstream Hollywood movie *Mandingo*, which starred my poor, sweet, real-life friend, boxer Kenny Norton—a genuine gentleman.

Back in my day, the BBC/white girl thing was not as popular; don't ask me why. For that reason, I don't recall ever having done a real hard-core scene with a black guy, the Long Dong scene having been fake. I have nothing against black guys. Some of my best friends are… well, you get the picture. I did, though, have my choice of casting, and I turned down certain guys of all colors and ethnicities. I was an equal-opportunity picky woman.

Johnny Keyes was one of the few really active black woodsmen back in my era. I never really liked him. I didn't find him attractive and I didn't like his personality. I did not form this opinion out of prejudice, which means "to pre-judge." I met him, I knew him, and we worked on films together. When I didn't do scenes with him, he started in on me that I was racist, which he harped on because I was a Southern girl (I had more of an accent back in the day). That pissed me off. He kept on it and on it and finally I snapped, "Johnny, I don't care if you're black, white, or green. I think you're ugly on the outside and ugly on the inside, and that's why I don't want to fuck you." That put an end to that.

Getting back to our filmmaking magic… in our film production, there was looping. They'd take a six-minute scene and stretch it for eighteen minutes or so. How? Just keep cutting and splicing and making copies of various camera shots. Watch our movies and look for it. I don't care who you are, you can't manage to make the exact same facial expression and turn your head in exactly the same way over and over and over again, with a passage of time in between. But they'd shoot a girl making her "cum face," then do some other shots, then come back to her and she's making the same damn face, at the same angle, with the same lighting. It's the same shot! The same went for the humping and pumping shots. Guys didn't always last that long, so they'd keep looping the guy plowing away over and over and over again, like he's the Energizer Bunny. They could make the guy go on forever. But it was an illusion; it was fake. But it served its purpose. People wanted scenes to last a certain amount of time and they weren't interested in guys with premature ejaculation.

The looping was also done with the sound. Again, the same thing happens in mainstream films. Actors go in later and overdub their voices in sections where the sound guy didn't pick up what they were saying loudly and clearly enough. They do it in a fancy recording studio with the film playing on a screen so the actor can match his or her voice perfectly to the movement of their lips.

Us? After we'd shoot a scene, the sound guy would pull us to the side and say, "Groan for me," or "Give me some dirty talk." We did it right then and there, two feet from where we'd just been filming. There was no video playback. It was all generic. Worse, it was so inauthentic. Sure, we'd be directed to make fuck sounds while we were humping away, but at least there was still a chance we'd lose ourselves in the moment and there'd be some realism to it. But imagine standing in a bathrobe with a sound guy and saying, "Ooo, yeah. That's it. Give it to me baby!" It was more sterile than phone sex. You had no one and nothing to play off of.

I was never around when they edited these things, but some of the people who did that job must have been stoned off their asses. John Holmes would be buried deep down my throat and I'd still be talking. What was I, a ventriloquist?! It was preposterous—and hilarious. But people watching porn must not have cared, or else they accepted that we were the only game in town. If someone came along and did things with a higher budget, they might have put a ton of companies out of business, but there was too much money to be made doing it on the cheap.

Sometimes when I see a loop I was in, not only can I tell the sound isn't synced up, I question whether it's even my voice. There's often no consistency. Hell, they might use my voice in a Vanessa del Rio scene and Vanessa's in one of mine. But who knew and who cared? It was crazy.

If I ruled the world I would have taken greater care when it came to these sorts of things, but if you put me on the spot and made me defend the way it was, my answer would be, "Why are you watching this stuff in the first place? To get off! So if you're watching it to check if the sound is synced up, or the bodies always match, or the camera shots are repeated, we must be doing a piss-poor job of getting you excited!" The genre does not exist for film critics. It serves a societal purpose of helping people masturbate, or couples get hot and get down.

This raises the question, "Did you watch your own movies?" The answer is yes, the dialogue parts. To me, that part was cool. I was pretending to be an actress. I never considered myself an actress—I was a *performer*—but when most of my clothes were on and I was talking, acting is what you would call it. I could fantasize I was on *Charlie's Angels* or something like that. That was the sort of fantasies *I* had when I watched my movies.

But the sex scenes? I was never comfortable watching them. They made me bashful. Ironic, I know. I had no problem doing it, but don't force me to watch it later. I could watch other people's scenes, just not my own. I was too critical of myself. I was critical of my dialogue scenes too, but that was in order to improve. But with my sex scenes, it was more a case of, "When I turn that way, my stomach creases and I look fat," or garbage like that. What the hell was I going to do about that kind of stuff? If the director said, "Turn this way," it wasn't like I was going to start arguing with him because it might not be perfectly flattering for me. I wasn't *that* much of a control freak. So if one of my movies is playing, I leave the room when my sex scenes come on, and then come back when someone else is doing it.

Porn sex and real-life sex have little in common, but that is less true today *because* of the movies we made. The pulling out and cumming on a girl's tits or face? If someone did that to me in real life back in the seventies, I'd have killed him. The dirty talk—when Ken did that to me, I hated it. But today, because of our films, guys and girls do that stuff all the time. I don't know if we should be thanked for that or chased out of town with a pitchfork.

Anal. Now every guy tries to get anal sex from a girl. Back in the day, it was a more exotic and rare thing. We took it mainstream.

Do I like anal? No. Did I do it? Yes, it paid more. I've always considered that hole a one-way street leading out. But an anal scene paid $200 more, which for me, back in the day, meant a lot. Of course, here's another trick of movie magic: it never lasted very long. If ever there was a time when they'd cut and splice film together, it was in anal scenes. Most of the girls felt as I did about it, so while we'd take the extra money, we'd only have the guy up there for two or three minutes or so, which would be looped and made into double or triple that time for the viewer. Two hundred bucks for three minutes of discomfort, back then, didn't seem like too bad a deal. Even so, I rarely did it. Most days I simply wasn't in the mood. Well, actually, I was never in the mood, but some days more than others. There may have been one or two girls who actually enjoyed it, but otherwise, the ones who did it more were just more prone to being short on cash.

I'm not into pain. That's why I never did bondage or S&M. Being a tall girl with big tits and that severe look of mine I would have been a natural for those sorts of films, but you can only simulate pain just so much. I wasn't taking a bunch of smacks to the ass or clamps on my nipples—no way, no how, no matter how much money was involved. Furthermore, since it was so against my nature, I was never a good enough actress to pretend I was into it.

There were a few actors who really did get off on that type of scene and I would sometimes watch their films or watch them do it live. It would be like watching a car wreck: you didn't want to look, but you couldn't help yourself. So long as I knew they weren't doing it against their will, I would be fascinated, wondering how they were wired that this sort of thing turned them on. I almost wanted to yell, "Cut!" and go up to them and ask them about it. It intrigued me. But it wasn't for me.

Girl/girl was pretty much mandatory. If you didn't do girl/girl back in the seventies and eighties, you might as well not get into the business.

Quite frankly, I didn't know anything about girl/girl sex before I started doing porn. I'd never been with another girl before. But it wasn't unappealing to me because women are beautiful, sexual beings. They're sensuous. So the idea didn't offend me. I didn't know what the hell I was *doing*, but I must have been pretty good at it because all the girls I worked with got off. I figured, who is going to know better what a woman wants than another woman? I just did what I liked done to me. It was the Golden Rule.

I enjoyed it. It's not a lifestyle choice where I did it and decided I was a lesbian or anything—not that there would have been anything wrong with that. And yes, after trying it on-screen, I did it off-screen as well. I'm not gay, though; I like guys still. I wouldn't marry a woman and have a committed relationship with one where I never had sex with a man ever again. But having sex with a girl is fun. I don't know if that classifies me as bisexual, but I wouldn't correct anyone if they accused me of that. I have no clue and I really don't care. Labels are worthless.

Did we fuck people we didn't want to? In my case, no. I might not have been crazy about John Leslie on a personal level, but once I set limits with John we were able to do scenes together. Sometimes, I used how I really felt about him in the scene. I've heard people refer to that as "hate fucking," though hate might be too strong a word for John and me.

Once, a director brought in a guy who absolutely, positively turned me off physically. He was new and I didn't know him from Adam. But he had what I call a jailhouse complexion—grey, pasty, pockmarked—just not a good-looking boy. He may have been the nicest person in the world, but I'd probably have to spend a month-long platonic vacation with him before I could see myself warming up to him sexually.

I pulled the director aside. This wasn't easy for me because I hate to hurt people's feelings, especially if they've done me no wrong. I said, "Look, this guy does not do it for me and I don't believe I'm that good an actress to fake it. It'll be a bust for all of us. I'll be miserable, he won't be able to get it up and keep it up, and you won't get a usable scene." The director hemmed and hawed until I finished with, "Just look at him. Now look at me. In real life, would you ever see the two of us together unless his daddy left him a billion dollars?" That finally did the trick. I can't recall if they sent him away or simply cast him in a different scene. In our movies, people were swapped around pretty easily most times, so I doubt I killed the poor fellow's career.

Do porn girls cum? Yes, about as easily and often as any other woman. Unlike the men, there is no standard for achieving orgasm. Like anywhere else, there are some women who cum in two seconds every time, some who never cum at all, and some who cum after four hours of diddling, but only in months with five Tuesdays. Me, I cum pretty easy and pretty often, much to the pleasure of the men I've been with. Is it one hundred percent? No, of course not. Does it make a difference if a camera is halfway up my hoochie? No, believe it or not. I learned early on to block that out. Don't ask me how, but I did it.

But here's the rub—or lack of it. The guys all have to have that precious "money shot," where they pull out and demonstrate they have indeed cum. Us ladies? We just get to groan. For the moviegoer, maybe we did and maybe we didn't. Only we know for sure. Yes, we know we have to be loud about it, and we know that when the guy is about to cum we have to make like we are cumming, too. With me, sometimes it was actually real—simultaneous orgasm. Many times I came before the guy. But the girls never got to cum *after*, because once the guy came, everything came to a screeching halt.

I, for one, would have liked to have my sexual needs taken into consideration, just like in real life. Off the set, if I was almost there and the guy was done, I'd expect him to be a gentleman and finish me off somehow. Ladies, demand this of your men!

But on camera, once the guy shot his load, everyone started breaking down equipment and moving onto the next scene. This pissed me off. On the rare occasion I didn't cum, I was usually pretty darn close, so shutting everything down really left me hanging. This was an irritant I dealt with time after time, until one day I just boiled over.

I was doing a scene with Mike Ranger, my best buddy and roommate. Mike and I were like brother and sister off the set, yet we were able to turn it back on and be lovers when the cameras were on and we were being paid to do it. Mike was great. He was an excellent lover and a total professional.

We were in a feature called *Anytime Anyplace*, and we played a couple of burglars. Nobody liked the director, which may have contributed to me finally having my "female orgasm catharsis," which was to come. Early on, we had an outdoor scene where we were live-miked. We finished the scene and they yelled, "Cut."

I, being the idiot that I am, assumed the mics automatically shut off. They didn't. Mike and I started chatting. I said, "I can't stand this little sweaty troll piece-of-shit director," and Mike agreed.

One of the crew came out and said, "Your mics are still live. He heard that."

I was embarrassed, but consoled myself by adding, "Well, it's true!"

But back to the female orgasm. Our next scene was the sex scene and it's a hot day in a hot room under hot lights in Southern California. In other words, it's a hundred twenty degrees and I'm supposed to be in sexual ecstasy. I'm dyin'. Mike's dyin'. But we're pros, so we get it on and do our thing.

Mike was one of those guys who could always give you a three-count before he came. This was incredibly important so the cameraman could capture the money shot. Like I said, he was a pro. He could stop and start on a dime; another thing that is so rare in real life and is another reason why there are such a small handful of great woodsmen in porn. These few guys were in every film, while it was more common for girls to cum and go from the business.

Mike did his thing, made his three-count, pulled out, came and, as always, the director yelled, "Cut," and everyone started closing up shop. No one knew or cared whether I had cum.

Maybe it was the heat, maybe it was my dislike for the director, maybe it was simply the straw that broke the camel's back, but this time I roared, "CUT, MY ASS! I'M NOT FINISHED YET!"

Mike looked at me and cracked up. I looked back at him and said, "Are you done?"

Mike said, "No."

"All right. Everybody, out of the room. We're finishing up."

No one thought I was serious, but Mike had my back (or shall I say, my front) and we shooed everyone out the door and locked it behind them, then pulled down the shades.

Did we keep going and did I cum? No! After lights, camera, and action were over, Mike and I would no sooner make it with one another than your average brother and sister. We did it on camera and nothing else. But I was making a point. If they'd have just let me go for another three minutes or so—which Mike would have happily done as well—I would have gotten off and been a happy woman.

What did we do? We toweled off, broke open some cold sodas, smoked a few cigarettes, and chatted. We'd hear the crew outside the door and when we'd be silent for a while, they'd start knocking to come back in. Dummies. Didn't they know we made sex sounds for a living? "Ooo, yes. Give it to me baby. That's it; right there. That's the spot. Oh, I just love it when you take me that way."

It was all for show, just like the overdubs we did for the sound guy. And these clowns bought it. They thought we were having Tarzan marathon sex when all we were doing was chilling out and unwinding. This went on for about an hour and a half until we finally got bored and let them back in. The looks they gave us! They thought Mike was the stud of the universe—which wouldn't have been far from the truth.

I'd made my point, but I only could have pulled it off with Mike, who was always up for fun and knew to follow my lead.

Oh, and one last thing—on the topic of sweaty, troll, piece-of-shit directors: There was a Hollywood movie about our Golden Age of Adult Entertainment entitled *Boogie Nights*. It wasn't bad. Paul Thomas Anderson, the writer/director (not to be confused with Paul Thomas, one of my old co-stars who later went into writing and directing as well) definitely did his research. Some of the characters were based on real people I'd worked with, such as John Holmes and others. The story lines—the porn girl who lost custody of her child—were mostly all based on real tales from our industry.

I was asked to work on the film. The offer was rather vague, but by that point in my life (1997) I wasn't interested in working cheap, and the offer was just that—cheap—so I passed. I say it was vague because it was unclear whether they wanted me to play the aging porn star, which would eventually be played by Nina Hartley, or to come on board as an advisor. I was often asked to be an advisor on projects having to do with adult films, but they always thought I would be so flattered I would work for nothing. Ha! You want me, you pay me.

One thing I had trouble with in that film is they cast Burt Reynolds as the writer/director. Burt did a fabulous job and the recognition he got for his acting in the film was well deserved. But even an aging Burt Reynolds looked *nothing* like the guys I worked with in real life. You want me to advise you on casting that part now (too late, I know)? Danny DeVito. *That's* what most adult filmmakers looked like back in the day. Most all of them were sweaty little trolls, and Danny would have been magnificent in that part. Of course, many of my contemporaries like Candida Royalle, Paul Thomas, Veronica Hart, and Jamie Gillis eventually went behind the camera and I would never describe any of them as sweaty pieces of shit.

When people look for bad news about adult cinema, they try to make a case that the girls are all doing it against their will. I can't speak on behalf of everyone; I can only speak for me. Some people thought Ken was forcing me to do things, since he was always on the set. Believe me, Ken never made me do anything, nor could he if he even wanted to. The only thing that came close to that with us was the swinging, and even then, it wasn't like he was forcing me at gunpoint. That was more a case of the person you're in a relationship with nudging you and nudging you about something until you said, "Fine, now get off my case!" If I'd have said no and stood my ground, there would have been no repercussions.

But other girls; who knows? For the ones I knew, it was never the situation, or else they never told me it was. Still, you have all these girls who do tell-alls later in life and they talk about people making them get into the business when they didn't want to. Whatever makes you sleep at night.

The other thing are the girls who later claim they got into the business because Uncle Normy raped them when they were eight and it screwed them up in the head. If those tales are true, my heart goes out to them; it truly does. But again, I heard little to none of that first-hand when we were doing films together, so perhaps I'm a little cynical. I'm sure it definitely happened to some women because things like that happen to women all the time, sad to say, and we all cope with it in different ways. Again, I'm sympathetic. But there are definitely girls who leave the business and have to tell some tale in order to live with themselves and their neighbors. Whatever gets you through the night.

Which leads to the mob. I'm told a lot of the companies involved in our industry have or had mob ties. What did I know about it? Nothing at all. I'm not saying that because I'm watching my back. I sincerely never met someone I knew to be in organized crime *when* I was in the business. I'd read later that this one or that one was alleged to be mobbed up, but it was always years and years later, and at that point it meant nothing at all to me. My end of the porn business never seemed that "organized" to begin with. It was a job. I did my thing, I got paid, I went home.

Did anyone ever threaten me if I refused to do something? Hell no! I turned down films when I wanted to, for whatever reason I chose, and no one tried to muscle me. No one got scary with me on the set if I didn't want to do something. A few times, some director would blow his stack and yell, "You'll never work in this town again," but everyone in Hollywood has heard that at one time or another, and just like Hollywood—which has almost as many mob rumors—it is rarely if ever carried out mob-style, if at all.

We weren't paid much, certainly considering how much money we were bringing in. But again, that never came off as a mobster thing—more like a cheap, greedy bastard thing. I'd bellow for more money and either I got it or I didn't. I never woke up to any horse heads in my bed. The business knew better than to treat me that way because I made them money, and in the end that's the only thing that matters.

All in all, the adult film business is a lot like mainstream Hollywood. Some of what you see is real and some less than real. It does what it sets out to do: make people hot. If it fails at that, it will be a hell of a lot less popular and lucrative.

One of my early glamour shots, wrapped in fur.

With Arsenio Hall and Alan Thicke on
Thicke of the Night, 1984.

Interviewing me gets a young
Oprah Winfrey in trouble.

On Al Goldstein's "Midnight Blue" in the 1980's.

With Redd Foxx: 'I'm Cummin', Elizabeth!'

Nice shot by photographer Cass Paley.

26

Goodbye Ken

KEN AND I WERE ARGUING ALL THE TIME. It was particularly disturbing when I found a picture of a woman with a baby who coincidentally shared Ken's last name.

Things started to click in my head. When we were in Maryland one time, he disappeared for hours, claiming he had to pick up mail. He would also make trips there every month.

Ken never admitted to being married and I didn't put this all together at first because things were so hectic in our lives. But I probably suspected deep down and didn't want to think about it. Maybe he was divorced. Maybe he was legally separated. What did I know? But the idea of his leading a clandestine life grated on me, especially if I was helping pay for it.

I also found a ton of pictures of him on 35mm slides having sex with a variety of women. It couldn't be any more obvious he was fooling around on me. But considering my line of work and the fact we both swung, the lines of what was acceptable and not had become blurred for me. The difference was, I never "dated" without him. When I did films, he was on the set and I was a professional adult actress getting paid. He knew all the actors I was with. When we swung, we were both there together. There were certain moral and ethical lines I did not cross. Not so with him. What I did know for sure, though, was just how unhappy I had become with this man.

I also wanted to stop going to swing parties. It wasn't really something I enjoyed. Ken wasn't using it for the purpose for which it was intended—to meet new people and get to know them first before fooling around. He just wanted to get a free piece of ass and it was getting to the point where it was disgusting me. I looked the other way while Ken got his jollies, relieved because it got him off and I wouldn't have to do him later. I may have been the only person to ever go to swing clubs for the purpose of avoiding sex. But now even that got tired.

We were even at a hotel one night when he said he was going to get ice and disappeared for a while. I caught him coming out of another room and said, "What are you doing in there?"

"The door was open so I wanted to peek in and see if everyone was okay."

"Yeah, sure." I didn't really care. And yet, on at least some level, I did.

Ken also got off on peeking in windows. He was a pervert. But as fed up as I was with him, we were living in California and I didn't really know anybody I could turn to or trust for help. Breaking up with a guy is often ugly for a woman. Men sometimes get violent or destructive. I had no real support system in place.

As my relationship was collapsing, my career was skyrocketing. I was given the moniker "The Marilyn Monroe of Porn," and since she was one of my idols I found it very flattering. It still says that on the cover of *Inside Seka*. *High Society* magazine wanted me to do a photo shoot in a tribute to Marilyn, so I asked for a particularly good make-up artist who they agreed to fly in: Fred. The shoot was in New Jersey. Ken came along, too, but didn't want to spring for another room, so Fred stayed with us. They paid me a decent amount of money under the condition that Ken was not allowed to be on the set during the shoot.

It was tense at best between us. One of the reasons for his being banned was I heard he was hitting on other girls. Besides, he was shooting pictures at the same time the pros were, which was throwing off all the lighting. It would take them twice as long to shoot because he was in the way. Unlike when I first began, I found I was much more relaxed without him there and the shoot went off without a hitch. But when the work was over we went back to the room and all hell broke loose.

Ken was really pissed off. I had just spent the day with this guy he didn't know—Fred. He insinuated Fred and I had been fooling around.

"Are you that dumb you don't know he's gay?" Meanwhile, poor Fred was standing there uncomfortably through the entire screaming match.

Ken knew he was slowly but surely losing control of me and was freaking out. That was the first time I told him he couldn't come on the set, and I was also starting to make my own friends. But he just kept screaming and yelling. I got fed up and told him I was leaving and he could do whatever he wanted. I started to get my clothes together. Ken and I always drove everywhere because we traveled with our dogs. That was another big joke throughout the business, because we never went anywhere without our three dogs.

In a frenzy, he suddenly grabbed my baby poodle and locked her in the car. I pleaded with him to give me my dog but he wouldn't. He was desperately trying to keep me there. He didn't think I would leave without the dog and he was right.

I did not know how much rage I had until that particular moment. He had a really gorgeous red and white Cadillac with white leather interior, and he clearly loved that vehicle more than he did me. I found a piece of two-by-four and started beating the Caddy and he was freaking out.

"Don't hurt my car! Don't hurt my car!"

"So give me my dog!"

Here I was, looking like Marilyn Monroe outside this sleazy hotel in New Jersey, and I started bashing it in.

One headlight gone.

He still wouldn't give me the dog.

The other headlight gone.

No dog.

I started wailing on the hood and then the mirror on the side. I said, "The windshield is next."

He still wouldn't budge. The Caddy was starting to look totaled.

At this point the police pulled up—two officers in one car. They looked at me and simply asked, "What's going on?"

I explained and Fred verified everything I said. The police looked at Ken. "Sir, open the car and give the lady her dog."

He started arguing with them. They didn't even give him time to plead his case. "Give her the dog!"

Finally, he relented.

The cops asked me what I wanted to do and I said I just wanted to get my stuff and leave. They stood there until I did just that. I didn't even look at Ken, and the cops wouldn't let him say a word to me. Every time he opened his mouth to say something they told him, "Be quiet. Leave her alone."

I left for another local hotel with Fred, who was trying hard to keep me together. I went back to California to a home that was in his name, in spite of the fact I was the breadwinner. I knew I only had a few days to get my life in order because he was back East fixing his prized car. But I didn't know what to do.

There was no communication between us at all at this point. I had all the locks changed on the house because I had no idea what he was planning. I was afraid for my safety. Actually, I was afraid for my life. He'd never beaten me or anything like that before, and I was a pretty big girl, but no one is tougher than a bullet.

After the second or third day I called the guys at Caballero, who produced Swedish Erotica, and they told me they'd send two guys over to help me move. The only problem was I had nowhere to go.

They sent two young guys with a big truck to help me get my stuff out of there. They were huge. Muscle on top of muscle. I'd never seen two fellows quite that size before. I was upstairs as they took the furniture apart. But I'd forgotten the garage door was open and I didn't hear a car pull up. I didn't think it would be Ken so soon, but it was.

For some strange reason, the first thing he did was throw his clothes in the washing machine. Why, I don't know. But he did.

When I heard the washing machine, I said to the guys, "What the hell is going on?" There he was in the garage separating his clothes to do a wash, like nothing in the world had happened.

"What are these guys doing here?" he asked.

"I'm leaving."

"You're not going anywhere."

"You're not stopping her," one of my protectors said with a "Don't fuck with me" scowl plastered on his face.

They asked me if I wanted the washer and dryer and I said, "Absolutely."

"But I have my clothes in there… ."

Ignoring him, they cut the line and pulled Ken's load out, unceremoniously dumping his soaking garments on the floor of the garage. "Not anymore you don't."

They picked up the washer and dryer and without a bit of effort loaded in on the truck. These big boys were not for the faint of heart.

Ken started to say something and one of the guys said, "You'll be in a healthier place if you just didn't say anything."

They proceeded to load the rest of my things in the truck. I had car keys in my hand for my little chocolate brown Spitfire convertible and they saw I was agitated.

"Do you want to drive?"

"No, I'm a little too upset to drive."

One got on the right hand side of the car and the other guy on the left, and they picked it up and deposited it on the truck. Just like that.

My dog, Yvonne, and the little Spitfire and I sat all loaded on the truck. Having absolutely no idea what lay ahead, off we went.

27

The Underground Railroad

THE SWEDISH EROTICA GUYS had an apartment they owned and let me use for free. It was gorgeous and in a nice neighborhood. It wasn't fancy, but everything seemed to be brand new. It was completely furnished down to dishes and pots and pans. They put my things in storage. This, of course, was in the pre-cell phone days so I was grateful there was a phone already hooked up. I settled in and for the first time I could remember, I was feeling lost. There was nobody else there; it was just me. No husband. No boyfriend. No real friends. And I didn't know my way around at all. I even got lost going to the supermarket. But as lost as I felt, I was relieved at the same time. And I slept a lot because I was emotionally and physically drained.

I had been paid pretty well thus far in my adult career, but foolishly all I had in my name was my little car. I had just begun sticking some money in a bank account, which Ken didn't know about, because after finding the pictures of his family I didn't trust him like I did in the beginning.

After sleeping for a week and realizing my funds wouldn't last forever, I called Fred. We talked and I told him what had happened. He said, "I wasn't going to tell you to leave the guy, but he's a jerk. I'm glad you did, though."

To this day, the thought of Ken just scares me. I feel he's dangerous and vengeful.

Fred told me if I came to Chicago he could help me out and I could live in his huge house in Barrington. I said "fine" and packed up what little belongings I had. The Swedish Erotica guys said they would take care of my car. I left most of my stuff in California and went to Illinois.

Fred picked me up at the airport and I had never seen a house like his before in my life. It was very reminiscent of a Frank Lloyd Wright. Fred had done very well for himself. He used to breed blue Afghan hounds and show dogs, which he was no longer doing at that point. And the make-up gig was very good to him, as he used to work with Rona Barrett, Fleetwood Mac, and others. In the late seventies and early eighties he was charging $500 a face, which in those days was a heck of a lot of money. He also worked a lot on adult sets.

He was a very interesting man and he found me very interesting. On my sci-fi film, *Ultra Flesh*, he put jewels over my eyes and I gave him various ideas regarding my make-up. He saw I paid attention to detail, which he appreciated.

And he desperately wanted to give me a make-over.

If you look at the pictures of me from the seventies, I had an older look. Fred made me appear younger and a lot more exotic and different than everyone else in the business—again. Very high fashion. If you compare the cover of *Inside Seka* to a later *Club Magazine* picture, there's a dramatic difference.

I moved into Fred's house and he made me start working out. I was also taking ballet lessons, along with singing lessons. I enrolled at Northwestern University to study diction and elocution. All of this helped me attain my goal of ridding myself of my Southern accent.

Fred was trying to bring me to a higher level, which would mean more pay. He was committed to updating my all-around appearance for the eighties. At the time, I didn't know how to do my clothes. I started getting manicures, pedicures, and facials. After three or four weeks, he posed to me that he wanted to be my manager. He said since I was living in his house and he was paying for all of this, we should have a 50/50 split. At this particular point in my life I was learning a lot and feeling better about myself. Film work kept me busy and kept my mind off things. Besides, I knew Fred didn't want to fuck me. At least not sexually. I wasn't in the mood for any sexual pressure.

At that point, I wasn't interested in sex unless it was on the set. After Ken, I just felt used. Fred was gay and did just fine on his own. His very pretty lover, Gary, lived with him. I liked Gary, but he wasn't happy I was there. Plus, he was just nuts. He was an extremely jealous and insecure man who didn't like that Fred was with me all the time.

Fred and I were on the way back from the gym one day when we stopped at a gas station convenience store for a pack of cigarettes. They had men's magazines and Fred was intently looking at one. I curiously thought to myself, "Why is he staring at a girlie magazine?" Then he actually bought it.

"Why are you looking at this?"

I started thumbing through it and he showed me an index card-size entry form to win a contest to "direct Seka's next movie." I had no idea what this was about, as I had never worked for, nor even spoken a word with *Club Magazine*.

"They can't just use your name like that."

The first thing we did was to call my lawyer to have my name registered and trademarked. I didn't own the rights to the picture they used, so I had no legal complaint there. But I called the magazine and asked, "What are you going to do when you have a winner and I don't want to do your movie?"

"We thought we'd talk to you afterwards."

I explained how bad it would make me look if they held the contest and I didn't go through with it, so I negotiated a price with them. They came back with some ridiculously low counter-offer and I sued them.

Nobody in the adult business had ever sued anybody. It was unheard of. I guess everybody was afraid to because they figured they'd never work again.

I retained a lawyer who was absolutely ready to jump all over it. He was hungry because he was on a contingency and taking a third. He also knew he had a damn strong case. The *Club Magazine* people thought I'd let it go, but I didn't.

Fred and I were ready to go before the judge when *Club* came to us and asked if we'd settle out of court. Fred demanded free ad space in the magazine, a retainer fee for a year, and multiple layouts for working exclusively for them, and that they could only use the shots of me once. Afterwards, I'd own the rights to every photo from that point on.

As for actual monetary damages, we agreed to settle it out of court for a dollar. The lawyer wasn't happy because he was getting thirty-three cents. But I gave him the whole dollar. I'm generous like that.

This contract had a lot of potential for real money. It also set a precedent for women in the business and raised the bar for performers to make money. It proved we could say no to things without the fear of being blacklisted.

I was the first person to take control of my destiny in this business.

Fred did a great job. I learned a lot from him and we had a great time doing it. But like every other man who had been in my life, he started to get greedy. And it didn't take long.

28

Let the Games Begin

THE METAMORPHOSES HAD TAKEN PLACE. Thanks to Fred, I looked and felt better than I ever had. Meanwhile, *Club Magazine* ran that little contest to direct my next movie, although to the best of my recollection they didn't use the winner the way they advertised. *Club* at the time also owned a company called Electric Blue, which produced R-rated films. They had been doing some work with Marilyn Chambers and they wanted me to do one of their Electric Blues for them. They did them in a numbered series and they were at 007, so I suggested they do a James Bond sort of thing, which they agreed to.

I think it got shot down because of the copyright and trademark on Bond. But they sent Fred and me to England because I don't travel alone. He did all the make-up and what was so cool is they paid me a really decent amount of money and flew us both first class to Europe, which was a pretty expensive ticket.

After we did the film—and there wasn't anything eventful about the shoot itself—we decided to travel through Europe. We took our tickets to American Airlines to see if we could go to Paris and Italy if we converted the tickets. They said we could do anything we wanted first class as long as we didn't exceed the mileage from England to Chicago.

The first stop was Paris and I fell in love with it. I was this little country bumpkin and amazingly, there I was.

We were sitting on the Left Bank having dinner one evening and this hot little blonde boy walked by and I just couldn't resist. I spoke no French. He spoke no English. It was perfect. He had beautiful blonde curly hair, big blue eyes, and was tanned and buff. Ironically enough, the friend he was with was gay. So Fred grabbed one and I grabbed the other and off we went. That was the event that snapped me out of my off-set abstinence after Ken.

155

The next night, Fred dragged me to the ballet. Frank Zappa was there and we had on the same Kensie sweater. He walked up, looked at me, and said, "Nice sweater." I was so tongue-tied I just nodded my head. He said, "What's up, Seka; cat got your tongue?"

"Well, you're Frank Zappa," I blubbered all over myself.

"I know that."

It blew me away because here was one of my all-time favorite musicians and he knew little old me. I was becoming aware I was famous to some degree, but didn't realize *how* famous. This was one of the first times it hit me. He told me to enjoy the show and that was that. Funny enough, I bumped into Frank again at the opening of "Dreamgirls" in New York a few months later and we both had on the same sweater again.

When we got home, it was business as usual. I went to the gym regularly and continued my elocution and diction classes.

Fred and I started a mail order company and part of the deal with *Club* was that I had a certain amount of ad space in both *Club* and its sister publication, *Club International*. It was a very strategic contract that got me so many ads on the right side of the page, in the middle of the page, and on the spine. It was based on how people paged through the magazine. I think twice a year I got the inside back cover. These ads paid off, since the mail order company took off quickly.

We started creating products like T-shirts, blocks of note paper, and coffee mugs. The mugs were cute. When you put something hot in the cup, a lip print and my logo would appear. We also had strip pens where you'd click them and my clothes would fall off. There were also used panties, key chains, and a fan club membership. Fans could even order a phone call for a certain amount of time with a first, second, and third best time for me to call on whatever day they wanted.

What was interesting about the calls was that when I made them, it would be mostly human interest questions. You'd think they'd want me to talk dirty or whatever, but I was pleasantly surprised. Most just wanted to chat. "Where were you born? Who's your favorite girl or guy to work with?" Even today it's the same. People want to know certain things about me because they don't believe everything they read. We also had pre-recorded sexy recordings they could get off on, and those sold very well because most people were intimidated to ask me on the phone to do that. We did custom Polaroid pictures. They got six pictures and they could ask me to wear stockings and garter belts, or however they wanted me to dress. As long as it wasn't too outrageous, I'd fill the orders.

I was extremely proud of it all, as I initially had no idea what mail order companies were about. I created something from absolutely nothing and money was coming in pretty well. Some wack-a-doos wanting things like clippings of my hair or pubic hair, but I figured, "Whatever floats your boat." I was also thinking, "I'm making really good money without having to have sex on screen." What a concept! It was like a residual. It was easier than making films. No travel. Nobody's B.S. I could actually use my time constructively—not only with the business, but by working out and taking all my lessons and classes to improve myself as a model, an actress, and a person.

I really wasn't dating much. I went out to dinner with one fellow occasionally, but it wasn't a heavy-duty romance. He was a nice Jewish boy who worked for one of the distributors that released everything from mainstream movies to X-rated. There was also a fellow who reminded me of the Marlboro Man. He knew who I was because my hairdresser, Chuck, and Chuck's lover, Cedric, told him about me. He knew about my career and it didn't bother him. In fact, he thought it was a pretty hot deal, since I was probably the only porn star in Illinois. Our entire industry was centered around L.A.

Over the years, it has intimidated some men. Even today, I see some guys sweaty, shaky, and finding it hard to talk when they ask me for an autograph. It's a strange feeling to have that effect on people. But he was just a pretty boy living at home with his mommy and daddy who were rich. I don't think he worked. His job was to be cute. I didn't really want anything serious, though. I had come to the realization that this was my career and I was very focused on myself and making sure I had money in the bank.

Fred made me start paying rent, which I wasn't opposed to doing, although this was on top of him taking 50% of my earnings for being my manager. He said it would teach me responsibility. But somewhere in the back of my head I didn't want to face the fact the numbers didn't mesh. I was the one earning most of the money coming into the house, I was paying him a salary already, and now rent. I rationalized that he did my makeup and devoted a lot of time to me and what we were trying to accomplish. We worked together for close to a year, but suddenly I noticed expensive wallpaper going up, and top-of-the-line carpet being ripped out and replaced. And he wasn't working nearly as much at his own gigs.

I may have been a country girl, but I could add. I also didn't have as much freedom as I thought. I always thought of him as my friend, but I was hearing way too much of, "I don't want you to do this. You shouldn't do that." I figured I had my own parents and didn't need him to be one, too.

Without his knowing it, I had found an apartment. One day I got up the nerve to address the issue, telling him we all needed our own space.

That was when the shit hit the fan.

"'You can't even find a place on your own!" he screamed. The whole thing threw him into a hissy fit. The truth is, he really didn't want me to go because then he wouldn't have control—just like Ken. But I moved that very day.

I didn't feel as alone this time. I had made friends through him. One fellow, Ronald, was also a gay hairdresser. Seems I made a habit of collecting gay hairdressers. He was an absolute crazy man in a good way.

I met a woman, Barbara, who was also gay. I had a lot of fun with her as well. I had this theory that Fred was trying to set me up with her, to keep me away from guys who could take me away from him. It didn't occur to him she was totally supportive of my independence, or that maybe a woman could take me away from him, too.

About this time, *Club Magazine* called to renegotiate our contract. There was always a signing bonus and a royalty check. We got to the meeting and things were a little tense between Fred and I. Peter from *Club* sensed this, but we worked it all out. Peter handed Fred one sealed envelope and me another. When Fred asked for my envelope, I told him no. I had the larger of the two, so clearly Peter knew what was going on, and I promptly deposited it in my bank.

Sensing things were going badly, I told Fred I wanted to see the books. He was very reluctant. He'd even started to keep his office locked when he left the house, which he had never done before. I don't think he realized that when we went to get our novelty items made, I took everyone's business card. I wanted to have the contact info handy. Little Grasshopper learned quickly. My wiser instincts had kicked in. I now knew whom to reach if I ever needed anything.

All the mail orders were being sent to Michigan Avenue, because it was a prestigious Chicago address. Fred would always go down to pick up all the orders. Now I was sending someone else downtown to beat him to the punch.

One day when he was gone, I checked the books. His little office was off of his bedroom and he'd forgotten to lock the doors. Lo and behold, I found two sets of books.

Even though I cut him a 50/50 deal, I discovered it was more like 90/10 in his favor. I was white-hot pissed off. I was extremely hurt, too, but knew what I had to do. I took the books and he came home and freaked out. I sensed a lawsuit was about to ensue as he realized I finally knew exactly what was going on.

Fred sued me for breach of contract, since I didn't put my *Club* check back into the business. But Barbara was a court reporter and was surrounded by lawyers. She worked for a Judge Bailey and talked to her on my behalf. She sent me to a criminal attorney named David Shippers, who was one of the best in the country. Subsequently, he was one of the men who worked with Kenneth Starr when he prosecuted Bill Clinton. He had also worked to write the RICO Act.

This was a serious player.

Fred had Jenner and Block, who were also huge. I had never dealt with attorneys before, but I knew I was in for the fight of my life.

I walked out of David Shippers' office after giving him a $5,000 retaining fee, took a deep breath, and said, "Okay, let the games begin."

29

Victory

THE BATTLE HAD BEGUN.

Although the business was mine, it was at the time named Fred Marks, Ltd. The court, however, legally turned it over to me until the actual trial. What I had to do was put 50% of it into an escrow interest-bearing account, and whoever won in the end was the one who got the business and the account.

Clearly, this was winner take all.

Money at the time was extremely tight. I had to run the company, take care of my bills, pay expensive lawyers, and put 50% away that I could not touch. Stuck out in the suburbs of Chicago, it was also pretty hard to maneuver back and forth to the city three times a week for endless meetings with lawyers.

It wasn't exactly the best year of my life.

I told my friend Barbara I desperately needed to find an apartment downtown. I wanted one with two bedrooms, as I needed one for my office. I also asked for a terrace, both for my little dog and because of my claustrophobia and needing someplace to get outside.

She found me just what I wanted, right in the heart of the Gold Coast of Chicago, a frou-frou neighborhood. Pleased with it, I ended up living in that building for twenty-five years. The following year, 1982, I bought it. Although the rent was extremely reasonable, it was still more than what I was paying in the 'burbs, and I also had to pay for parking.

It was all an additional strain on me. I couldn't shop for clothes and had to watch what I bought at the grocery store and make sure the rent got paid. An awful lot of Friday and Saturday nights were spent home alone because I just didn't have the money.

I knew Fred was out clubbing but I didn't want to put myself in any kind of jeopardizing position. He didn't play by the rules, so I didn't know what he could conjure up as far as my activities and who I was socializing with. I thought it was best to stay quiet and be by myself for the most part. It was like being in solitary confinement for a year and a half.

I thought Fred was a friend and had been proven wrong. The whole situation was extremely disheartening. I didn't mind giving him half my earnings because of all he had done for me, but I saw this as pure greed and his not giving a rat's ass about anyone but himself. I'd sit across the room from Fred and Gary and wanted to rip their eyes out. Fred always wore sunglasses because it was like someone playing poker, not wanting to show his hand. The lawyers actually made him take off his glasses one day. Fred was like a clear piece of glass. No emotion. Nothing. Gary was the polar opposite. He was highly emotional and didn't really know how to play poker, if you will. He would get upset at the questions and try to place all the blame on me. I was attacking his lover. He was like a puppet—he'd do anything Fred told him to, even if it meant perjuring himself. Gary thought Fred was emotionally stronger than me, but he had never seen the likes of me before. One of the things that always get me through life is my tenacity. I'm like a pit bull. I don't give up until I'm done, I win, or I'm dead.

With all kinds of depositions and legal maneuvering, it was extremely draining and I got very thin during this time. It went back and forth, forth and back over months, with my finding out more things Fred had done. Because of his familiarity with the law, David Shippers tried the unusual strategy of going after Fred under the RICO statutes. Under RICO—usually reserved for Mafiosos and other organized crime figures—there are five charges and you have to prove three out of the five for a winning case.

In my head and in my heart, I felt I was going to win, but it was overwhelmingly exhausting and there was always that doubt things could go wrong. Consumed by this legal battle, I had to hire more attorneys to handle what few movie contracts, appearances, and entertainment business I was able to squeeze in. I really didn't have the time or energy to wholeheartedly pursue my career. One of my lawyers, Charley Witz, was crazier than a loon, but quite nice. Very eccentric. He would make you nuts with his dotting every i and crossing every t. Incredibly precise. It was nerve-wracking, but he did teach me how to read legal documents.

And boy were there documents.

One of the few positive things that came out of all this was there was a ton of publicity. It went AP wire to wire, *USA Today*, the *Wall Street Journal*, and all the other newspapers from coast to coast. You couldn't pay for that kind of publicity. I was doing TV interviews with Larry King, Phil Donahue, and all kinds of morning shows from New York to L.A.

Larry and Donahue were both very respectful. I was nervous with Larry the first time because I always watched his show and liked him. But he was very pleasant. He doesn't try to jackpot you and pull one over on you. He gave me an open invite to come back, and I did several times.

It was kind of interesting, as I was doing interviews on my legal situation instead of on the adult entertainment business. I was an entertainer using the RICO Act to sue someone on criminal charges as opposed to civil charges. Nobody had ever used the RICO Act in this manner. The possible outcome was the loser facing triple damages, attorney fees, and getting jail time as well. It involved wire fraud on the telephone, mail fraud, as well as charges for cooking the books.

After one of the depositions, Fred and Gary left and Mr. Shippers suddenly shot me a triumphant look. "This is a slam dunk. We have five out of five."

I saw the light at the end of the tunnel, but it still was far from over.

Mr. Shippers sent Fred's lawyers a letter proving we had, in fact, proven the five counts. He wanted to know if they wanted to go to trial or settle out of court. I'd already invested a year and a half of my life and probably spent an easy $90,000. Back then that was a fortune, besides all the bookings I lost because of being so involved with this.

The first response we got back was they were willing to spend $2,000 to settle out of court and they wanted half the money in the escrow account. That was pretty stupid. Then they came back with another offer that was just as outrageous. By the time the third offer came I knew I had won, and knew it was in my best interest to settle rather than go through another long, drawn-out trial, which probably would have been another year. Plus, there was a lot of money in the escrow account.

They wanted to settle for $10,000. I would keep the business and all the cash in the account. At this point I felt I had been rode hard and put up wet. I was done. I took it.

I finally convinced myself I was satisfied, although deep down I wanted another five or ten pounds of flesh for what had been done to me. He had completely redone his house and driveway with the money from our business. But I felt like I had been stuck in mud this whole time. I didn't want another year of anguish. I was content with my decision, and also vowed nobody would ever own part of me again. I could continue with my life; I had grown up once more.

The business' name was changed to Pearl Productions, Ltd. I got the name from the late, great Janis Joplin and her first solo album, *Pearl*. As I started to piece my life back together, I heard through the grapevine that Fred and Gary were very sick. They were early AIDS cases. Nobody knew much about the disease at that time. They were in and out of the hospital with pneumonia. Both died within the year.

I can't say I was happy Fred was dead. I knew and liked all his friends and family, and they suffered. Nobody should have to suffer that way. But I wouldn't say it bothered me either. The visual I had in my head was of the house falling on the Wicked Witch of the West, with Dorothy—Dottie—Seka—me—watching all the Munchkins dancing around. "Ding, dong, the wicked witch is dead... ."

Getting press for using RICO to get justice.

30

A New Four-Letter Word

AIDS. Fred and Gary drove it home for me, but while they were some of the earliest cases I knew, talk of the disease was spreading like wildfire throughout the adult industry.

For those not old enough to be sexually active in the 1980s, let me take you back. Take what we know about AIDS today and imagine a time when we knew *nothing!* Absolutely nothing. In some cases less than nothing. Every day we were being pelted with new information, much of it untrue: It only happens to gay guys. You get it from toilet seats. You could get it from oral sex. You *couldn't* get it from oral sex. Condoms protect against it. Condoms provide no protection at all. There were those saying the whole thing was a crock and it didn't exist at all! Or that it was a massive conspiracy to kill gay people. You name it, we heard it, and by "we" I mean the adult industry. We probably heard most of it before anyone else because we had sex for a living. You're damn right we were listening. Again though, the problem was, what do you listen *to?*

We had always been into getting tested on a regular basis, but that was for the clap and herpes and things like that. We girls also kept up on pregnancy testing as well. But picture a time when there was no test for HIV or AIDS. That's what I lived through.

Initially, it was called "the gay disease." Did that give us all a sense of relief? No. The girls all did girl/girl scenes. Did "the gay disease" cover that, too? We didn't know. We doubted it did, but nobody knew anything for sure.

Some of the guys were gay, believe it or not. A greater number were bi or else occasionally did "gay for pay"—straight guys who did gay porn when they needed the extra dough.

Gay guys in straight porn? Sure. Premature ejaculation is always a concern. If a gay guy can manage to get it up and keep it up, he is often a good bet to perform well. He'll be on top of a girl, reading *Blueboy* magazine, bored out of his skull and lasting for hours. It works.

But once "the gay disease" came around, it was a witch hunt. Certain guys were shooed off sets and blacklisted. Some were gay or actively bi, while others were merely "suspected," and that was enough to kill their careers.

Then we had our first fatalities. Some guys we swore were straight as an arrow passed away. Then some girls. Things were getting freaky. Along with these events were the ever-changing theories from the news and medical community. Everyone could get it. Or maybe we all already had it and the entire world was coming to an end. It was madness.

Some folks slept right through the whole thing. Mr. and Mrs. America, married and monogamous for decades, tended not to worry as much. But us? We were on the front lines, baby. An enraged God was gonna smite us all for our perversions. We was all gonna die.

John Holmes' death hit me particularly hard. John and I did so many scenes together. We were paired together as often as Tracy and Hepburn. But John's death left as many questions as answers. We all knew he did drugs, but which ones? When? How much? Did he use needles? Most of us didn't think he did. I never partied with any of the other actors in the industry, so as well as I knew John, a lot of those tales were just second-hand stories to me. I didn't know what to believe. And he went so fast. That was the part that freaked me out the most. It made me wonder—and to a degree it still makes me wonder—if it was even AIDS at all. I'm not saying AIDS doesn't exist, but for most people the incubation period is fairly long and the painful slide to nothingness horrifically drawn out. John seemed to go in a matter of weeks. How was that so?

But worst for me was realizing how often I'd been with John. And some of the others who died—the girls, too. Now if someone screened a movie I was in and I saw John or one of the others, it was like watching a horror film, like I was watching the prediction of my own death.

I started turning away jobs. A lot of us did. Others, on the other hand, were in denial. There was so much misinformation that if you were the eternal optimist, you could con yourself into blocking out the bad news and clinging somehow to the reports that the whole thing wasn't as bad as it seemed and it only happened to "other kinds of people." Some thought since we all knew each other so well, we were in a protective little bubble. But most of us had been with at least one person from the business who had it, so how was that theory supposed to make any sense? There were also the "death wish" people who claimed they simply didn't give a shit;

life was a crapshoot anyway and any of us could walk outside and get hit by a drunk driver on the way to the corner store.

Me? I wanted to live. The idea of condoms protecting you from infection started to gain more and more traction. But the powers that be who ran the industry tried a few films with guys wearing condoms and the feedback wasn't positive. By and large, guys didn't like to wear those—guys in the audience, I mean. After the Pill came out, every girl was on it and condoms gathered dust on pharmacy shelves. Most guys in mainstream America got used to going bareback and they liked it. Watching pornos with woodsmen in rubbers was a buzzkill for them. Most non-industry folks were less paranoid and scared than we were, so they really didn't want to start using them.

Another strange thing was that as more people became aware of AIDS, the more XXX product they wanted. Masturbation went up! No one ever got AIDS from jerking off, so bring on the porno and have yourself a safe sex party! The disease was cutting into the amount of new product being produced since it was cutting into the acting pool, but all our old stuff was being converted to Beta and VHS and people were watching it at home. In the eighties, everyone went out and bought a home video system. Gone were the red carpet premieres. Adult movie theaters began closing. Who wanted to be harassed by local cops for jerking it in a public theater when you could watch our stuff in the privacy of your own home? Of course, we actors saw none of the new profits. We got paid to work on that film one, two, three, four years ago, and the fact that now it was playing in half the bedrooms in America didn't make us one thin dime. Even when we tried negotiating for a piece of "the back end"—a percentage of the video sales—we never saw a penny. Creative accounting. None of us had the cash to take those guys to court to prove we were owed more money, so our only option was to keep working or get a job waxing cars.

With the advent of home video, the industry expanded. More new girls and guys came in. When people like me and others started turning down jobs, even more came in. Those of us who took a tiny bit of false comfort in the fact we were a little community of actors who all knew each other and who we'd all been with, had that thrown out the window. We'd show up on set and we knew no one—it was all newbies. Fresh meat. People who could have been carrying any damn disease.

But I was still Seka. I was still a star. It wasn't an ego thing; it was a business thing, period. Like any other company in America, I knew how my stock was doing on the market.

I got more demanding. If I was going to risk my life, I was damn sure going to die rich. I haggled with people like crazy. I was asking for fees no other porn actor had ever asked for before. And I was getting it. As soon as I'd get it, I'd ask for even more the next time.

But I was playing with fire and I knew it. Not only did I start asking for ridiculously high fees, I coupled that with demands for my personal choice of co-stars. That worked pretty well, since the people I wanted were also big names who had been on the scene a while and had nice-sized followings as well.

But then I took it too far—or exactly as far as I should have, depending upon how you look at it. Not only did I jack up my fee and demand final casting, I also insisted everyone wear condoms. It was a Mexican standoff. The industry and I had a gun on one another and someone was going to blink. I'd been winning these battles for a while now, but it was finally time for the ol' gunslinger to get it right in the heart.

They turned me down. I'd set the bar too high. But you only do that if you know you can afford it. Affording it had nothing to do with money in the bank, though, at least for me. Affording it meant I was sick and tired of playing Russian Roulette. I wasn't going to budge on the condom issue, which was now even more important to me than the money and the casting. And if I didn't get my way, I was more than happy to walk away from it all.

When they finally said no, I was still on the top of the porn world. I was still box office gold. But if it didn't matter to them, it didn't matter to me. I'd walked off jobs before and now I was ready to do it again. I never knew where I was going when I did it in my early days, and I had no idea where I was heading now. But it didn't matter. I was getting out alive.

Some of my Club Magazine shots from the 1980's, courtesy of photographer
extraordinaire Suze Randell.

With Ginger Lynn.

31

Art

FOR A WHILE, I wasn't doing films except for *Club*'s R-rated ones. But I was doing plenty of photo shoots for three different photographers: Dennis Scott in Chicago, Suze Randall in L.A., and Joanie Alum in England.

I used Dennis when I first came to Chicago. He also shot for Australian *Playboy* and has always been very highly regarded. Some photographers have a knack for shooting food or nature, while others really know how to shoot people. In my opinion, these three are masters at shooting women. Suze and Joanie worked for *Club Magazine* a lot and when the publication asked me to model for Suze, I said absolutely, because she did gorgeous work. None of them wanted to give up the rights to the pictures, but I ended up retaining the ownership of the transparencies because otherwise I wouldn't have done them. At the time it was unheard of for a model to wield such power.

Suze was a riot to work with. She was very motivating and had the best make-up artists, stylists, and set designers. You would go in and there was nothing you'd have to do but have your make-up and hair done and walk out in front of the camera. That took a lot of the stress off getting ready for a shoot. She always had great music playing, which was helpful. To be in front of a camera with nobody saying or doing anything is kind of boring. She had this chair that looked like an old school desk with wheels she'd put on it to roll around the studio. She'd just be flying around on this contraption. Suze was an interesting-looking woman, too. She had the clearest, bluest eyes, with extremely short, curly hair. And her British accent was so expressive. You could hear the enthusiasm in her voice.

It was an experience working with her because she'd work very quickly. Using four or five cameras, she'd shoot a roll of film and her assistant would just hand her another one. Keeping up the energy and pace, everything would just click and work very well. Of course, those were the days before digital cameras. We'd have Polaroids and check the lighting and make-up, but once she started shooting, everything was "brilliant, sparkling," and all those other catchy British phrases. She'd shoot one hundred or so rolls of film and there were thirty-five pictures on a roll of 35mm slides. There would be literally 3,500 pictures shot. The reason you did that was if you could get two or three good pictures from a hundred pictures taken, you were happy. When we would finish the shoot, she would have the film developed. She'd mark the ones she liked and send me the pictures to edit, as I had final approval. Then I'd send them to *Club*. It was a wonderful experience.

Suze was like a painter. I don't know if you could use Monet or Renoir as comparisons, but like them, she'd set the stage to take the photographs. The lighting had to be just right for the subject to look her best. If she made you look good, it made her look good. She used jewel-toned colors. Really rich emerald greens. Cobalt blues. Ruby reds. Even the make-up artist had to be the very best. She used Alexis Vogel. Alexis's father photographed more *Playboy* covers than any other *Playboy* photographer to date. Like a photographer uses lighting, Alexis used her make-up and brushes. She works for the crème de la crème of Hollywood such as Pamela Anderson, Jay Leno, and the *American Idol* participants, just to name a few.

Many photographers were frugal and would use their own vehicles, but Suze wouldn't do that. She'd lease a Ferrari or a Rolls Royce. Everything was extremely highbrow with her. And she treated everyone with respect. Not just the model, but the make-up artist and her assistants. It made it easy for everyone to work because they all got along. She eventually built an empire and today does films as well. Her daughter Holly was just a baby when I was being shot, and now she's also in the business. Suze, like Dennis and Joanie, loved the work we did together and none of them felt they were selling out because they were shooting nudes for adult magazines.

Dennis was quite different in the way he did things. He was much more of a romantic. He would have music playing—whatever the person in front of the camera wanted. I preferred a little rock and roll or jazz. But he was much quieter. He doesn't talk a whole lot in general. When you see his work, you can tell a true romantic had done them, because the lighting is softer and the settings he chose were dreamier. There was a famous book Dennis did called *Four Faces*, with pictures of Veronica Lake, Gloria Swanson, Marlene Dietrich, and another legend from that time.

I always liked Marlene, so we redid that famous picture of Marlene, down to the cigarette holder and gloves from that time period. I've had people look at that shot and say, "That's a great picture of Marlene Dietrich." I'll tell them, "That's not Marlene, that's me." He was a master with lighting, as were Suze and Joanie.

Joanie was a gorgeous woman. Just beautiful. She was really tall, willowy, and youthful-looking, with that Bo Derek kind of hair. She dressed very hip. Joanie was married, but I can't remember her husband's name. Very up. Vivacious. They flew me to work with her. I thought, "How am I going to get in front of this woman? She's too gorgeous."

It was intimidating for me to take my clothes off in front of pretty women. Joanie looked like she should have been in front of the camera; she was just striking. Like Suze, she was very vocal and physical. But unlike Suze, who sat in her chair most of the time, and Dennis who was very quiet, slower paced, and methodical, Joanie would be up on six to eight foot ladders shooting down on you. Or she'd be on the floor or shooting from around a corner. Her body would be as contorted and twisted up as the person in front of the camera. You can always identify one of her pictures by the way they are posed. I don't think I ever hurt as bad as after the first day I shot with her. She'd like to get you all scrunched and twisted up, and you'd think, "How in God's name is this going to look?" But they were always great photographs. Her husband was in charge of this cone-shaped light she called her "pussy light." This was back in the days when women still had hair on their genitalia. She'd put a little bit of oil on your pubes and he knew just how to hold the light to get just the right amount of illumination there. You never heard him say a whole lot of anything. I truly believe he didn't want to make anyone uncomfortable, like an onlooker or anything like that. He was very much a gentleman.

They were all totally professional. They never came on to their subjects. I eventually did date Dennis, though. One night he said, "Why don't you come on over? I'll order some dinner and go through the pictures." We always liked each other and there was a good chemistry there and things just happened. I loved him to death. He was a nice man. But I don't think either of us was ever in love with the other. It was something safe. I knew what he did and he obviously knew my story. At the time, I was the only nude photography he was doing. I enjoyed my time with him but knew it wasn't going to amount to much. I can't even remember us breaking up. There was never an argument or anything like that. I got busy at one point and we just stopped seeing each other.

When I look back at these pictures I started doing from about 1980 on, I just love them. It wasn't that the prior ones were bad, but the photographers simply weren't of the same quality. In a way, these pictures preserve not only my youth but also a time in history. It's a documentation of life.

When I think about it, now that I'm in my fifties, I've spent literally half my life in front of a camera. This, of course, puts pressure on me. When I leave the house, just to go down the street, I refuse to let people see me looking bad. One of the reasons is you never know if someone is going to take your picture and publish it somewhere. I want to have my hair looking nice. I always wonder why people walk around in dirty clothes with hair looking like it hasn't been washed in a week. I've even seen people shopping in their bedroom slippers. I guess some people feel when you get to a certain age there's no reason to take care of yourself, but I feel you shouldn't let yourself go. I've had some bouts with keeping my weight in check and I hate it, yet I never reach a point where I think, "Okay, so I'm overweight. Big deal. This is my 'new normal.'" I don't think this is being egotistical. You should keep it together. To have the entire world think you look good for your age makes you feel better about life in general.

Those three photographers spoiled me for anyone else. Working with them was a high point in my career and in my life. Even at shows I work today, people will walk up and ask me to sign those pictures. I get requests via my website for certain shots from the *Club* years. None of the pictures for *Club* at that time were hardcore. Today, there are all kinds of books that present nudes as art. But if it's in an adult magazine, it's regarded as pornography. If those very same pictures I did were taken out of those publications without anyone knowing where they came from, most people would say, "That's a beautiful photo." But since it's in *Club*, they frown upon it. Perception is everything.

I will go to my grave believing the human body is a beautiful thing and these pictures hold up as art. Looking back at these shots I'm extremely proud of the work I've done.

Some of my Club Magazine and glamour shots from the 1980's,
courtesy of the fabulous Dennis Scott.

Posing me as Marlene Dietrich

Looking like I'm ready for a roller disco.

Dietrich again.

Getting wild

32

Good Times

LIVING IN DOWNTOWN CHICAGO, I was the toast of the town. In the mid-eighties there was hot nightlife and no matter where I went, I didn't have to wait for tables or on lines. I was invited to all the new nightclubs and didn't pay for a drink or a meal. I was having a ball.

I even hired a PR person. Pornography was such a hot topic and a lot of the attention given to me was about my case. I had the balls to use the RICO Act and won, so I was continually doing TV talk shows from L.A. to New York. Meanwhile, the mail order business was doing very well and I was still working at *Club*. For once, life didn't have any rough spots.

There was a nightclub called Limelight that had a big opening in Chicago, which was hyped for a couple of months. Everybody wanted to get into the event. Special invitations went out to certain people to enter first, because there were lines down the street. There were tons of limos. It was an old Shriners Hall, which was kind of gothic looking in a way. Neat rooms. VIP areas. I went and it was absolutely one of the craziest nights ever in Chicago. As the doors opened, the flashbulbs start going off. There were so many flashes you couldn't see anything. It took like forty minutes to walk up the stairs because I was literally blinded. My friend Ronnie, who was my hairdresser at the time, was with me and we didn't get home until five o'clock in the morning.

Champagne was flowing like water. Anybody who was anyone was there. Oprah Winfrey, all of Chicago's pro athletes. It didn't matter which team: the White Sox, the Cubs, the Bears, and the Bulls. Even other club owners were coming in. Restaurant owners. Magazine editors. And an awful lot of networking. It was overwhelming because everybody wanted to talk to me.

181

I had never really experienced anything like this. I was used to autograph signings and appearances, but this was different because these were press people who could take me to other levels in my career. I was proud that I didn't have anyone telling me what to say or what to wear. I was on my own now and it felt like the first time leaving home without answering to anyone.

I also went to the International Film Festival and it was full of people from all over the world. Dolph Lundgren was there and I went out with him once. He was a very good-looking man and we all know he's built very well. But very strange. He was extremely quiet and shy for someone who wanted to take me home. At the time, he had just broken up with Grace Jones, because in bed he kept comparing my nipples to hers. I guess he had a thing for nipples. Oddly, for somebody who had a body like his, he always tried to cover himself with a robe or a towel. There wasn't anything wrong with him at all, believe me. He looked like a Greek God and was one of the best male specimens I have ever seen. The whole date, as well as the sex, though, just didn't live up to my expectations. He called again the next time he was in town but I told him I had a prior engagement. I tried to be nice.

I also met Matt Dillon at Limelight. He was a lot of fun. And a hottie. He came over and was talking to me for a few minutes and I was in the mood, so I said, "Do you want to get out of here?" He quickly responded, "Yes." Simple as that. Big difference between men and women: when men go out, they wonder if they're going to get laid. When women go out, we *choose* whether we're going to get laid.

We went to my place and went at it for a couple of hours. He was getting very relaxed afterwards and started to go to sleep. I basically did a boy thing and said, "Look, you need to get up and put your clothes on and go back to your hotel. I'm not your mother. I'm not going to clean up after you." He didn't get pissed off, but he had a look like a little hurt puppy. He was certainly good at what he did, though.

Gary Busey, on the other hand, was a train wreck. The door guys at the China Club said Gary wanted to meet me and go to a hockey game. I was exhausted, but said I would. I can't say whether I did it because it was him or because it was a Blackhawks game.

He was not a pleasant person at all. He took me out but paid no attention to me whatsoever. When he was ready to leave, his crew wanted to go out. He said, "We're not taking you home. You're going with us." And he said it belligerently.

I said. "Fine," and walked right out of the car.

Twenty years later we worked the Hollywood Collectors Show and he came up to my booth and was looking around. I said, "Gary, how have you been?" He said, "Do I know you?" He seemed fried. It wasn't worth the effort to remind him about our "date."

I didn't really have a boyfriend at the time, per se. I knew by then most guys weren't asking me out because they wanted to know me. They were asking Seka out and to see if they could score. It didn't affect my view of men in a bad way. I didn't really want a relationship at the time anyway. I was having too much fun to be tied down. If I wanted to get laid it wasn't difficult for me to do; I could just ask. No fuss, no muss.

I think every person goes through a period where they're single and feeling completely free, as well as free of guilt. For most people, it happens when they're in high school or college or shortly thereafter. For this eighteen-year-old wedding night virgin, that time was now. Call me slow, but I finally got around to it and it felt good. I was old enough to know it was just a phase, but I soaked it up and was happy while it lasted.

I also went out with Billy Connors, the pitching coach of the Chicago Cubs. I'd visit him in the off-season in Florida and I'd spend a couple of weeks at a time with him there. Even though we were intimate, we were really good friends. I'd go to spring training once in a while. The players treated me wonderfully. They were gentlemen. And that's when the Cubs had some ball players who could really, really play, even though they unfortunately never made it to the World Series. I've always been into baseball, so I went to a lot of games in the summertime.

Guys like sports, I like sports, so I was always a fun date even if it didn't morph into sex. Through Billy, I got to know the Cubs, but sports is a small world in any major league city, so I got to know White Sox players, Blackhawks, Bulls, you name it.

When you're a porn star, there's rarely any neutral ground. People tend to either love you or hate you. I remember seeing big Horace Grant of the Bulls in a restaurant. Such a tough guy on the court, but a sweetie off of it. As I approached, Horace rose from his seat and pulled a chair out for me like a proper gentleman should. He was sharing a table with Scottie "No Tippin'" Pippin. Scottie, who fans thought was the nicer guy, not only didn't acknowledge me, he turned to Horace and said loud enough for anyone to hear, "Why are you being nice to *her*?" Like I was some sort of disease.

Horace immediately straightened Pippin out, saying, "You need to shut your mouth. You're in front of a lady. She's a very nice woman."

I had an almost identical thing happen with Otis Wilson of the Super Bowl Shuffle Bears. Otis was a darling, but again, one time he was out with a teammate and the teammate immediately thought he could talk to me like a piece of trash and Otis nearly came to blows with him. It was always a mixed blessing. Fame got me close to wonderful people like Horace and Otis, but notoriety made others think they could treat me like I was subhuman.

There were always celebrities in Chicago shooting movies because of the architecture. On screen, it passed for any number of American cities. I was asked to play myself in the Jessica Lange movie *Men Don't Leave*. She played a divorced woman with two children who was financially strapped, and her two sons were trying to help her with the money situation. They took a VCR to sell to this fence who had all these VCRs and TVs. One of the movies playing on a TV was a Seka film. So they brought me in to recreate a porn scene. If they thought about it, all they needed to do was ask a film company for a three minute clip, but instead they had me on the set for a couple of days. It was kind of fun watching real Hollywood in action, especially after all that casting couch bullshit that never turned into anything real.

The actors were very nice. Down to earth. Just pleasant people. As always though, it's the producers and people behind the scenes—the decision makers—who give you attitude. Because I had done adult films, I was not looked at as a real actor and it made them think they could take liberties. "How about a blow job?" "How about us getting laid?" I'd look at these creeps and say, "I wouldn't fuck you if you were the last man on Earth." What did they think I was going to say? "Okay, drop your drawers. Do me right here."

I wasn't afraid to speak my mind anymore, but it was hurtful. I could understand if it's Joe Average. Guys come on all gross and sexual to girls in clubs all the time. But when it's people in the movie or entertainment business, I'm just like, "My God, how ignorant can you be?" They know how the business works. Adult stars are no different than anyone else. The disrespect bothers me. There are plenty of Hollywood stars who get naked on screen, and they wouldn't talk to them like that. But they feel with someone like me it's okay. Ironically, in the adult business, producers wouldn't think to do this. Not to me anyway. If they wanted to get me laid, they wanted to get me laid on screen so we could all make money. But I guess that will always happen. People can be very brazen. They still do that stuff to me. Because you've had sex on camera, they feel you'll spread your legs for anyone. I may be a very sexual person, but they think you're some indiscriminate sex-crazed nymphomaniac.

There's also the power game. They have the power, and Hollywood is teeming with girls who want to be movie stars. They'd never dare proposition Julia Roberts or someone like that, but before Julia Roberts was Julia Roberts, who knew how many of these lechers she had to fend off? But with a major adult star trying to cross over, it was like trolling for little starlets again, 'cept I didn't play.

Rock stars treated me with far more respect. During that time, I was always invited to Aerosmith and Rolling Stones concerts. They would call and say, "What are you doing?" One time I was in Virginia visiting my family and I got a call from one of Aerosmith's sax players, who asked if I'd come to their concert in Chicago. I told them I wasn't home and they said they'd be in Virginia in two days. They gave me backstage parking and passes, great seats, and rooms at the hotel. Not one band member ever hit on me. I think they get hit on so often by so many chicks that they know what it's like.

Steven Tyler was absolutely fabulous. A total gentleman. Very funny. Very polite. They liked my films and when they were on their tour buses they played porn.

When the Rolling Stones were in town they'd pick up my tickets. They had a huge bus that would take certain people to their concerts. I'd hop on the bus with some of the band members. One evening we were out there a couple of hours early. They had a big tent set up with pool tables, pinball machines, and a nice buffet laid out. Ronnie Wood was playing pool and his wife came up to me and said, "Would you do something for me? Ronnie loves you to death. All he does is talk about you. Would you please go over and give him a hug?"

It was a huge thrill for me. I walked over to him, gave him a hug and a little kiss on the cheek. His wife stood there as his mouth hung open. He couldn't say a word. And she knew he'd react like that!

Mick Jagger's security pretty much kept him to himself. All you'd get from Mick was, "Thank you for coming to the show." Very polite, but nothing more than that. He does about an hour and a half workout before the show just to warm up his muscles, and then a long cool down after, so there's not a lot of time for chit-chat. When you're at that level of performing, you don't need a lot of hustle-bustle before a show. You need your head clear. When they're on tour they're usually so busy doing interviews and such.

Keith Richards is not only funny looking, but just plain funny. A very nice guy. I've been going to see the Stones for thirty years, and as long as they keep going, I'll keep going.

All in all, this period was a fabulous time. Everything seemed right with the world. But as good as it was, little did I know what the coming years had in store for me.

With Bon Jovi, 1987. Slippery When Wet, indeed. The band used to hide out and get their hair styled in my apartment in order to avoid the paparazzi. And in the eighties, that was a lot of hair.

With Aerosmith's Steven Tyler.

With my favorite singer of all time, Roy Orbison, and his
great guitarist Bucky Barrett, 1985.

With Mötley Crüe.

33

Seka Versus the US Government

DURING THE 1980S under the Reagan administration, the government was coming down hard on the adult entertainment business. They were trying to close down dance clubs, bookstores, and doing stings on movie sets. Everybody on the set got busted. The feds were even pulling magazines off of newsstands, and I'm talking mainstream magazines like *Playboy* and *Penthouse*. And if they weren't being removed from the stores, they were told to cover up the flesh.

I feel it was an issue of freedom of speech, which is what this country was built on. I'm against censorship, period. If you don't like something, don't order it. Don't support it. Turn the channel. Whatever. But don't try and shut it down.

In some European countries where pornography and/or prostitution are legal, there's less rape. There's tax money to be paid and the government makes out. Again, nobody's being forced into watching or doing anything.

The Meese Commission was trying to show there was violence and rape in pornography. They were painting us as Satan's helpers trying to destroy the moral fabric of America. Hell, you couldn't even show an erection in the newsstand nudie mags. And most of the plots of our movies were so inane you couldn't take much of it seriously to begin with.

But they sure were out to get us.

Different adult film actors and actresses were asked to go to Washington to give their point of view on the industry. John Westin was one of the lawyers fighting to show that this was a First Amendment issue. He knew that as one of the leading names at the time and being someone who was fairly well spoken and not intimidated easily, I was a good candidate to speak for them. I said, "Absolutely. I would be more than glad to be part of this."

Seka was about to take on the U.S. government.

I had been told to wear "court attire." I guess they were worried they'd have a group of us looking like strippers. I showed up in an Yves St. Laurent double-breasted jacket with matching knee length skirt, with a crew collar, short-sleeved red sweater underneath, and shoes and purse that matched the suit. But there was just a touch of cobalt blue showing them there was something to be reckoned with. It was very understated, but a definite high-powered corporate look. I could have passed for one of the lawyers.

As I walked into the impressive and imposing marbled halls of Washington, D.C., I realized the gravity of what was going on. I was on Capitol Hill, for Christ's sake. Nonetheless, I felt powerful and proud to be fighting for our freedom. I sincerely felt Attorney General Meese and his cronies were wrong. They were violating my rights. In fact, I was there to fight for everyone's constitutional rights. If you don't fight for what you believe in, you no longer live in a democracy. It becomes a tyranny of sorts.

Mr. Westin sat down with a group of us. Adult actress Veronica Vera was there, too. He told us what to expect. He was a very capable, excellent lawyer who kept me calm. He didn't try to manipulate us. He just readied us for what might be coming, telling us if we feel like we're stumped and need a little extra time to think, repeat the question back to the person who asked.

We were sitting at a table on these big, long, mahogany benches. There were huge, gargantuan double doors going into the hearing room. You're the size of an ant in comparison, but I didn't feel that way even when I was summoned and the doors opened.

There had to be fifty to seventy-five reporters and media people inside. The lights of the camera flashes and video cameras were blinding. But I felt like I was walking on sunshine. There was no way I was going to let this crumb of a man, Ed Meese, make me feel ashamed. He wasn't my father and I wasn't going to let him scold me.

They asked if I saw drugs in our business. I told them there may have been, but I didn't see it. I wasn't going to lie. They had this image of us all sitting around shooting heroin and snorting coke off each other's asses. Nothing could be further from the truth. We were worker bees, blue-collar types. We didn't push papers around in an air-conditioned office. We were sweaty, athletic, and at the end of a sixteen-hour day we were physically dog-tired. If we were doing drugs that whole time there was no way we could perform.

They asked if there was anything I did on film that I didn't want to do. "No," I said honestly.

After many negative questions trying to paint me into a corner making my industry look bad, they clearly saw they weren't getting anywhere. I told them I liked what I did and I did it because I wanted to. That wasn't exactly the answer they were looking for. There was an awkward pause. Dead silence.

It was around this point, I got hot under the collar and said, "Look, Eddie... ."

John Westin kicked me hard under the table as if to say, "This is the Attorney General!"

I looked at John and said, "Well, that's his name, isn't it?"

Meese sat up rigidly in his chair looking startled, like I had offended him. I brought up *Gone With The Wind* and commented on the scene where Rhett Butler broke the bedroom door down and ravished Scarlett. Just because you didn't see the actual act, didn't he rape her? All you saw was her face going "No, no, no..." but her body was saying "Yes, yes, yes..." This was a critically acclaimed classic film, but I didn't see anyone attacking it because it had a rape scene in it.

He didn't respond. I tasted victory. He was speechless.

I was pretty much dismissed after that. They hadn't gotten what they wanted from me. The anti-porn people never did and never will.

There was a ton of press after this and much of it portrayed me positively as someone who didn't back down. In fact, I don't remember a negative word written about me in particular.

The Meese Report ultimately met with much controversy. It was criticized by some of the experts whose research was utilized. They claimed their results were distorted and were incongruent with the final report. Some believe Meese minimized evidence indicating pornography is not dangerous, and others regard the commission members as a pre-selected cohort of anti-pornography zealots. The report was criticized by many inside and outside the pornography industry, calling it biased, incredible, and inaccurate. Ultimately Meese himself, as well as other members of the commission, such as Father Bruce Ritter, met with personal scandals.

Meanwhile, this little country girl had taken on the U.S. government and stood her ground, taking on the big boys. I walked down those halls of justice and felt like David. Goliath had been slain.

PORN STAR "Seka" testifies before Senate committee on pornography in Washington Tuesday. Seka, who has performed in over 30 adult movies, advocated stiffer penalties for the pornographers who prey on children.

Before the Meese Commission. No, I am not describing the size of John Holmes.

With Kay Parker and Annette Haven in DC for the Meese Commission.

With my former co-star Richard Pacheco testifying before the Meese Commission.

In DC during the Meese hearings.

Testifying in front of the Meese
Commission with Veronica Vera.

I look pretty classy when I'm testifying
before Congress.

34

Stripper

TIMES REMAINED GOOD. I was on a roll. Between the mail order business and working for *Club Magazine*, I was making a decent wage. But having stopped making films was beginning to hit me in the wallet.

In film, I started out making two, three, four hundred dollars a day. By the time I stopped, I was the highest paid actor in the business. I won't say how much I commanded, but suffice it to say it was cushy.

I missed that dough. It was funny, though, that because of home video, almost no one knew I'd retired. If you asked people five or six years after I retired who was the biggest porn star in the world, many would still say it was me. Porn lives on a helluva long time. It's got the half-life of uranium. And people don't mind seeing the same film or the same scene over and over and over again. Yet, we had no residuals. My films could sell hundreds of millions of copies and be played billions and billions of times, yet I'd never see another red cent.

One day the phone rang. It was Chuck Traynor.

I knew Chuck. Everyone knew Chuck. Chuck was the guy who gave the world Linda Lovelace. He then married Marilyn Chambers, whom I got to know quite well later on, although I never actually worked with either Linda or Marilyn.

Most all the world knows *of* Chuck Traynor. Linda Lovelace wrote a scathing book about how Chuck brutalized her, forced her into porn, beat her, made her turn tricks, and literally held her prisoner. Is any of it true? I have no freaking idea. Truly, I do not. Within the industry, I heard rumors both ways, some claiming it was all gospel truth, and others claiming Linda's tales were exaggerated beyond belief. And since I never saw any of it with my own eyes, I have no opinion whatsoever. When I got friendly with Marilyn, Chuck's name came up but there were never any confessions similar to Linda's, which doesn't really mean anything one way or the other.

I did meet Linda once, although it was a surprise meeting for both of us. I was booked on a talk show—I believe it may have been The Richard Bey Show, though I could be mistaken. It was around 1988 and Linda had just written her book and was out promoting it. Me, I was simply making a TV appearance, or so I thought. I used to get calls all the time to appear, usually to discuss the adult industry. Some folks like Phil Donohue, Oprah Winfrey, and Larry King were quite kind, while others, like Morton Downey, Jr., had me on as a human punching bag. Either way, I usually got little to no prep, nor did I need it. I think pretty fast on my feet and it was never an issue of worrying they'd booked me to discuss astrophysics, though I could sure as hell discuss black holes and big bangs.

So there's Linda Lovelace trashtalking Chuck, which was perfectly fine with me because no one really liked Chuck. But then she went after the entire industry and everyone in it, which would include me, which prompted me to fight back.

She was rambling on and on that she was forced to do everything she did on film and she had no idea what was going on, ever. I've heard this sort of stuff from a lot of people after they leave the business and it never fails to piss me off, particularly when I know it's crap. I perked up and said, "If you had no idea what was going on, why did you ask Al Goldstein, the publisher of *Screw* magazine, to babysit your pets when you were filming?"

Linda snapped back, "If I knew you were going to be on this show, I wouldn't have shown up."

I can't argue that I had, indeed, been sprung on her by surprise. Hell, no one told me Linda Lovelace was going to be on the same panel, either. They had us in different dressing rooms and we were even kept from each other in the green room. I suppose it was more to keep her off-balance than me, 'cause I could care less. But I definitely struck a nerve. As it turns out, I was reaching deep into my memory for that Al Goldstein anecdote— so deep that I actually got it wrong! For which Linda should have been eternally grateful. I knew Al, and I knew he told me something about him and Linda and dogs. Seems when Linda disavowed the industry, Al found not one but two movies Linda did where she had sex with a dog. Geez! And here I was, turning down scenes with humans I didn't like.

So Chuck Traynor calls me. By this time, he's divorced from Marilyn Chambers as well and now, according to him, he's married to some stripper named "Bo," like Bo Derek. I don't know Bo from Bo Diddley, but whatever. Traynor tells me I could make tons of money stripping. I blurted out a loud laugh. To me, strippers were dancers. I'm no dancer. I mean, I could dance at a wedding reception or a crowded nightclub, but I was not a skilled pole dancer.

Chuck kept pushing. More and more strip clubs were opening. Adult film stars were being asked to headline. It wouldn't be like regular strip club action where I'd be working the pole with half a dozen other girls and hustling lap dances. It would be like a stage show and I would be the feature attraction. No, check that. He wanted me to be the opening act for his new wife, Bo.

Opening act?? Moi?? And again, who the fuck was "Bo"? I knew Chuck was a hustler and I realized he was trying to hustle me.

"Chuck, I never heard of any 'Bo,' and unless she's the real Bo Derek, she ain't headlining over me. You know and I know if I show up, everyone in the audience will have paid to see me, not some no-name."

This went on and on and Chuck was persistent, even when I called him on his bullshit. He got down to talking numbers. I thought for a moment, and then came out with the most outrageous price I could conjure up. The point is, I really didn't want to do this. I'm not a dancer, and even if I could learn how to do it, I didn't know if I even wanted to. So I handled the negotiation as I did at the end of my film career. Since I didn't really want to do it anymore, I asked for the sun, the moon, and the stars, expecting to be turned down.

Chuck said, "Okay."

Shit. Now I had to do it. Off I went to beautiful Rochester, New York. I was goin' on the road.

When I got to Rochester, I met Bo. She was stunning. She looked nothing like Bo Derek—she was a dark-haired beauty with a killer bod and was younger than me. I hated her. Ha! Worse yet, she could dance. Boy, could she dance! She really was a star-attraction-level dancer, but no one knew her yet. But they knew Seka and that's what sold the tickets, just as I predicted.

Chuck booked me to be the featured performer-of-the-week at a number of venues and we drew big crowds, filling the house each show. They wanted six shows a day, but I demanded no more than four, as each set was about twenty minutes and it was grueling work.

I had steamer trunks full of costumes and gimmicks and I'd get enough bookings to be on the road for two to three months at a time. I had elaborate costumes made. There were huge capes with my name written out in my handwriting with bulbs that lit up. I had a top hat and tails that were mirrored to go with the songs. My tapes were also custom made to go with each of my outfits. The set would start out with *Singin' in the Rain*, with my umbrella lit up and flashing underneath, which would lead right into *It's Raining Men*. I also had flash paper that made sparks of fire for two seconds, along with a magic cane that expanded when you held it a certain way.

I began doing a comedy act before the show. I would come out un-announced, dressed as an old woman, sort of like a white Moms Mabley. Guys wouldn't know it was me at first. I'd tell dirty jokes and stories, making fun of this slutty girl, Seka, they'd all paid to see. It was a riot. I swear, I was doing everything in my power to entertain them and distract them from noticing I couldn't dance a lick. I could strut my stuff. I was a show-man. I did everything I could think of to dazzle them with flash.

When I first started, it felt incredibly weird to take my clothes off on stage. The guys would hoot and holler and I felt very bashful and would almost want to crawl under the stage. Odd, I know. But it was so differ-ent from doing movies. On set, I would be around eight or ten people at most, all of whom I knew, some quite well. On stage, I didn't know any of those people. And the people from my movie days wouldn't clap and shout when I dropped my drawers.

It was kind of cool to work in these big, big places. They'd hold two or three hundred people, with a mob standing outside for the next show. After each set there would be a designated area cordoned off for guys to take pictures with me. There were times when they'd have to actually cut the line so I could get ready for the next show. After my performance, I'd go back and finish the pictures of those I didn't have time for the first go-round, and there would already be new people coming. It was a really good feeling to know I had that many fans.

I'd work Monday through Saturday, travel on Sunday, and start the process all over again the following Monday, just in a different city. Half the time I didn't know where I was. Sometimes I'd wake up in the hotel and have to look at the matchbook by my bed to see what town I was in. I felt beat up after a while.

While I was on stage, I was thinking of how much money I'd be mak-ing selling the pictures and merchandise after the set. Or, "This show will get me to Mexico." I tried to do most of my dancing in the summer months so I could go to Mexico, St. Maarten, St. Croix, and other places I loved in the winter. I'd call Chicago and find out if it was warm yet and if it wasn't, I'd just stay longer until it was. If I needed more money, I'd call my secretary and tell her to pay my credit cards off and I'd get back to stripping.

Although I obviously preferred to be lounging on an island, I enjoyed doing the shows. And I never, ever thought of the audience or fans as losers. These were the folks who paid my bills. Stripping does give you an empowering sensation. There's an excitement knowing that people are there just for you. It does a lot for your ego. The only thing was, it never mattered how many times I went on a stage, I was always scared to death before I went out. I didn't want to disappoint people.

They always gave me bodyguards to go to and from the clubs to my hotels. They'd drop me off and pick me up every day. After the show they'd go with me to the area where we'd do the photos and autographs with the customers. They'd always give me these huge, gigantic bodyguards who were generally bouncers at the club.

There was this one black fellow we called Tree. He was the most massive man I'd ever seen. And his partner was pretty big himself. When I'd walk between them, nobody could even see me. The late actor Michael Clarke Duncan from *The Green Mile* was one of my bodyguards in Chicago. He, too, was one helluva big man.

Sometimes people would try to reach out, touch me, and grab a piece of clothing when I was walking to the autograph area. That was pretty scary. The security guys would just take their arms, push them back, and practically project them across the room. There was no intention of hurting them, just to get them away. There was one club in Chicago that was so packed we didn't know how they would get me on stage. But I had some bodybuilder friends there who said they'd help me for free. They were dressed up in leather and KISS-like make-up, with spiked armbands and dog collars. It was quite a scene as they carried me above the crowd as I lay flat and felt like I was floating over the masses. If anybody started to get too close they would smack them with those spiked armbands.

Eventually, I stopped working with Chuck Traynor. While I can't say exactly how he treated Linda Lovelace or Marilyn Chambers, I can say this: he's an asshole. That came out rather quickly in our relationship. He treated Bo like shit and I didn't like it. I may not have seen anything illegal or worth calling the cops about, but an asshole is an asshole, period, even if there isn't a law against it. He tried treating me that way and I stopped him in his tracks. That put an end to that, but still, I found him unlikeable and he was making an otherwise pleasant experience unpleasant, and who needs that? Life is too short. Besides, while he may have introduced me to the field, once I'd gotten my feet wet, offers from others kept rolling in. I'd get by.

Most of the other girls at the clubs were really nice—*and* they could really dance. A lot of people have this concept that strippers are real bitchy to each other. But they'd knock on my door and ask me if I needed anything. They'd also want to know how to become a feature performer and get into the adult business. I basically recommended they do something for *Playboy*, *Penthouse*, or *Club* as opposed to films. The porno industry can be cutthroat, and if you're just doing magazines you'll work alone. You didn't have to worry if you like a partner or not.

I'd get offers to go out after the gigs. Some rock band would be in town like The Fabulous Thunderbirds, or good local bands. We'd both be playing at the same time so they couldn't come to the show. They'd send flowers and invite me to go out clubbing. I got to meet Roy Orbison that way because we were in town at the same time. He was my absolute favorite performer. I still have a picture of us together.

From time to time there would be female impersonators who would come in dressed as me. There is no better compliment than someone trying to emulate you. I would make them get up on stage with me and it was hysterically funny. Some of my greatest fans are gay men. At the time there weren't a lot of gay bookstores where they could watch gay movies. A lot of times they went to see *my* movies with John Holmes. After all, he had the biggest cock around. Even today I have a lot of gay members on my website. I've even had recent appearances where on certain days gay men would predominantly come and see me. Some would swoon, "Oh my GAWD, it's Seka!" Packs of gay men crowded around me. The same with lesbians. I think I cover all bases with my fans.

As my film career got smaller and smaller in the rearview mirror of my life, attendance started to drop in the clubs and ultimately the bookings dried up. But in spite of the grueling nature of it all, some of the best times I ever had were when I was stripping.

During my dancing days, at the infamous Frank's Chicken House in NJ, posing with some deranged fan. OMG, it's comedian Jim Norton!

With baby-faced Jim Norton in the 1980's. How did he get into a strip club? He looks about 12.

A pit stop during my dancing days with the crew of the USS Honolulu.

On the USS Honolulu during my dancing days. No, I did not dance on the ship, at least not professionally.

With a fan and my dancing co-star, Bo, Chuck Traynor's last wife, in Niagara Falls, Canada.

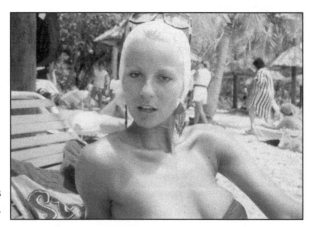

Relaxing between gigs in St. Maarten.

35

Sam the Man

I WENT TO SEE SAM KINISON at the Vic Theater one weekend in Chicago. It's a beautiful old theater with gilded artwork on the walls, opera boxes on the side, and graduated seating. It had been converted into a nightclub and performance palace. Bands and comedians would come in and they even had a series where you could watch classic movies while eating snacks. It was a great venue because of the ambiance and the type of unique programming presented.

I heard Sam was not only hysterical but also irreverent, which certainly appealed to me. But I didn't know much about him except he was an ordained minister and the church he started was near the theater. I was invited to the performance and not only had backstage passes, but a great little opera box on the side of the stage. I was with a couple of friends and it was V.I.P. treatment all the way.

Suddenly, out comes this large, roaring, straggly redheaded man in an overcoat with his cap turned backwards. Most of the comedians of that era were dressed a hell of a lot better. It was like seeing a heavyset Columbo on stage. But seeing him storm out and seize the mike was like an instant jolt of energy. The place went wild. It was just amazing to watch how he worked the crowd. He literally started screaming and it made me jump out of my seat. I started to laugh uncontrollably. When I get extremely tickled like that, I can't get my breath. I couldn't stop laughing and was making a honking sound to the point that he stopped the act, looked at me, and he actually started laughing.

We were getting ready to leave when one of Sam's people came over and said, "Sam would like to meet you." I said, "Cool, but my friends have to come, too." I didn't go anyplace by myself if I didn't know the person. Besides, I figured "share the wealth"—my pals wanted to meet him, too.

We went backstage and were hanging out and hitting it off. It was a really interesting chemistry. I felt very comfortable, like I had known him a long time. It wasn't like, "I'm Sam and you have to worship me." He was just very down-to-earth.

"We're going out. Would you like to come with us?" he asked.

As I had nothing to do, I said, "Why not?" It was a group of his friends and his manager Elliot Abbott, a really nice man. He helped Penny Marshall put together *A League of Their Own* and was a big time agent.

We went out on the town in Chicago, hitting what felt like every nightspot. It was amazing how people flocked to him. Sam was very cordial to everyone, but he never neglected me that evening, which I found kind of refreshing. He wasn't treating me like just another groupie. I didn't mind that he wasn't a traditionally attractive man. Looks were never a big thing to me anyway. I'd rather have a man who can hold a conversation. Sam had unbelievable charisma and was highly intelligent.

I ended up spending the night with him, and with Sam it was all sex, drugs, and rock and roll. I had certainly done my share of partying, as many of us had in the eighties, but this ex-preacher sure took things to a whole new level.

He stayed in town that week, with his next show scheduled four or five days later in Fort Lauderdale. Elliot asked if I wanted to go. "Sam really likes you. And he hasn't felt like that towards someone in a long time."

I figured, why not? It was a trip to Florida on someone else's dime. Plus, there were a lot of drugs around.

I never did drugs as a kid. When I got married, Frank got me to try pot and I continued to smoke up once in a while, though I was never what you'd call a stoner. Hell, I never really liked to drink much. When I'd be booked for industry events and meet-and-greets, I'd force myself to hold a glass in order to fit in. I never knew what to order so I'd ask for a screwdriver. To this day, I hate those things. Eventually, I started to enjoy sunny morning mimosas when I was living in California and would lounge around on my days off by the pool and Jacuzzi. Later on, I learned to appreciate fine wine.

When I was on set, I was always straight as an arrow (my girl/girl scenes aside). I knew cocaine was becoming popular, but I never saw any being used at work because it would have screwed up filming and wasted precious time. In fact, I never tried it myself until after I'd stopped doing films and after I'd been asked about the topic before the Meese Commission. But like most others of my generation, I eventually gave it a try and liked it on occasion. But at this point in my life, it wasn't a driving passion or hobby.

So we went to Florida and I was told to have my bags packed and Sam's guys would take care of everything. I didn't have to worry about checking in or anything. Sam did another spectacular show, which led to another spectacular evening of partying and drinking. That was a continuous thing.

We were told after the show to pack a bag for a couple of days, leave the rest of the stuff at the hotel, as we were going on vacation to a beautiful little island called Cat Cay right outside of Florida. It sounded like fun, but this was where reality started to set in.

He suddenly demanded, "Put my stuff in a bag." I didn't like being spoken to like that, but let it roll off my back, figuring he was springing for everything. Besides, he just wore a t-shirt, sweat pants, tennis shoes, an overcoat, and a hat anyway. It wasn't like there was a lot of packing to do.

As we headed out, I noticed everyone was getting a little edgy because they couldn't bring their stash, since Cat Cay was technically outside the U.S. But knowing that everyone was going to want their drugs, and having big boobs like I do, I put about fifty Quaaludes under one breast, and about a half ounce of cocaine under the other. Nobody knew I had it, but I figured they'd want it and I was doing them a favor.

I put on a tiny little bikini to distract the agents. It worked like a charm. We got on the boat with no problem.

The island was small and quaint, with the natives quite friendly. There was one restaurant and the only transportation was little golf carts. I thought it would be a very relaxing couple of days.

I couldn't have been more wrong. When we got in the room, Sam was already going, "God damn it, nobody's holding!"

I said, "Hold on a minute, Sam."

I lifted up my top and out dropped the drugs.

He just went wild. "Oh my God, how did you do it?"

"It's easy when you have boobs like this."

All was right in the world.

We went to the restaurant and they had this local cocktail that was just amazing, and we were flat out wasted from it. We asked them to make us up a batch of it. They made up eight or nine half-gallon milk jugs filled with this stuff, which I called the Cat Cay Kitty.

After dinner, we all grabbed our jugs, hopped on our golf carts, and went crazy zipping around the island. We decided to go skinny dipping, swimming nude at night with absolutely no fear. Who knew there were sharks there?

Crashing several carts in the jungle area, we basically wrecked and abandoned them. We ended up lying on the beach naked, which wasn't a pretty sight for most involved.

Over the rest of our vacation we slept, partied, and even squeezed in some deep sea fishing. It was quite a couple of days.

It seemed to me we had become boyfriend and girlfriend, since he asked me to come to his next gig in Vancouver. "I really want you to come. You don't have to worry about anything. You don't have to pay for anything. I haven't liked anyone like you for a long time. It would make my day if you came along." In spite of his religious background, he loved the fact I was an adult star. He had seen a lot of my movies and was a fan.

On the way to Sam's next gig, our limo was driven to a private Lear-jet. That was the preferred mode of transportation for Sam, as it was the least amount of hassle. It couldn't have been planned better, with the door of the limo opening almost simultaneously with the jet's door. I was like, "Wow," and not a lot of things impress me.

Sam did his show in a 12,000-seat venue and we were right back to partying like rock stars. Lines of cocaine on every coffee table in the suite. And Quaaludes. It was like those were the snacks. I was surprised there weren't butlers with silver trays passing them around. We had a line of cocaine, half a Quaalude, and a cocktail just to start the evening, which we called a "rocktail." I have to admit, it was fun.

After Vancouver we were told to pack a day bag. But getting Sam out of bed was an absolute chore. He was not a very willing participant. I rolled him over and said, "Get your ass out of bed and get dressed now!" I had to lay his clothes out for him like a kid, but that wasn't too difficult since he always wore the same thing. I was told Sam had become my responsibility as far as getting him dressed and ready.

We piled into another limo and were taken to this absolutely drop dead gorgeous yacht. We were going boating for the afternoon. There were fifteen or twenty people there. I thought they had rented it, but the actual owners were there. I was talking to a pleasant gentleman about music. This was around when "We Are the World" was out. I told him an Earth, Wind, and Fire tune I loved was much better and would be a more appropriate anthem. Interrupting the conversation, I asked him, "Do you happen to know where the lady's room is?" He gave me directions and I walked into this huge private state room. It was comparable to a beautiful hotel suite. The entire back of the bed was lined with Grammy awards.

I'm not normally a nosey person, but I looked at them, and they were all made out to Earth, Wind, and Fire. He didn't tell me he was Maurice White, the founder and leader of the band. When I came back out I laughed and said to him, "Are you amused with yourself?"

He said, "That was probably the nicest compliment I've ever heard."

Sam loved Baileys on the rocks and Saki. Back at the hotel, Sam was downing a ton of Saki. We were all partying again and I knew we had to go to Seattle the next day. We partied until the wee hours of the morning, but I was trying simultaneously to pack. We had new hundred dollar bills for each line of cocaine we were doing. God forbid we should use the same one.

I went around the room afterwards, picking up hundred dollar bills, wiping the cocaine off, and straightening them out. There had to be four or five thousand dollars in my hand. I walked over to Sam and he said, "Are you fucking crazy?"

"What do you mean?"

He said, "Keep it."

"But it's your money…"

"Just keep it."

He didn't have to ask me again.

Sam woke up in a gnarly mood. We went from limos, jets, and yachts to a beat-up old station wagon for a short ride to Seattle. But getting him up was a nightmare.

"Leave me alone. I want to sleep."

I got all the bags together and set them outside the room. "Sam, come on. We've got to go. You can sleep in the car." He put a pillow on my lap and slept the whole ride down.

We didn't have to leave the hotel to get to the venue. There was a servant's area that led backstage. But it was about five minutes before show time and he was still sleeping. This was becoming a real job. Well paid, but a pain in the butt. When you're in two hotels a day and partying like a rock star, people are going to be grumpy. But when Sam got vicious, he'd curse like nobody's business. "What the fuck's wrong with you, bitch; can't you see I'm sleeping?"

Not very nice.

I felt obligated to everyone else to get him where he had to go, but I was pissed off because he was ungrateful I was actually helping him keep his career on track. I finally got him up, dressed, and had him brush his teeth. Everybody was looking at me. They were all nervous and sweating. It was literally thirty seconds before the show and the place was packed. He pulled himself together, walked out, and brought the house down.

Standing there next to Elliot, I said, "I want to quit now."

"It is taxing, isn't it?" he said, laughing in relief.

I said, "My tenure is done."

All of a sudden in the middle of the show I heard Sam calling me out. He was standing in the middle of the stage waiting for me.

"Elliot, I don't want to do this."

But I wasn't going to humiliate Sam by leaving him just standing there. So we do this little back and forth off the cuff, and I'm holding my own with him. The fans liked me, too, and people were standing up screaming my name. I think Sam was jealous because I had popped the crowd and they kept screaming for me even after I left the stage. So he started yelling back at the crowd, "Shut up! The bitch is gone." He wasn't a happy camper that I had stolen his spotlight.

We were going back to L.A. right after the show on another private jet. He was still grumpy, sleepy, and of course had done too much drugs and alcohol. Not too many words were exchanged between us because he was pissed off. We were flying into John Wayne Airport. He kept asking me for cocaine and Quaaludes and I didn't have any. Hell, we had used them all up. He had a bottle of Baileys in one hand and a cup of ice in another. I didn't like his attitude so I just tried to get some sleep and ignore him.

When we got off the plane, Sam suddenly started screaming at me. He was yelling in Sam Kinison fashion how I had woken him up and there were no more drugs. He was coming down, and coming down from drugs is a terrifying experience and not a pretty picture.

I grabbed my suitcase and was trying to get it over to the side where I could call a taxi just to get away from the whole scene. But he kept dragging one of my bags and pulling it away from me. Meanwhile, he had me cornered next to a pay phone, screaming in my face, "You ungrateful bitch!"

Fed up, I looked at him and said, "Eat shit and die, Sam."

He grabbed the suitcase and told me he was keeping it.

"I just want to get away from you. Keep it."

I got a cab and went to my friend's house to try to regroup and figure out how to get my other suitcase. I was so exhausted I probably slept for two days.

When I finally reached Sam, he told me to come to his house and get the bag. Now he seemed to be in a perfectly good mood. Billy Idol and his girlfriend were there and obviously Sam had gotten his "medication." He apologized for being an asshole and I said, "Look Sam, I'm staying with friends and I need to go back to Chicago."

He sounded like a little kid when he asked, "But will you see me again?"

I said, "Yes, if you behave yourself."

I didn't hear from him for a month or so.

Sam had been on *Saturday Night Live* and they went ballistic because he didn't stick to the script. But he got such a great response from the fans that they wanted him back. I got a call from Elliot and he asked me, "How would you like to be on *Saturday Night Live* with Sam?"

Sam had demanded me or else he wasn't going to do the show. I think it was his way of apologizing. They must have wanted him badly enough because it was a go.

Everybody was very nice and extremely pleased with me because I did exactly what they wanted. I acted like a total professional, getting there on time and seizing the opportunity. My part was to feed Sam grapes along with the Church Lady. I was in a sexy nightgown and they obviously wanted to exploit my popularity. The audience found the contrast between me and Dana Carvey in drag hilarious. It was a great moment. I also came out at the end with the entire cast. I was shocked to hear Don Pardo announce, "We had another wonderful show having Sam Kinison back, but the best part of the show was having Seka on."

I didn't hear from Sam after that. I guess it was too big a blow to his ego.

The Sam Kinison roller coaster was too scary for me to ride. I genuinely loved Sam and cared for him. It was fun, it was exciting, and an experience most people will never have in their life. Plus, I got a lot of publicity out of it.

When I heard Sam died, I was truly sad. I tried to reach Elliot to find out what had happened but couldn't get in touch with anyone. Basically I knew what the public knew. I heard he had cleaned up his act, which made it even more tragic.

He was one of the greats, right up there with Lenny Bruce and Richard Pryor. And an unforgettable part of my life.

With my boyfriend of the time, Sam Kinison, hosting SNL 3-15-86.

Classic Sam.

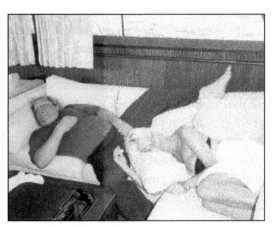

Lolling around Cat Cay in a boat with Sam Kinison, in between "rocktails."

36

Patrick

PATRICK WAS A VERY TALENTED BLUES harmonica player who also fancied himself a photographer. He was about five foot seven with long, red, wavy hair that went down to the middle of his back, which he always wore in a French braid. He was very Irish looking with a fair complexion, freckles, and really, really pretty soft milky brown eyes. I was an inch or two taller than him, but the height difference never bothered me. For whatever reason, I usually dated men who were shorter than me.

We met at Kingston Mines, a blues club in Chicago. It was a jam session. He knew who I was, but I had never seen him before. I thought he was really cool because he played harmonica, had that long braid, a great laugh, and was very popular. It seemed that everybody in the club knew him. What was there not to like?

We started hanging out, partying, and soon enough, dating. It was the same old sex, drugs, and rock and roll, only with a steadier partner. I thought he was a serious artist because he kept saying he had an album deal coming soon. He envisioned himself a Bruce Hornsby type.

I had to go to L.A. for a photo shoot and he wanted to come along. He had some friends there and also had golfing on his brain. While I was working he golfed and socialized. And out of nowhere one night he asked me to marry him. And he kept asking. He was in love.

In a drug induced haze, I said, "Sure, why not?" It seemed like a well thought out decision at the time. Besides, I just wanted to go to sleep and shut him up.

Unbeknownst to me, while I was at the photo shoot, he arranged for a minister, a marriage license, the whole nine yards. I have a friend who still lives in L.A., and Patrick asked if we could have the wedding in his backyard.

I got back from the shoot and he told me, "We're getting married tomorrow."

Now, I liked him well enough. But was I in love with him? Not quite.

I woke up in a stupor, barely realizing I was about to be married again. With all the partying, I'd had maybe five hours' sleep in three or four days. I stood in front of the minister in a fog. When he asked, "Do you take this man to be your lawfully wedded husband?" I didn't even absorb it. I felt several people poke me, abruptly jolting me back to reality. It was then I uttered the incredibly romantic words, "Yeah, I guess so."

That should have given me a clue right there.

After the "I guess so's" were pronounced, we had what you might call a reception, with lunch served to the eight or nine people present, including my make-up artist, hairdresser, and a couple of other friends. As they ate, I went into the bedroom and slept through the whole darn thing.

When I woke up hours later, most everyone was gone. A dream wedding this wasn't.

I had a couple of other things to do in L.A., so Patrick headed back to Chicago, where he said he'd move his things in while I was out of town. When I got back to Chicago, I was horrified to find my whole house rearranged. There were all kinds of shady-looking people in and out of there at all hours of day and night. It didn't take me long to figure out my musician/photographer husband was actually a drug dealer. That's why everybody in that club knew him. Was I ever pissed he was dealing from my house! I was terrified of losing my home. Despite rumors, I'd only been married once before, and Frank sold pot, so here I was again, reliving the worst parts of my life on an endless loop.

When Patrick referred to it as "our house," I corrected him, firmly. Things went downhill awfully fast. I wasn't too polite to anyone who walked through the door, which was not doing his business much good. Ultimately, I would get disgusted and pick myself up and leave my own place.

One day, I looked at him and simply said, "I want a divorce."

I went to my lawyer and told him what I'd done and he said, "Oh my God, what's wrong with you?"

I replied, "I'm crazy; what do you want from me?"

Patrick truly thought he was in love and told me he'd contest the divorce. He was using a lot and was in just as bad a condition as I was, for my partying had gotten way out of control, although I never had a desire to deal. Too dangerous. Soon after, Patrick was summoned to my lawyer's office, where I had all the papers ready to be signed. But he said, "I'm not signing them."

I lost it. I angrily stormed over to him, picked him up, and literally threw him against the wall. When I'm angry, it gives me crazy strength.

"Sign the papers or I'm going to break your fucking legs!"

He said, "You're threatening me. You're threatening me and we're in front of lawyers."

"They're my lawyers, dumb ass, and I'm paying them. Do you think they're going to squeal on me?"

So he signed.

And just like that the marriage was over. The whole thing lasted six weeks and we were in each other's company for about three.

It was one of the things that made me realize I needed to get straight, and fast. The next time I saw him, we bumped into each other on the street and he had grown a beard, gained about fifty pounds, and just looked terrible. I barely recognized my ex-husband.

37

Careful...
They May Screw You

I'D LEFT XXX FILMS, I did the stripping thing for a while, I still did the *Club* magazine work and the mail order business, but funds were dwindling. My opulent lifestyle was eating up all my cash, but I didn't want to give it up without a fight.

The film business never stopped calling me. My videos were still the rage. Other, younger stars had come along, but my name continued to bring in audiences and sales. Instead of just saying no, I kept up my game of asking for far too much money, as well as so many other conditions, in order to make them hang up the phone. But while AIDS lingered as a concern, other factors kept teasing me to come back. Sure, money was number one, but other things, such as creative control, played in my head. So long as they still knew I could make them money, the industry seemed willing to give me a wide berth if I ever wanted back in.

I decided to make my own movie. It was a challenge. It was almost like giving birth.

In that era, I can't remember any woman but Gail Palmer raising money, writing, directing, editing, and getting a distribution deal before the first inch of film was shot. But it was something I needed to—and somehow knew I *could* do.

I started writing *Careful, He May Be Watching* while I was traveling quite a bit with Barbara. She knew the lawyers to go to in order to draw up the agreements, and the people we needed to raise money from.

I wrote it out in longhand on a legal pad, as I didn't really know how to put it into script format. For that, I hired Richard Pacheco, whose real name is Howie Gordon. He was an actor I had worked with and I really liked him a lot and still do. He was one of the few guys in the business I felt was extremely sensitive. Even though he got paid to get a hard-on on demand, he personally wasn't a hard-on. I was even friendly with his wife and kids. He always had a tablet with him and would be writing something, so I knew he was the right man for the job.

I gave the plot a little twist—something I had not seen or heard before in XXX. I played both leading ladies: a blonde named Jane Smith, and a redhead named Molly Flame. Jane was an ordinary housewife and Molly a porn star. And they both liked to watch adult films. It turned on Jane's husband, an airline pilot, whose favorite porn star was Molly. What he didn't know was that Molly was actually his wife, because I wore a red wig and dyed my pubes red to match the red hair. As was my philosophy, the carpet always has to match the drapes. In the scenes with Jane, my pubes were blonde. Come to think of it, that may have been the first and last time that's ever happened in any movie, period. Hell, today's adult stars barely even have pubes at all, except for maybe a little landing strip.

After a few years off, I worried about my looks. Mainstream actresses battle aging, but can rely on lots more tricks than we ladies who go naked all the time. Nudity is unforgiving.

One of the things that set us apart back in my day from the adult films of today was our natural bodies. When you saw someone like me or Kay Parker, really busty gals, we were all real. No implants, please! No ass implants, no big collagen blowjob lips, no nothing. And people could tell, especially after the passage of time when our films are compared to more modern fare. Most of the implant girls never even try to look real and natural. That's when we really get appreciated by the guys who considered themselves porn connoisseurs. Still, as we age… lemma tell ya, big boobs follow the laws of gravity. They drop like wages in a recession. I also have to compensate when I step on a scale. I carry around forty pounds of boobage.

I was never a purist, per se. I will not rip on girls for getting work done. But I had a different challenge. People had certain expectations about my body. My body was my signature. My pride was that I didn't want to have anything done where fans would say, "Oh look, she had her boobs done. They're larger now and they're up around her neck." If I was to have anything done, it would be for maintenance sake only. If a doctor couldn't make me look the same as I always looked, I wasn't interested.

Some girls go in with the best of intentions, but the doctors screw up and they come out looking like Outer Space Barbie. I shopped around and shopped around. I knew I needed help—my knockers were speeding toward my knees.

I had my babies lifted—not enlarged, just lifted. A few years later, I had to do it again. Finally, on round three (long after *Careful*), I got them raised again (I treat them like a draw bridge), along with a face lift and a tummy tuck. I go to doctors today and they're amazed at how good a job my surgeons did. They have to search all over me to find even the slightest hint of a scar anywhere. As natural-looking as can be. My breasts still hang down as large natural breasts tend to do. When I lie on my back, they splay out toward my armpits rather than reaching for the ceiling like they have magnets in the nipples. Again, if I never told anyone, no one would ever know, which is the whole idea... until now.

Being a woman, I wanted to make the film a little more romantic than standard adult fare, but for commercial purposes I realized I had to appeal to the hardcore audience and make it hot as well.

Mike Horner played my husband because he looked like the airline pilot-type—very Superman-ish and extremely clean cut. He was a nice guy and I wanted to work with him. What was great about running my own show was I didn't have to reject anyone. I just cast people I liked and respected on a personal level. And those who I knew could do the job.

Shanna McCullough was also in the movie and I loved her. She was very pretty and lollipop sweet. But when you needed her to be nasty, she could be a hot little girl. I think it gave a lot of depth to her character—to appear one way and be able to completely turn it around.

There's also a scene where Shanna plays an airline stewardess and one of the passengers is Whoopi Goldberg's mother. Howie knew Whoopi very well and he made the introduction. Whoopi was a complete unknown at the time. She asked me to send her demo tape to my agent friend, Sy Sussman, to get her started. A week later, Mike Nichols signed her to her one-woman show on Broadway and the rest is history.

Since I helped her out, Whoopi even let me stay in her home once her career got going. She's nutty as a fruitcake, but in a good way. She's naturally funny, but intense. The lady's extremely well read and well-spoken. I don't think you can be a really good comedian unless you're an intelligent person.

When Whoopi bought herself a red Porsche and pointed to the car she asked me, "Can you believe that? I can't believe that car is all mine. And it's all paid for!" She was just so excited she finally made the big time after struggling for years. God bless her.

I was invited to opening night of her show on Broadway. Ironically, the Kennedys, James Earl Jones, and other celebs were dressed to the nines and sitting behind us, while I was in the front row with jeans and cowboy boots. Whoopi actually said we were sitting up front because we were the ones who helped her on the way up. That's loyalty, and I'll never forget her class and pure heart.

Whoopi had a tour bus and asked me for my posters because she wanted to put them on the inside of the vehicle. She thought it was funny when they took it for a wash that people would think it was my bus and not hers.

Once she was sick and hospitalized in Chicago. I don't recall exactly what was wrong at the time, but she had to cancel her run. I visited her in the hospital like a good friend. I told a pal of mine who ran a great restaurant to bring her and the hospital staff some food. I made sure everyone was well fed. Even in L.A. we'd pass each other in our cars and pull over and chat. She never once ignored me. I think she's a super comedian, an excellent actress, and a good human being.

Anyway, I told Whoopi I needed some extras for the movie and she said, "Hey Mom, you want to be in a movie?"

Just like that. She simply sat on the plane. It was a non-speaking role where she was supposed to react to the pilot and the stewardess having sex, which they weren't actually doing at the time. You just saw her and the rest of the extras rubbernecking to watch the action that was supposedly going on.

Kay Parker was also in the film and I always loved Kay. She is just a wonderful woman—very kind and sincere and extremely thoughtful to everyone. I've never heard or seen her be unkind to anyone. She's also quite graceful—just a class act.

I hired Ronnie Webber, my hairdresser at the time (I went through a lot of hair and makeup people over the years), to do my hair. And I put him in the movie as a hairdresser, too. He's a funny, funny man.

It was a pleasure to have a cast where I liked every single person on a personal level without having to compromise on quality. With all the pressure on my shoulders, it was nonetheless exhilarating. I even raised the money for the movie in a week. Watching it all come together felt like a triumph.

This isn't to say there aren't some bitches and bastards in the industry. In my previous films, there were some people behind the camera I couldn't stand. One boom guy, in fact, purposely cracked me on the head one day just to get my attention and tell me something. I almost ripped his throat out. I refused to go back to work until they got another guy. They pleaded with me. It was some guy who did legitimate films and thought we weren't real people, we were just porno actors. But here I could pick and choose my dream cast and crew.

Or so I thought.

I had extreme confidence in everyone I personally hired from the lighting people to the camera people to the directors. This wasn't one of those cheapo weekend shoots. But on a project this big, you still had tech people who came on the recommendation of others.

Everything was going pretty smoothly but then came a bump in the road. A lot of the crew was union. From their work in "legit" films, they were used to overtime, double time, triple time, and golden time, which is a lot of bucks. I respect unions, but the problem in any situation is when only one set of workers is unionized. I would have died and gone to heaven if we porn actors had ever formed a union. A hell of a lot would have been different. But we weren't, so to treat certain people one way and the rest of us another just wasn't going to fly. This came up on every XXX feature ever filmed and the tech guys knew or should have known the score. This wasn't a union gig; get used to it. If you don't like it, leave.

But since I was a woman, these guys thought they were going to outsmart me. I told them I'd take care of them and they'd be paid for some overtime, but we don't do triple time, golden time, and all that stuff. It's not a three or four million dollar movie. But they figured they would hold me up.

I knew this was going to happen. I don't know why, but I had an innate sense or something. So I had a couple of people hired as gophers keeping an eye on the reels of film. Nobody else knew about it but me, nor did anyone even know who my spies were.

Even though I was in front of the camera trying to perform and make it all look as hot as possible, I was simultaneously thinking about who was trying to rip me off and how. Not an easy gig.

When I wrote the checks, the crew told me the overtime pay wasn't enough. "We have two rolls of your film," a pair of men exclaimed, thinking they had me over a barrel.

I smirked and said. "You think so? Open it.'"

"If we open it, it'll expose it."

When I insisted, they were shocked to see it was blank. At my insistence, my posse kept their eyes glued to the real reels and hid them in my car every time there was a break. It was like a scene out of a caper movie.

Careful did really well, and was even nominated and won some industry awards, but I never saw a dime because I kept getting told it didn't make any money. Although I knew that was bull, I didn't have the means to prove it. They made money on it for over twenty years. I was just plain ripped off. Screwed if you will, on camera and off.

When the smoke cleared, I had some investors who needed a write-off and they certainly got one. But not being able to pay some people their money back was painful for all of us involved.

It took years of fighting to get my movie back, and now I own the rights and have re-released it. We re-mastered it, added some new footage that had never been seen before, and it's doing fairly well. Video-X-Pix is doing the distribution. It's the same people that did *Inside Seka* and I trust these folks very much.

Some people may find it odd that creating a porn flick is something one would take pride in. But from where I'm sitting, *Careful, He May Be Watching* was an accomplishment. To me, the film was better than most X-rated flicks out there. I don't know whether I'd call it art, but it was certainly professional and entertaining.

Completing a project on that scale showed me I could do anything I set my mind to. But getting ripped off like I did ultimately made it all bittersweet.

Careful, He May Be Watching, my next-to-last film, which I wrote,
produced, and co-directed ... as a redhead!

...And as a blonde.

About to get down with my
favorite lady, Kay Parker.

Making out with co-star
Shanna McCullough.

One of my favorite woodsmen, Mike Horner.

I cast myself as a porn star.
Quite a stretch.

38

Amok

AFTER THE MOVIE WAS RELEASED, I had investors down my throat, a distributor that wouldn't show me the books, and a partner in Barbara who I butted heads with every step of the way.

Life was wonderful.

Barbara had been a good friend to me. A few years back she helped make me aware of what "Dead Fred" was doing to me, and even found me the lawyers to go after him. But we just weren't seeing eye-to-eye on anything related to the film. Ultimately, we ended up in court. It wasn't as bad as my previous knockdown, drag out fight with Fred, because Barbara was a good friend of mine and I didn't want to go the Fred route. And it wasn't that she was dishonest—she wanted to do things a certain way but didn't know the adult business. Barbara didn't understand what was involved in the distribution of an adult film and how to deal with the industry. I knew these people. I knew how they worked. I knew their M.O. In her legal world, everything was black and white, but in the adult film world, where everything was "grey," you were playing with their bats and balls. I had nurtured this project, but she wanted to change the rules in the middle of the game. It was an ongoing battle with her and it hurt me because we had always been so close. I was pissed off, as our friendship was crumbling.

To get the books, I had to settle with her out of court for $10,000. This was an awful lot of money to me at the time, and another hurdle for me to go over. But I just didn't have the strength for another long, drawn out court battle. Even worse, it ended our relationship, and that hurt me a lot. I was very sad. It was like mourning a loss of a loved one. I pretty much lost faith in humanity.

At the same time, the investors kept calling and asking if there were any profits, and the only thing I could report to them was "No, there weren't." All the reports I received was that the movie hadn't made money even though it won awards. When I would ask to see why it was showing a deficit rather than a profit, I wasn't getting a response. When I asked my accounting people to take an overview of it, they basically looked at me and said these guys are bigger than you, they could hide anything they want, and I should decide whether I want to spin my wheels or leave it alone.

I left it alone.

With everything I'd been through in the business, I just felt defeated. This was a new sensation for me. I had found producers, wrote it, edited it, shot it, and gave it to people in the industry who I'd made a lot of money for. I worked with Caballero before and just expected more from them.

I ended up running amok. I didn't give a flying fuck about a whole lot of anything or anyone. In spite of everything that had happened to me in my life, I always had faith in people, but this was the last straw. I decided everybody was horrible and I didn't want to see all the ugliness. I wanted to be numb.

I went clubbing. Drinking. Drugging. I had partied before, but now I was drinking heavily and doing a lot of cocaine. Sometimes I'd stay up for four or five days straight partying. It got me really skinny.

It was the era. There was lots of coke, lots of partying, and lots of drinking. When we would get ready to go out for the evening, we'd do a big line of cocaine, half a Quaalude, and a vodka on the rocks. Sam Kinison called that a rocktail and I kept up the name in his honor and eventually his memory. But I always felt I could stop if I wanted to.

Since I'd made my comeback with *Careful*, the adult world thought I was back for good. But now everything was being shot on video and I was being offered significantly less money. If they weren't going to pay me what I wanted, I couldn't see the point in doing them for less.

I wasn't on any schedule and had no routine whatsoever. Time meant nothing to me. Sometimes I'd just find myself at an airport with a carryon bag, looking at the board, seeing what was available, and pointing to the first destination that struck my fancy, saying, "I want to go there," and I'd be gone two to three months. My secretary would do my mail order business and I'd be somewhere warm like the Dominican Republic, Costa Rica, or Mexico. Anywhere there was an ocean and sand.

When I ran out of money, I'd call Chicago and simply say, "Put more money in my checking account."

On other occasions, I'd visit my family back East. My Uncle Tom liked to speculate on real estate and he and I bought a farm in Virginia together, which we held onto for a few years and then sold. I would hang out there and garden and visit with old friends and just not do a whole lot of anything. I never really told my family much about my lifestyle or career, and they didn't ask. They knew about the adult films, but never really questioned me about any of it. They saw I paid my bills and as far as they knew, everything was fine. But anybody who parties like a rock star doesn't reveal much about what they're doing, and I didn't either. I may have appeared to them to be happy, but I certainly wasn't, or I wouldn't have been doing the amount of drugs I was doing.

It turned into a three-year blur. I still had the mail order business, the *Club Magazine* shoots, and some stripping here and there, but all in all it was one big, outrageous party. I'm sure I did certain things I don't even remember. Even in my drug haze, I did manage to meet some truly interesting and talented people. Brilliant musicians like Buddy Miles, and blues greats Sugar Blue and Big Time Sarah. Not only were they fabulous performers, but they also turned into true friends. I remember seeing The Rolling Stones when Sugar opened for them in Chicago at a huge outdoor concert. Sugar played the famous harmonica part on their big hit, "Miss You." I was on the Stones' bus with him. Sugar was very nervous because it was such a large audience and it was *The Stones*! But in spite of the stage fright, he was absolutely awesome. Very few men on this planet can play the harmonica like Sugar.

I just couldn't handle a serious relationship. Instead, I had fuck buddies. Whoever was convenient at the moment. The flavor of the day. I'd get what I wanted and tell them to leave. I didn't even want them to spend the night. I didn't want to wake up next to anyone or talk to them. I didn't want to feel anything since I didn't believe in people anymore. I didn't give a flying fuck about any of them. I don't remember most of their names.

There was an adult actor named Jerry Butler who stated in many interviews that I went into rehab for a year. Not true. Nobody goes into rehab for a year. I've never even been in rehab. I'm the type of person who says, "When I'm done, I'm done." Could I have used therapy and rehab? No doubt. What made me decide to stop, though, was my life was out of control, especially my business life, which was in trouble. I couldn't understand why this was happening, but I simply hadn't bothered to pay attention.

One day, I just put down my drink, put down my doobie, put down my straw, and blew the cocaine off the mirror. The air became clearer. It was time to get myself back together.

39

Old Strippers

MOVIES WERE OVER, but I still occasionally did appearances. I went down to Tennessee for an autograph session at an adult book store and was picked up at the airport by two promoters. Prior to the appearance, they told me what was expected. I was just supposed to sign and pose for pictures with the fans. Sounded easy enough.

I asked them to take me to the store so we could set up. There was a six foot-long table with a curtain in the front and a backdrop. But they kept acting sort of strange. When I asked what the backdrop was for, they said "Oh, that's where you get naked and take pictures with the guys."

I said, "That's not what the deal said. I'm not going to do that."

I was told I had no choice. It was what the customers expected. I'm sure they had a lot of girls who came down and did that—there were tons of pictures of performers on the wall. What made it seem shady, though, was having the big black curtain there so guys could feel me up. It wasn't simply that it was beneath me. If they told me in advance, at least I could have decided whether or not to do it. What pissed me off was the deception, the attitude that as an adult actress I was such a whore they could do anything they wanted with me without so much as a "how do you do?" And on top of it, they wanted 50% of the picture money.

I said, "I'm not getting naked. And you're not getting anything."

They were trying to be tough guys, attempting to bully me into it. I wasn't going for it. They said, "Well, the gig's off."

They turned around, walked away, and I said, "Are you at least going to take me back to the hotel?"

"Find your own way."

And I did.

I started walking out of the store to grab a cab when this large, round, jolly fellow with thinning red hair came into the store. He said, "I saw you

229

were going to be here today and I wanted you to come to my club. But I didn't know how to get in touch with you."

I had heard of his place and it was supposed to be pretty nice, upscale strip joint. We went back to my hotel and he informed me, "We'll pay for your room for a week so I'll have time to advertise you. I only want you to do two shows a day for four days." He also said I could keep all the photograph money.

Some five years and several pounds since I'd last stripped, it didn't sound like the greatest idea in the world. Hell, I didn't even have "proper stripping clothes" with me. But I needed the money.

I knew I wasn't in dancing shape. Once I stopped doing coke, the pounds grew back on and then some. Even back in my prime, I was nervous and scared about live shows. Any dancer who tells you otherwise is lying. I would always think, "Are they going to like me?" But I would get standing ovations just for walking out. It was a feeling of power. Sometimes I'd even see guys jerking off in their seats. For whatever reason, it didn't seem sleazy to me. I was amused they would actually have the nerve to do this at a live performance in a room full of people. Hell, I could get a guy to do anything I wanted from the stage. If I wanted him to jump out of his seat and walk on stage for me to do a lap dance, he'd do it. I had fans actually come and bow down in front of me and say, "I am not worthy." That made me uncomfortable, since I'm just a regular person, but it wasn't like it was my idea.

But did I still have it? I wondered nervously as we wrote the out contract on a napkin.

The club was packed the entire four days. The owner asked if I would hang around between shows to just talk to customers and have a drink with them. Since he had been so gracious, I didn't mind at all. I had already told the bartenders that when the customers bought me a drink, put very little alcohol in as I didn't want to get hammered.

They had a designated corner table for the owner and me. I had on a mini-skirt with high heels and a low cut blouse, but was well aware I didn't look like the Seka of old. Yet the customers were exceedingly nice and flattering to me. That was until one guy put his hands on the table. Kind of leaning on his knuckles, he said, "Would you mind standing up?"

Not knowing his game, I obliged him.

Looking me up and down in a disdainful sort of way, he suddenly blurted out, "Why would I want to see a fat old porn star?"

That cut me deep to the bone. He had been intentionally cruel and it was devastating.

It always hurts me when fans have this unrealistic expectation that thirty years later a Seka or a Ginger Lynn won't age. That we're like that image on a seventies screen or in a magazine centerfold from a quarter century ago. We all get older. Have they looked in the mirror to see how *they've* aged? This fellow wasn't exactly Mr. GQ himself. But it does hurt your feelings. It makes you doubt yourself. You wonder if everybody feels that way or if they're just feeling sorry for you and that's why they're coming by.

I didn't know what to say, nor did I even have the chance to respond. The owner sort of lifted his finger and suddenly two huge bouncers grabbed the guy. "You're never allowed back in here again. Don't even try."

Sitting in the dressing room prior to my set, I thought this was one of the stupidest things I'd ever done. The customer's cruel comments kept playing through my head. It was all I could do to walk on those pumps up to that stage. I was totally self-conscious. I was actually grateful the club was not well lit.

But when I got up there, the audience was so warm and responsive. And very kind. When they were giving me tips they'd say things like, "Thank you for being here. I love your movies." Some said I looked *better*. One or two even said it was *nice* I put some weight on. Who knows, maybe they were prompted by the owner to say it, but it helped alleviate the feeling of not being good enough anymore. Without our fans, we're nothing.

My Aunt Merlyn and my Uncle Doug were my favorite relatives and since they didn't live that far away, they picked me up at the hotel. I hadn't seen them in a long time and they drove me to the airport. It was wonderful being with them as they had always been so supportive of everything I had done.

Getting on that plane, I actually felt good about my little misadventure. What had started out as a horrible, horrible time turned out to be an eye-opening experience. I saw how cruel people could be, but left feeling really loved and appreciated.

40

Heads I Live, Tails I Die

WHEN YOU'VE SPENT MUCH OF YOUR LIFE living on the edge like I have, any particular decision or action can be life or death. August 27, 1990, was no exception.

I went to the Alpine Valley Music Theater near East Troy, Wisconsin, to see the great blues guitarist Stevie Ray Vaughn. I was a huge fan of his so it was well worth the ninety-or-so-minute trip from Chicago to see him. I had been given all-access passes by some friends I knew and immediately went backstage. They had a hospitality suite with a buffet spread for guests and it was sort of like a meet and greet, with the band members hanging out and socializing. The band knew who I was, since I was kind of the "It Girl" for rock and rollers in those days.

This was the first time I met Stevie and I was thrilled because he was one of the most dynamic blues guitarists who ever lived. I was awestruck and nearly speechless during our brief conversation. He seemed like an old soul, much wiser and insightful than his years. His eyes held great depth. And that came out every time his fingers touched the strings of his guitar. Not much was said, but I remember how gracious he was. "Thank you for coming. I appreciate it."

He was clearly a man of few words, but I sensed his sincerity. I knew from being around a lot of musicians to give him space, as he was about to get on stage. Some performers are nervous and quiet moments before show time and I didn't want to be intrusive and put him out in any way. I certainly didn't want to come off like a doting fan, although that's exactly what I was.

Amazingly, Eric Clapton, Buddy Guy, Robert Cray, and Stevie's older brother Jimmy Vaughn were also backstage, and as much as I respect and admire all of them, I'd come to see Stevie.

233

It was one of the most amazing blues shows I had ever seen, and I felt privileged to be there. Hell, it was like a musical orgasm on stage. Truly memorable.

After the show, I innately knew he'd need to come down. The adrenaline had to be through the roof and I knew that feeling, so I tried to stand back and respect his space. The worst thing you can do in a situation like that is to be goo-goo over a star.

Everybody was kind of mingling around backstage. Somebody suddenly said to me, "We're getting ready to go back to the city by chopper. We can get you back sooner than by car."

A cold chill ran down my spine and the hairs on my neck stood up. Maybe it was a premonition. Or maybe it just wasn't a good night since I knew how foggy it was. But as much as I wanted to, I listened to the voice inside telling me, "Don't get on that helicopter."

I declined the generous invitation. How many people would have turned down a chance to share a helicopter with a major rock star and his crew?

I drove back to Chicago. It wasn't until the next morning I learned the chopper had crashed and all aboard were killed, including Stevie Ray Vaughn.

I was devastated. The whole thing shook me to my core. One of the most magnificent true bluesmen was gone at the peak of his powers. It was like a relative or friend dying. You know you're never going to hear that person live again. A recording may be brilliant, but it's just not the same. I don't claim he and I had some fabulous friendship—we'd only met that night and hardly spoke at all. That would have made it so much more ironic if I had joined him on that flight and perished as well. Think of the erroneous conclusions people would have drawn.

The experience affected me deeply. It validated that I should always listen to my "inner voice." I think we all have that innate ability to know what we should and should not do. Now, whenever I have an inner battle over something, I try to listen to myself and do whatever I think is right. Had I not that night, I wouldn't be here today.

41

Hot Dogs

I HADN'T DONE A FILM IN SEVERAL YEARS. And when you don't work in the adult industry, you are looked upon as a has-been. I also wasn't exactly in the best shape of my life. I had let myself go and was embarrassed to be seen in front of a camera. I actually wasn't doing much of anything but staying at home, worrying about bills, and eating.

Once I realized I wasn't going to make films, and the modeling dwindled down, I started to look for jobs. The porn legend was about to join the "real world."

I still had my looks and personality, but to find a good job with benefits and to make my house payments was virtually impossible. Everybody in Chicago knew who I was. It would have been okay if I was a real, full-time stripper, but for "legitimate" jobs, people didn't want an ex-porn star.

I'd go into a normal bar, ask for work as a bartender, work for a week and a half, and then they'd tell me somebody was coming back from sick leave or whatever. None of it was true. The owners would hear who I was and didn't want "my element" around.

So I figured the strip clubs would be the way to go, since it was "my element." I eventually did find a job at The Crazy Horse in Chicago as a daytime bartender. I never actually went to bartending school. I pretended I knew what I was doing and read my little bartending book. I had big boobs and was blonde, and if I bent over enough they didn't care what drink I put in front of them. Eventually, I learned how to be a good bartender.

Did I think this was a come-down from my former red-carpet, autograph-selling life? Believe it or not, no. It simply followed a pattern I'd been on my entire life. When I needed money, I worked. Each step along the road, I'd go as far as I could and then something would force me to completely change direction and start at the bottom again. At Ken's, I was just a cashier in a dirty bookstore. Eventually, I became management. In the film biz, I was the new girl doing cheap loops, and then worked my way up to being the star. Stripping was about the only thing I'd ever done where I came in at the top and worked my way down! I needed some bread and bartending did not hurt my ego one bit. It was honest labor and I got paid.

I still looked around for other opportunities. On some job interviews, I'd be recognized and they'd get excited about hiring me, but eventually a customer would complain that a porn star was serving them and they'd let me go. "How could anyone think of hiring somebody like her?" I had to be a whore, a hooker, a lowlife. It was okay to look at my films and fantasize about me, but not to have me out in public. It was almost like being an animal in a zoo. You could look at them but not let them loose. It really pissed me off big time because I had become a good bartender. The bar tabs would go up three or four times when they heard I was there. The zoo had a new attraction. But they'd come up with some absurd reason to let me go and I knew why. I went through this same scenario five or six times.

Sometimes the bosses would ask me to do things they'd never ask anyone else. They'd have me work New Year's Eve. When they'd split tips, they'd cheat me in spite of the fact I was doing more business than they were. One New Year's Eve, I quit because management was literally screaming at me. I had totally cleaned up after my shift, but now they were demanding I do the work of the rest of the staff. Meanwhile, we were in the middle of a snowstorm and I wanted to get home in one piece. They told me if I didn't like it I could leave. In spite of desperately needing the gig, I told them to go fuck themselves and walked out. The only reason I could think of for being treated like this was because of what I had done in the past. Also, it must have made them feel oh so powerful to push around a former porn "star." Once you've been on a pedestal, everyone wants to knock you down.

Some of the girls who got out of the adult film game changed their appearances and their names in order to never be found or found out. I couldn't care less about that. I sincerely wasn't ashamed. The way I saw it, it wasn't my problem, it was everyone else's problem. My only problem was they were letting their problem *become* my problem.

A customer named Paulie came into the bar one night and said he loved my movies for years and years. He told me if I ever needed a job I should get in touch, and handed me his card. He owned hot dog stands inside of Home Depot. So I went to work selling hot dogs. He told everybody that Seka was working there and it was great for me because it was just this little hot dog stand and all kinds of characters would stop there. They'd want to talk to me and the added bonus was that the hotdogs were really good. All the contractors came in at night. I'd sell literally $2,500 worth of hotdogs in a shift, but I only got $10 an hour plus tips. Regardless, it was better than bartending.

It bothered me tremendously that I had allowed myself to be in this position. I had made some terrible business decisions. But I was willing to pay my dues to get back on my feet.

Ironically, I had a good time. Firemen would visit in all their gear and get hot dogs just because they wanted to meet me. Ditto the police. And these people who came in were wonderful. They thought it was the best thing since sliced bread that I was making a hot dog for them. It was probably the safest job I ever had, since there were always cops and rescue squad people there to see me.

Most of the people I worked with were Latina women. They were pretty and sweet. They'd watch their p's and q's and did they ever work their asses off! I felt bad for them because they put up with a lot more crap than I would at a job. They didn't have health insurance and had large families to support. I don't think I could have worked with a nicer group of women ever. They were very gentle, sincere, and caring. They weren't judgmental of what I had done. As long as you pulled your weight, they were great to you. They saw I didn't expect to be treated any differently than they were and they respected me for that.

Their plight made me think of the choices I had made. Whether I had picked the easy or hard road in life as an adult actress, at least I had choices. Since many of them were illegal and barely spoke the language, their options were limited, to say the least.

I enjoyed seeing people from all walks of life coming in. It was the full spectrum of society from very high end folk getting out of limos for a hot dog, to normal people going about their lives. You never knew from customer to customer how the conversation would go or what would happen. Nine times out of ten customers who recognized me were totally respectful and friendly, but whenever there was a problem it was usually the women who were jealous and spiteful.

I got really good at it. I could hold four hot dog buns in one hand and make four hot dogs at once. It may have been an odd thing to be proud of, but that's me.

The job was physically hard, though. I was in my forties and on my feet and in the heat for six or seven hours straight. I'd get home and couldn't move. The girls had warned me that the owner's girlfriend was a real bitch. They were right, too, because she tried to make my life miserable because her boyfriend liked me. She spoke to me in an insulting way and tried to make me do demeaning things she wouldn't dare ask anybody else to do.

I was never a person to lie down and be humiliated. As far as I'm concerned, you judge a person on who they are and if they keep their word. I wouldn't put up with rudeness. And slinging hot dogs wasn't a career. I told him one day, "Look, I can't work for your girlfriend and I know you're not going to give her up over me. I quit."

I knew at some point these jobs weren't going to work out. It was just a means to pay some bills. I was now in my mid-forties and had to once again figure out what to do with my life.

42

Matthew

ONE OF MY FAVORITE PEOPLE in the world is my cousin Sarah Jane. Although she's about nine years younger than I am, she's always been like a sister to me. And considering I don't speak to my own sister at all, she's someone I need so very much in my life. Pretty, smart, and kind, you could not find a better surrogate sister in the world. With her thick Radford, Virginia, accent, I'm sometimes the only person in the room who can make sense out of what she's saying. I would do anything for her. We've been to hell and back together.

Sarah had two children, Meredith and Matthew. Both were beautiful inside and out, with olive complexions, dark hair, and dark eyes. Matthew was the sweetest little child, while Meredith was the feisty one. He had a silent strength about him, while Meredith would tell you whatever was on her mind. And in her twenties, she still does today.

Since Meredith was able to walk and talk, everyone in the family joked that she was my child because she's so willful. She's strong, outspoken, and stands up for herself. Wearing her heart on her sleeve, behind the bravado, she's a very tender person. And the capper is she's very, very bright.

I was always Aunt Dot to these children, as well as to all of my cousins' kids.

When he was around the age of fourteen, Matthew started to get headaches. He was an amateur wrestler at his local high school. He'd come home and tell his mom he couldn't get rid of his headaches. Sarah figured it was from the intense body contact and exertion. However, it persisted for weeks.

When the doctor looked in his eyes he told her simply, "Something isn't right."

And it wasn't. They found three brain tumors. He had brain cancer.

Sarah was divorced from the father of her kids but he was still in their lives. When they got the news, the whole family, and even the community, rallied in support of them. Aunts, uncles, cousins, neighbors, friends, classmates, and everyone in between helped them with whatever they needed. We cleaned the house, did the lawn, took care of the laundry, went shopping, and took a load off poor Sarah. We saw the sadness in Sarah, but she stayed strong and did whatever she could to help Matthew in his fight. I don't think I ever saw her break down once through the whole ordeal.

She drove a couple hundred miles each way for radiation treatments and chemo. Matthew didn't want to stay in the hospital, and she promised him he'd never be alone. For a couple of months, Matthew would be able to basically go about his life. I'd fly in from Chicago and take him to his favorite restaurant. It wasn't so much going out to eat, but us all being there together.

On top of everything, it was a financial drain on them. When I asked if there was anything she needed, she answered honestly, "Well, we can always use money." So I sent what I could. Considering I worked at a Home Depot slinging hot dogs eight hours a day, I didn't have an abundance of that.

When I told the owner of the hot dog stand what was going on he said, "Okay, we'll set up outside and sell hot dogs for a dollar each. We'll do a fundraiser for him. And if people want to give more, they can."

We raised two thousand and change in one afternoon. That's a lot of hotdogs.

For the most part, everyone was very nice about buying a hotdog or throwing some money in the jar. But there're always rotten apples in the bunch. One guy said. "Why in the hell would I want to give a porn star money for her nephew? That's just ridiculous. Go beg from someone else."

I got very angry, but a split second later I realized how sad it was that this man had no compassion whatsoever.

Later in the day, a woman just stood there staring at me and said, "You spread your legs all these years. Why don't you spread your legs again?"

She gave me the strangest look as if she was expecting me to say something hostile, but I figured why waste my breath on someone like this? I simply said to her, "Why don't you just walk away?"

When the smoke cleared, though, I felt really, really good. Not only had it been a financial success, it was heartwarming that people who didn't know my Matthew were willing to dig into their pockets to help someone literally a thousand miles away. It gave me back some faith in humanity.

We did another fundraiser at The Big House restaurant in Chicago, where I had known the owner for years. It was a Sunday afternoon and she called all our musician friends—Nan Mason, Bob Salone, Frank Deron. Buddy Charles, Carla Valenti and many other well-known Chicago performers. Other community leaders and business people donated items for a silent auction like TVs, a spa day, and dinners at different restaurants. Joey Mondelli's chef, Armando, from La Scarola's restaurant, donated a home-cooked dinner to the highest bidder. The support was overwhelming. These were all friends who came through for me when I most needed them. Each and every one of them passed out fliers around the neighborhood, told everyone they knew, and asked for five-dollar donations. There were also tip jars around that were filling up with cash, but even more amazing was the fact that person after person kept walking over to me with envelopes with cash in them. Even the musicians who donated their time and service and weren't making a dime came over and handed me money. I broke down and cried several times.

In spite of the sad circumstances, it was an amazing show and they purposely picked out uplifting, funny, and poignant songs about people loving and caring for each other. "Time in a Bottle" was one song I remember being performed. And tunes about love took on a whole new meaning, since this time it was a love between an aunt and her dying nephew.

Unbelievably, I walked out of there with almost thirteen thousand dollars.

For several weeks, bar and restaurant owners let me put a jar out with a picture of Matthew on it where their patrons could put in money. I'd come by a few days later to pick them up and it was overwhelming to me that these jars were full. I'd send large checks in Matthew's name, and Sarah was also just blown away by the whole thing. It helped them out a lot. The thankfulness that came from Matthew alone meant a lot to me.

"You really do love me, don't you? Thank you for everything you have done for my mom and my family." He was a very selfless child.

Lelo and Frank of the Italian restaurant Topo Gigio helped me get in touch with the Make-A-Wish Foundation. By this point Matthew knew he was dying and I knew there were things he wanted to do. He wanted to go to Disneyworld to go on the Aerosmith ride. He loved the band and amusement parks. So Make-A-Wish brought Sarah, her ex-husband, Meredith, and Matthew there for four days. Whatever Matthew wanted to do they took care of it and it was a beautiful experience.

Matthew also loved the Dallas Cowboys, while his sister Meredith is a Washington Redskins fan. Washington and Dallas play each other twice a year. I called my ex-boyfriend Billy Connors of the Cubs and asked if he knew anyone in the football world. He asked me to give him a couple of days to see what he could pull off and he called me back with four tickets for the game. Not only that, Matthew had a pass to be in the Cowboys locker room. His favorite player was Emmitt Smith. Emmitt gave him his Super Bowl ring to wear during the game. Matthew met all the guys and was just thrilled. He was in a wheelchair at this point and it was very exhausting for him, but it was just a wonderful day. That young man could not thank me enough. But I didn't need to be thanked. I was just happy I had been in a position to do it.

The last time I saw Matthew was on July 3, 2002. He was bedridden. He said, "Aunt Dot, I love you. I'm really getting tired now." I knew what he meant. I walked out of the room and broke down. At that point it was a waiting game. I got the call the next day that he was gone.

Sarah, Meredith, and her husband were in the room when it happened. They all needed to say what they had to say to him. Rather than dying alone in some hospital hooked up to machines, that's the way it should be.

After he died on July 4th, I took a blanket, a small cooler of beer, and walked up the street to grab a nice, grassy spot where they were blowing off fireworks. The sky was so crystal clear. It was like a celebration of his life and a sendoff at the same time.

Matthew had asked Sarah to have me pick out a song for his funeral. When the music started to play and everyone heard rock and roller Joe Cocker's voice they looked at me like I was nuts. The song was from a CD called *No Ordinary World*. It's a ballad called "On My Way Home."

By the end of the song there wasn't a dry eye in the house.

43

The Last Garter

I RETIRED AND UN-RETIRED as often as an aging prizefighter. I was like Al Pacino in *Godfather III*—just when I thought I was out, they pull me back in.

When I started in adult films, I got paid peanuts, like everyone else. Then I raised the stakes and the industry went with me. I raised my wages to the point where I ran myself out of the business, and I was glad. But even once I'd done that, even once I left and then came back to do *Careful*, which I felt was my swan song, they kept calling. It was like a bad romance. I'd name a ridiculous figure, they'd turn me down, and I thought that would be the end of it. Some time would pass and they'd call again and we'd dance the same dance once more. In my heart, I knew the day might come when they'd say yes and I'd need the money enough to call their bluff.

The numbers I'd quote were far more than any other single venture I'd moved into after acting. And there were certainly times I wondered where my next paycheck was coming from or how I would pay my mortgage. It was like a game of chicken.

In the middle of all that was AIDS. By the 1990s, the world finally started to have some semblance of agreement on what it was, what caused it, how you got it, and how best to prevent it. Tests were finally developed.

One day, everything came together just as I'd feared and hoped. A company was willing to meet my price. They agreed to my demands for creative control. They allowed me to cast who I wanted. I would only do sex scenes with people of my own choosing. Everyone I did those scenes with would be tested for HIV, and even then, they would still be wearing condoms. I never thought anyone would accept my terms, but they did, and I needed the money so much I had no sane choice but to go along.

The film was called *American Garter*. Like *Careful*, it was very story-driven and practically soft-core—a couples' movie, as they were called. It was done on film instead of video, so it looked classy. They got Henri Pachard to direct, and Gloria Leonard was involved in the production as well. I'd never worked with Henri before, but I liked everything I'd heard about him from others I knew and trusted, and I'd always liked and respected Gloria. It looked like there was nothing for me to complain about, no excuses for me to use to get out of doing it.

Check that—there was one thing. I'd gained weight. I was pushing forty and I looked it, at least in my own eyes, despite having had some work done. I started working out and dieting and lost the worst of the weight, but when I looked in the mirror, I still wasn't satisfied with what was looking back. I was in MILF territory, which I had trouble coming to grips with. That term hadn't quite been invented yet, but there were girls like Kay Parker, Juliet Anderson, and Georgina Spelvin who'd always done those sorts of roles. I wasn't sure I was ready for that yet. I think lots of mainstream actresses feel the same way, kicking and biting their way into middle age, still wanting to play ingénues and romantic leads with hot young guys and not being regarded as a cougar. Now that was me, and I didn't like it one bit.

There was something else I should have known from all the years I'd been in the industry—everyone lies. Yes, they paid me what they promised, and yes, I got the casting I'd asked for—good guys I could count on like Randy West. But when it came to condom time, the hair flew.

First, they conveniently forgot I'd insisted upon it. Yeah, like I'd forget a thing like that, right at the height of AIDS awareness. We fought. And fought. And fought. I wasn't going to do a scene with a penis unless it was covered in latex, and if they didn't meet their obligations, I was walking off the set and I knew if we went to court they'd be the ones in breach of contract, not me.

Would you believe they thought they came up with a way of "meeting me halfway?" I never would have dreamed there was a way of "sorta" wearing a condom, but they found it. Of course, this didn't come from any discussion with me—I'd already drawn my line in the sand. But when they "agreed" with me, we got started on my first sex scene and when it was time for insertion, I looked down and there was this little rubber thing on the very tip of the guy's cock. I'd never seen such a thing in my life. It wasn't like I didn't know what a condom looked like—the men I was sleeping with at the time were all wearing them. But nobody ever wore anything that looked like this. It was so funny looking I didn't know whether to laugh or scream.

"What the fuck is this?!"

"It's a condom."

"No it's not! It's, it's… It looks like a fucking yarmulke!" And it did. It looked like it was made for a penis having a Bar Mitzvah.

"It'll work; trust us. It's rubber; everything will be okay. And best of all, the audience will never know."

I stomped off the set. This wasn't Gloria or Henri I was fighting with. They were actually on my side. It was the suits—or what passes for suits in the porn industry. The money guys who ran the show.

"Don't piss on my shoes and tell me it's raining. You can call that a condom all you want; I say it's not a condom. A condom covers the entire penis. That thing will fall off the moment he enters me."

They debated me. More than anything else, they kept saying, "But this way, no one will know he's wearing one."

"Listen, everyone should wear a condom unless they're in a long-term, committed, monogamous relationship. I *want* the audience to know he's wearing one!"

I never would have dreamed it, but I'd just given my first Safe Sex Public Service Announcement. If they'd had the cameras rolling, they could have shown it on TV or in movie previews. And it would have worked a helluva lot better than the kinds of homogenized spokespeople who were already doing them. I had become associated with sex, and if someone like me said it, unscripted, people might have taken it more to heart. I never set out to be the spokesmodel for safer sex, but I believed in it and I would have done PSAs in a heartbeat. But America didn't want to see someone like me with a message like that, unless I was already riddled with AIDS and speaking from my deathbed. I believed in what I was saying because I didn't want to end up like that. I liked breathing too much! Life is good! So is sex, so what you do, if you have any sense at all, is try to combine the two—life *and* sex. Condoms help with that.

Henri and Gloria cheered me on. "Give her what she wants!" It worked. If you watch closely, you can see the condoms in my *Garter* scenes, and even if you can't because of some angle, trust me, they're there.

Garter was not a big hit, unfortunately. If it was, perhaps I would have "un-retired" a few more times. But *Garter* would be the last—my final XXX feature in which I'd have real sex.

Did I miss it? No. The phone continued to ring, but it wasn't just that they wouldn't meet my price. The industry continued to change, and not for the better. *Garter* was practically a throwback, with people like Randy, Ona Zee, Mike Horner, and I involved. Literally no hardcore was being done on film. There was either soft core—no erections and no penetration seen—or there was hardcore. Most hardcore was becoming almost totally plotless. Many of the old players were disappearing, and not just the ones in front of the camera. I'd get calls from people I'd never heard of. Fly-by-nights. It used to be we all knew each other—not just the actors, but the entire industry. Now any punk with a video camera was a filmmaker, especially in porn. With home video and the Internet, the industry had grown too large. And it wasn't some big corporate thing. That might have actually been better, believe it or not. I'd go to return people's calls and the number would be disconnected. That sort of thing didn't happen with Time Warner or Sony.

With more product, there were more actors. I didn't know these people from a hole in the wall. I wouldn't know who to ask for or who to avoid. There were always a few bad eggs who would pass through the system—crackheads and crackwhores who did one or two films, got a bad reputation they richly deserved, and then faded away. You knew who they were. We had our own little "minor league" system. Now it was all minor league. With people like Randy West, Annie Sprinkle, Debi Diamond, and Ginger Lynn, you knew you were with people who at least cared about themselves, and by doing that, they cared about you, health-wise. But many of the kids I met who were just entering the business in the nineties and beyond seemed to have a death wish. They didn't give a shit if they lived or died, just as long as they could say they were a porn star.

The industry didn't do that to them. They did that to themselves. A small handful like Jenna Jameson and Lexington Steele have lasted, while most haven't. I got out alive. That's the most important thing.

44

Radio Star

I ALWAYS ENJOYED DOING RADIO. But I never imagined I'd become a radio host in a major market.

I had been a guest on several WLUP Chicago radio shows, including Steve Dahl and Gary Myers' show. Steve was the guy who crushed thousands of disco records at Comiskey Park in support of rock and roll. They'd call me at like six o'clock in the morning and ask me dumb stuff like, "What are you doing?" I'd tell them I was sleeping or cleaning the apartment. I guess they found it interesting that an adult movie star would have a normal life. They were huge shock jocks on "The Loop," so it was good publicity to be on with them. They liked me so they weren't slamming me.

I did a New Year's Eve show with them at a club called Park West, where I was in a hot tub the entire show (talk about getting pruney). Steve, who was totally loaded, would climb in and out. At one point, he was on stage with an electric guitar in his hands when he started drunkenly stumbling backwards towards me. I was in there thinking, "We're going to fry because he's going to fall into the hot tub." I was right. At the last second somebody grabbed it out of his hand right before he fell in. That would have been some way to go.

At one point I was the "den mother" for the Kevin Matthews Show. He'd say, "Let's call the Den Mother," and I'd come into the studio. You never knew what he was going to do because he'd fly by the seat of his pants.

He would do fundraisers for a Catholic orphanage he was fond of. Believe it or not, he called his charity barbecue contest Beat Kev's Meat. There were some pretty good cooks out there and he'd have celebrity judges. One summer, he asked me to come out and help the event draw better, along with celebrity hunter and fisherman Babe Winkelman. He was sort of like the Brawny Paper Towel guy. They'd have an auction with things like a guitar from Mötley Crüe or a painting from a gallery. Dinner was served under a huge tent. Kev would ask me and Dave to take this big fish bowl around asking for donations for the orphanage but we were toasted, having been drinking all afternoon. The priest was pretty drunk, too. It made for an interesting day of fund-raising—the porn star, the priest, and the outdoorsman teaming up.

Kevin kept remarking I had a good voice for radio. I finally said to him, "Make it happen." And he did.

It was Saturday nights from 10 p.m. to 2 a.m. and it was called "Let's Talk about Sex." At first I was like, "How do you fill up four hours of time?" I dreaded dead air. The first night I thought, "This is going to be the longest night of my life." But I was absolutely wrong. The phones just lit up. I also had guests like the gay women who wrote *Diamonds Are a Girls' Best Friend*, a book about women's softball. Johnson and Johnson had actual doctors on who specialized in sexuality. They could ask any of us questions. I remember one question in particular. A caller wanted to know, "Where was the strangest place you ever had sex?" My immediate thought was the famous *Newlywed Show* segment, so I said, "In the butt." We all cracked up.

Although it did get wild at times and we had an awful lot of fun, we didn't think of the show or treat it like a shock jock gig. A lot of the questions were from people with legitimate problems. Women worried about keeping things interesting and fresh, while men were more worried about whether they were cumming too soon. It was very satisfying because we actually helped people with good, solid advice from folks qualified to give it. We covered a lot of ground. We made them feel open and at ease. We didn't have licenses on the wall. The intimidation factor was taken away. There was no judgment on our end.

We welcomed just about anybody who wanted to come to the studio. We had dominatrixes with their slaves. We'd spank people. Restaurant owners would bring foods that served as aphrodisiacs. Of course, everybody who worked at the station wanted to watch the show because we always had naked people there, sort of like Howard Stern.

We even had a big pajama party one New Year's Eve. Some people came in trench coats naked underneath, because that's how they slept. Marilyn Miglin, who sells the fragrance "Pheromone" and all kinds of perfumes and creams for body care, brought gifts for us to give to various callers. She'd talk about how important it was for both men and women to take care of their skin to look their best. Another gentleman owned a chocolate company and he'd do giveaways as well. There were all kinds of business people who had giveaways to offer, which helped build the audience because everyone liked something for free.

One time The Rolling Stones were in Chicago prior to heading out to Berlin, Germany. My co-host Stan Lawrence handed me an envelope and I opened it on the air. There were tickets for me and another person to cover the Stones in Germany for the Loop. I was so excited I could have died.

In Berlin, it was balmy with a light breeze blowing. It felt very upbeat. But as soon as we walked into the stadium, there was no air moving. It was like being in a mausoleum. It was eerie.

A big security guy took us around. I walked out on this platform—a big concrete slab. There were oceans of people before me. The security guy said, "You're standing right where Hitler stood for the Olympics." A chill went down my spine. It was a frightening feeling, like he was in that stadium. I said, "Move me now. Get me out of here." I was visibly shaking.

I knew one of the Stones' crew guys and they used to have these light and sound towers. My friend Janet and I were watching the show from up there. The lighting guys were always interesting. They had these gargantuan boards and buttons. I couldn't imagine how they knew what to do, when to do it, and do it as smoothly as they do. The one fellow was sitting there doing the lights and was rolling a joint. He motioned for Janet and me to come up. They took our hands and put their hands over ours and showed us how to do the lights. He was very coy about this as he slid out of the chair and I automatically slid into it. There were about 90,000 people in the stadium and I was mesmerized by the whole thing. Suddenly, I realized the two guys were gone. They were five or six feet behind us getting stoned and they were laughing their asses off at how freaked out we were.

I knew the Stones' music and I told my friend, "The end of this song is in about ten seconds." I knew that would call for some dramatic lighting. I didn't know whether to shit or go blind.

About a second and a half before the end of the song, these two guys swooped in and took control of the board to finish. I think it was the biggest rush I'd ever had.

Honey West and Alex were men who lived as women—they had all their boy parts. Alex really looked like a woman, but Honey looked like a big man in drag. The flamboyant duo were doing a play in Chicago called "Vampire Lesbians of Sodom." We'd do theater ticket giveaways on air and it was always an experience having them on, since they'd say the most outrageous things. The producer/ director of the play asked if I would consider being Honey's stand-in as the dreaded Succubus. Hence my stage debut came out of doing radio as well. That was difficult for me because standing on stage having to deliver lines with thirty other cast members wasn't my forte. But I was a trouper and did my best, and got a nice response from the audience. I would do two shows Friday and Saturday, and then run in and do a four-hour radio show.

The checks from the play were bouncing, though. Finally, I got tired of working my ass off and not getting paid so I quit. However, it was a great experience.

It was an exciting time for me. Although the pay wasn't particularly good, it did help my career to be on the air for three years. I hadn't made movies for quite a while and it did boost my exposure. This helped my mail order business and such. It also meant a lot to me that I was publicly perceived as someone with talents beyond just making adult films.

Although we were on only once a week from 1994 to 1996, our numbers were bigger than guys like Danny Bonaduce, who was on every day and syndicated. But since we were about sex, they never would syndicate us. I also think because I had been in pornography, the combination of Seka and sex wasn't what they were looking to promote. Different businesses would want to advertise with us, but the station was concerned some of their customers could potentially complain about being on a "sex show," so it was always a struggle.

My co-host was African-American, and I was the token female. To this day I think they had us on just to cover their asses with affirmative action. There was never real support or promotion for the show. It had no room to grow. I got tired of being told "No" when I wanted to do promotions like Kevin, or even when I wanted to do charity work for The Rainbow House, which is a safe house for battered women.

One day there was a pink slip in my mailbox saying they didn't think the show was enough of a success. I was asked to clean out my locker. Thus ended my radio career.

To this day I get emails from people telling me they used to listen to me on The Loop and that they wished it had never gone off. And I miss it myself. It was one of the most interesting and rewarding things I've ever done.

I loved the Cubs and the Cubs loved me.

In the first home I owned all by myself, Chicago, 1986.

On the radio. Literally.

I smoke. Don't hate me.

Chicago nights with my
hairdresser Ronnie Webber.

45

"It's Your Wife..."

I MET MY NEXT SERIOUS BEAU, who I'll call Jim, back when I was stripping in Chicago. Little did I know we'd have an on-again, off-again turbulent relationship for over a decade.

He owned an adult bookstore and one night he asked me to go to dinner. He seemed like a nice enough guy. Maybe an inch shorter than me, he had dark hair and eyes. A quiet man, I couldn't help but notice he rarely smiled. Jim was impeccably dressed, though. I don't think I ever saw him without custom made suits, shoes, and shirts—he definitely dressed to the nines. He always took me to great places to eat and was quite intelligent. All in all we had a good enough time.

I started to like him, although nothing physical happened for quite a while. He was the perfect gentleman. Eventually, we did sleep together and the relationship got more serious.

On Valentine's Day, I was sitting in my bathtub getting ready to go out to dinner with him when the phone rang. There was this girl on the other end going wacko crazy. She shrieked that she was Jim's girlfriend. I told her that if she were his girlfriend, he'd probably be going out with her instead. I didn't think anything of it and didn't even ask him about her. I just figured it was some crazy chick he'd been seeing and she was pissed off because he wasn't seeing her anymore.

When we went out that evening he gave me a beautiful pair of gold and diamond earrings. We had a really nice time, came back to my place, had sex, laid around, talked for a while, and he left. Everything seemed right in the world. I should have known better.

We continued to see each other and all of a sudden I didn't hear from him. He just dropped off the face of the earth. I had no clue what was going on. None of his friends would tell me where he was, so I figured he didn't want to see me anymore and didn't know how to say it. I liked him a whole lot, but it wasn't like I was madly in love. It didn't crush me, but I was hurt by the way the whole thing had been handled.

I decided I needed to go about my business and my life. Since we didn't hang out in the same circles and I wasn't close with any of his friends, it became almost out of sight, out of mind.

Two years passed and while bartending at The Crazy Horse, out of nowhere he walked into the club. He didn't make the least bit of effort to explain his disappearing act.

"What the hell happened to you?" I demanded.

"I had a lot on my mind and couldn't be distracted." End of story.

He handed me an envelope saying, "This is for you," and walked out just like that. I was stunned from the whole scenario. Later that evening when I was home alone, I opened the envelope and found a shitload of cash. I thought, holy crap, what's this for? Guilt money? Being naïve once again, I didn't question anything and even let him back into my life.

Things got a lot more heated up in the romance department and he decided he didn't want me working as a bartender. "No girl of mine should have to work," he told me. He announced he would "take care of everything" if I quit. Hey, sounded good to me. I figured if I could lie by the pool and go shopping, that was a lifestyle I could grow accustomed to. I was tired of schlepping drinks and busting my ass to make a living. I left my job and he did exactly what he said.

At the start, it was wonderful. I was always dressed sharp, and shopping became my new job. But it was hard reaching the man. Also, if I went out of the house and did something with my friends, he would act crazy. "Where have you been? Who have you been with?" I didn't go out with any other guys, but he never believed me.

Generally after a date, we'd end up at my place. After all the festivities were done, he'd inevitably say, "I have to go."

Finally, I questioned him. "Why do you always have to leave?"

He confessed he had to check in at a halfway house every night. He said he had been to jail—for what I didn't know, and didn't want to know. This was one of the reasons he had been AWOL from our relationship all that time.

I accepted that. But then we'd take trips to places like Vegas and Florida. If he was on parole, how did he pull that off? I never stopped to consider that, nor did I feel he was lying to me… until that same girl called one night and asked, "Is my husband there?"

I handed him the phone and said, "It's your wife."

He turned ten shades of white.

He walked into the other room and I could hear the heated conversation. When he came back out I said, "Maybe you should go."

I was more disgusted with myself than my lying lover. From that night on I didn't see him for several months. When I did finally hear from him, he said it really wasn't his wife; that it was some girl who had wanted to marry him but he refused. Stupid me believed him, or at least wanted to believe him. I honestly think part of the reason was I liked the lifestyle he provided me.

We started going out again, which proves you don't always get wiser as you get older.

A disco we liked was always jam-packed so we had the same table reserved every night. But one evening he was acting very strange. Suddenly he spilled his guts that he was, in fact, married, and the divorce was coming and she was collecting evidence for the case. "Don't be surprised if pictures of us turn up," he said. He glanced at some shadowy figures across the room as if they were spying on us. Just great. It all started to feel very cloak and dagger.

When it was good it was good, and when it was bad, it was really bad. I realized I wasn't dating the most reliable guy in the world and even though he didn't like me to work, I started to look for another job. Although I had become an experienced bartender, I was coming up empty as far as job offers. I truly believe he put the word out that I was his girl and he didn't want anyone hiring me.

His wife ultimately did leave him during one of our vacations and cleaned out his bank accounts. But all I thought was, "Yay, he's not married anymore!"

In addition to not wanting me to work, period, he didn't want me to have anything to do with the XXX business, even though he made a living off people like me with his own bookstores. With me not working and him being in a fight to the death with his ex-wife, money started to get tight. Our lifestyle started to get cheaper and cheaper. Checks were bouncing. I continued putting on weight since all I could do was wait around the house for him to show up.

Things started to disintegrate. Our sex life was dying because I had gotten disgusted with everything that had gone down—the lies, being made to feel like a caged bird, my own feelings about my weight and my looks.

I went to his home one day and we got in an argument over the bills. He snarled at me, "Why don't you get out of my house, you fat-ass cunt?"

Very nice. I said "Fine, that's the way it'll be."

And just like that, I ripped his key off of my ring, flung it into the middle of his yard, got in my car, and drove off. From dancing to bartending to hot dog vending to radio—nearly fourteen years of my life—all wasted on one lousy man who wasn't even available most of the time.

I haven't seen him since.

46

Daddy's Gone

MY DAD WAS STILL LIVING IN VIRGINIA. With a frugal lifestyle, a pension from the Army, and Social Security, Dad was pretty set financially. But he was still a heavy drinker and smoker. When I would visit him, he'd walk out, buy a bottle, sit in the park, and come back drunk.

He had a one-bedroom apartment on the ground level. Some of the kids in the complex would take advantage of him when he was sauced. They'd steal from him and even beat him up and knock him out. So he decided to live with his friends, a lovely couple named, believe it or not, Bud and Lou. The lady, Lou, was tall, thin, and striking with a chiseled jaw line and face. She had the most pleasant disposition. Bud, her husband, was this short, round, good ol' country boy who didn't have a whole lot to say.

At Bud and Lou's house, my father's mini-strokes started. He no longer had the use of his left arm or left leg. Falling out of bed, he'd often hurt himself, but I knew his friends loved him and for the most part he was being very well taken care of. If Dad needed something, Bud would literally carry him. But when he kept having these strokes one after another, they just couldn't keep taking care of him because they were old and also not in the best of health.

Dad asked me to put him in assisted care living. He actually liked the place we found for him. At least he wouldn't be hurt, beaten, or have his things stolen. He was a resident for a couple of years. He stopped his smoking and drinking there, and I pushed him around in his wheelchair, enjoying our time together. But gangrene set in on his foot, and I knew he didn't have long. He was also riddled with cancer—lung cancer and bone cancer. I wanted to stay to help more, but I had to go back to Chicago. I remember the last thing he said to me. "Whatever happens, do not let them amputate."

I said, "Okay, Dad, I won't."

My father was prepared to die. He had made peace with that. He started taking care of his arrangements a long time in advance to insure that his children would not have to bear that burden. Dad made me promise we wouldn't pay any more for the funeral than what he provided.

Soon after, I got a call from the nursing home. The brief conversation turned into one I'd never forget.

"We need to amputate part of your father's leg."

"That is not his wishes," I argued.

"But he's in a lot of pain."

"Give him more medication," I insisted.

"If we do it'll probably kill him."

"It's fine with me if you give him more pain medication."

"Ma'am, you do understand… ."

"Yes, I do. The man wants to go out with some dignity and peace."

The next morning they called to tell me he was gone.

I knew my father had loved me unconditionally. I wished we had more time together when I was growing up, but our relationship was typical of how divorce was handled back in the day. Try as I might, I couldn't bring myself to blame him or say, "Oh woe is me," because of him or anything he ever did or didn't do for me. Even with my porn career, he felt whatever you do, you should do it with dignity. I could have sold chicken shit and my dad would have been proud of me.

It was pretty tough on me, but at the same time all his papers were in order. No fuss, no muss. My dad was always very logical that way. I had to go to Virginia to help make the arrangements. There was my brother, whom I'd never had a good relationship with since the family deserted me when I was eight. He was talking to Tom, the funeral director.

As executor, my brother said, "I already picked everything out."

"We'll see how it goes," I replied.

The director said, "We're up to $25,000."

"That's not going to happen," I emphasized. I pulled out the insurance. "Show me what this is going to buy."

It might have been $5,000 at most. What they offered would be simple yet dignified. My brother was not happy about it. I told him he could pay out of his own pocket which, of course, he wasn't willing to do.

We had a graveside service with very bad weather that day. There was snow, snow, and more snow. We couldn't actually bury him for nearly a week because the ground was too frozen to dig the grave. The weather fit my mood and my sense of loss. More than anyone else in my family, I miss my father the most.

Believe it or not, these are candid shots of me washing my uncle's car in Virginia in the early '90's. (right and below)

My sister, Christmas Eve, 1986.

My brother Ray.

My mother. Gotta love the beehive.

With my Uncle Hardy, the
Baptist minister. A great man
who never judged me.

47

Webmistress

I'D RUN A MAIL-ORDER BUSINESS FOR YEARS, which was promoted by print ads, mostly in *Club Magazine*. But as time went by, magazines turned to e-zines and almost all mail-order businesses moved to that new-fangled thingy, the Internet.

Two close female friends bugged me for the longest time to do a website. They believed in me, felt there was a market for it, and put up the money which I didn't have at the time. Since I'd been out of the public eye for quite a while, I feared it would blow up in our faces. Making matters worse, neither of my partners was wealthy. I didn't know how or even if I could pay them back. We had to buy all kinds of equipment and pay strangers good money to get it off the ground.

We started out by getting my pictures from *Club Magazine* and scanning everything. It was labor intensive and I didn't know jack shit about it. Hell, I didn't even have a computer. My nephew bought me one to start the site. The *Club* material I had was mostly R-rated and I didn't have much new material to put up. I wasn't sure people wanted to see a fat old broad, since I was about sixty pounds heavier. I had become complacent and just didn't care.

I was very hardheaded and wanted to protect my image as best as I could. It felt like I was being pressured to be out in public before I was ready. Unlike my partners, I was also concerned with copyrights and registrations and "minor" things like that.

It was extremely tough and slow in the beginning. It seemed like it took forever to even get a single member. Complicating matters, someone else had the www.seka.com URL and I didn't know how to get it back. They had pictures of me on there and they were even saying they had my signed pictures for sale. But I was fortunate that on Google my www.officialseka.com was climbing in the rankings. I eventually hired a lawyer who cost me five grand I really couldn't afford, to win the rights to the domain name www.seka.com. The folks originally behind it just kind of went away.

When the income started trickling in, I saw it did have possibilities. It became my job, my focus, and my passion. I would be up practically all night going on different search engines asking people to do a banner exchange. I had Yahoo Groups and did anything I could to try to get the name out.

It finally began to grow and was doing well enough where I was able to relax somewhat and pay my bills. None of us were making any "real" money on it, though, because it was split three ways and the others also had their day jobs to focus on.

I wanted to give the girls something for their troubles, but just couldn't pull money out of the business at the time. I would pay for meals, entertainment, and business trips. But one of my partners wanted more control and seemed to be scared to give us space. Maybe we'd "run away," I don't know. For example, I had the opportunity to go to Florida to basically hang out. She wasn't too thrilled with that nor did she like it if I had a relationship or even a casual tryst with someone. It always bothered her tremendously. She was just very jealous and insecure.

As deeply indebted as I was to them, I knew this partnership just wasn't working. Eventually, lawyers came into the picture. I ultimately offered to buy them out. With one of the partners it worked out amicably. The other, of course, felt rejected. But I had found a way to make a living for myself again. And now I didn't have to answer to anybody else.

One day I got an e-mail from a company called AEBN and they wanted to do a custom theater on Seka.com. That's pay-per-view where people can go in to look at videos. I get a cut as an affiliate whenever someone clicks on and watches a piece of a movie. And if they don't want to watch me, they can go in and watch whoever they want.

As owner of the site, how do I feel about making money off someone *else* having sex? Well, people have been doing it to me long enough, so it doesn't feel exploitative. And unlike most in this cutthroat industry, I try to help my peers. I will always give an actress advice on where to get content, advice on who is honest in the business, and how to protect themselves legally.

I've always wanted the site to have style and class, without having to stoop to just going all out to get people's attention. My vision for the site is to portray myself with dignity and respect. I won't put violent sex on it—no choking and gagging. That wasn't a part of what I did to begin with. It's not something I personally like because I think it's degrading to women—unless, of course, it's something they're actually into. But I don't think it's very sexy. I don't even think it has a lot to do with sex. I think it has everything to do with control.

I get comments like, "Why don't you have more anal? Why don't you have more S&M?" Yet I stick to my guns with what I have up there. My own footage is tame in comparison to the rest of the industry.

I fully realize there are people who are always going to look at the site as nothing more than smut. And I know better than to argue with someone whose mind is already made up. But I honestly don't see anything wrong with someone escaping online and getting away from his or her problems for a bit. And if they get off on it, maybe that release is actually something positive rather than perverted or dirty. But who am I to judge these things?

The bottom line is I now have a job behind a computer keyboard rather than in front of a movie camera. And at this stage in my life, that's definitely a blessing.

48

Desperately Seeking Seka

OUT OF NOWHERE, I got a phone call from my friend Joey Mondelli, who owned an Italian restaurant named La Scarola's in Chicago. He said two foreign guys were looking for me but he wouldn't tell them anything.

"We told them we didn't know where you were, but if they came back in a few days we'd see if we could find you."

I have some very protective buddies.

Turns out these two Swedish fellows named Christian and Magnus had been conducting interviews about my career because they were doing a documentary on me. They looked everywhere but couldn't find me. Seems I was their "favorite."

Travelling around the world to track down an adult film star seemed a bit odd even to me, but I gave Joey permission to give them my number. When we finally spoke they had really heavy accents and I couldn't understand much of what they were saying. I met them at La Scarola's. I wanted to screen these fellows to see if they were legit and just what they were offering.

Both were in their early thirties and very European-looking. One was kind of blonde and a little balding. I wouldn't say they were terribly attractive; both were average-looking guys. But their personalities were just sparkling. They had on big, heavy coats with red and white Arabian-looking checked scarves. They were all bundled up for our cold Chicago winter. All the while, Joey kept his eye on them.

They spoke enthusiastically and I was flattered. I liked the idea of the documentary so I asked, "What are you going to call it?"

"We think the best name would be *Desperately Seeking Seka*, because that's exactly what we have been doing here in the States."

They told me about the people they had already interviewed like Veronica Hart, Ron Jeremy, and Ron Sullivan, who is better known as director Henri Pachard. And now they wanted to interview me. But when they told me the miniscule amount of money they were able to pay, I blurted out, "Be real!"

We eventually agreed on a price that was actually more than a couple of hundred bucks. Since Seka was desperately seeking some cash, *Desperately Seeking Seka* was a go.

They needed to come by my place to photograph me for the project. Feeling self-conscious about my weight, I figured I might as well film at my house where I felt most comfortable. I cooked them a nice dinner and the stage was my living room.

I thought they did a nice enough job, although they didn't ask me anything I hadn't been asked before. They were pretty pat questions like, "Who was your favorite male co-star? Who was your favorite female co-star?" It was actually kind of boring answering the same questions I'd heard so many times over the years. But I had the money in my pocket and did my best to appease them. I honestly didn't think much would come of the project. Here were two guys going back to Sweden to produce and distribute a low-budget film. They seemed professional enough with the cameras they were using, and were certainly determined, but the idea that it took them a year to find me made it seem like, "How big could it really be?" It wasn't like I was Howard Hughes or something. I never went out of my way to not be found.

I didn't even try to pursue royalties or anything. Plus, in my negative state of mind, I didn't think anybody would even remember me.

Sometime later, they called me about the possibility of doing an appearance for them in Thailand at a film festival where it was being screened. It was a pretty big deal because few films shown there had such strong sexual themes. I was excited about going since I'd never been to Thailand and it sounded exotic. But I got shot down when they were told by the festival board they were not allowed to bring in any of the interview subjects because of the nature of the film.

It was ultimately well received there and it gave the film some momentum. Apparently it did well at various other festivals, and with the nice response they got a U.S. deal with an American distributor. The funny thing was that when I got the movie in the mail I didn't even watch it for the longest time. I had no rights to it or any money on the back end. To me it was already over and done with. When I finally saw it, it kind of felt like it was more about the adult film industry itself than a movie about me. But it was a good enough film with some real substance to it.

About four years after I'd finished shooting it, I got a call from a company out of New York called The Disinformation Company. They wanted me to promote *Desperately Seeking Seka* here in the States. They wanted me to hit bookstores and even dangled the bait of TV appearances for me. But once again, the money wasn't great.

I told them I would do the publicity tour if I got one dollar from every DVD they sold. It sounded more than fair to me since they were selling them for thirty dollars a pop at that point and it *was* all about me.

"No, we can't do that."

I said, "See you. Goodbye."

They kept calling me back trying to make a deal. My answer was always the same. "I want a dollar per DVD sold." They offered ten cents per copy. Eventually, the big sports went up to twenty cents. I said I wouldn't do it unless I got what I wanted. I reached a point where I didn't even pick up the phone when they called.

There was no bad blood with the Swedish filmmakers themselves, since they understood where I was coming from. They allegedly had some money issues with the same distributors. Ironically, the film did pretty well at first. But I don't feel I sold myself short. The money I got came in awfully handy and they happened to have been two really nice guys. And I did get something out of it, as they did a hot link from their website to mine, which helped my site grow. But later I saw the price of the video drop dramatically because they didn't have anyone to promote it properly. You can now pick it up on eBay at around $5 a pop. So much for the glamorous world of documentary filmmaking.

Reunion time with Joey Silvera.

John Leslie and I patched it up at the end.

Paul Thomas never changes.

Candida Royalle makes the best films!

Serena co-starred with me in my first feature, "Dracula Sucks".

Pity me, I never got to work with Peter North.

The new generation: Seymore Butts.

With Cousin Stevie of "Family Business" With all those hot young things surrounding him, he still prefers an old established firm like me!

What a line-up! Ron Jeremy, Seka, Georgina Spelvin, director Henri Pachard, Marilyn Chambers, Christy Canyon, and director Roy Karch, 2007.

The two biggest stars of the late 70's/early '80's: me and Marilyn Chambers.

Nina Hartley. Yeah, I did her.

Decades later with Veronica Hart, who I helped break in, co-signing a *Seduction of Cindy* poster.

With one of the "new kids", Taylor Wane.

With Ginger Lynn in 2010.

My dream threesome: Randy West and Herschel Savage—two nice Jewish boys.

It ain't Grauman's Chinese Theatre, but I'm immortalized in front of the Hustler Store!

Here's a raunchy bunch: TT Boy, Randy West, Amber Lynn, Seka, Herschel Savage, Veronica Hart, Randy Spears, Ginger Lynn, (front) Kylie Ireland & Nina Hartley.

With Amber Lynn in Seattle. The puppet's name is Maurice.

49

On the Road, Fully Clothed

ONE OF THE WAYS I PAY THE BILLS these days is to go on the road to a variety of fan and industry conventions to sign autographs and sell product. It's a combination of heaven and hell.

I don't mind being on the road as long as I'm making money. At the Adult Video News (AVN) show—the "Academy Awards" of adult entertainment—they want you to come out and help draw people to their booth, but "we don't have money to pay you." This is a multi-billion dollar industry, mind you. So I won't do one unless a company working the event contacts me and offers me a fee.

One year John Holmes' widow, Laurie Holmes, who worked under the name Misty Dawn, contacted me about a signing at the AVN show. She worked for one of the sponsoring companies and she agreed to my terms so I figured I'd give it a shot. I'd never met her before and she turned out to be a very nice girl. We talked about John quite a bit and she knew I was one of the few people in the industry who continues to defend him. She was madly in love with him and still has to fight every day against people ripping off his estate by taking his name and likeness and putting it on t-shirts and other merchandise. I can certainly relate to being ripped off, so we hit it off famously and it was a good time.

Arthur Morowitz of Video-X-Pix is a wonderful guy and I was glad to see he was also at the event. Unlike many in our industry, he's just plain honest. Whatever he says he's going to do, he does. He's also fun to be around—just a nice man.

When I heard he was getting ready to leave and it was so busy that I had yet to see him, I made my way over to him. He was talking to somebody so I waited for a minute, but had to get back to work. When he saw me he gave me a big smile, pulled me over closely, and said, "Do you know who that is standing next to me?" I had no idea whatsoever. It looked like a little old man with a cane. His hair was completely white and he was pasty and unhealthy looking. But there was a certain way he moved his mouth that made me finally recognize who it was.

"Holy fuck, say it ain't so!" I thought I was absolutely going to crap my pants. It felt like I had seen a ghost. A chill actually ran down my spine and stayed there all day long.

It was Ken.

He started to say something and I simply went, "No, don't do it," and just turned and walked away. To this day, the man sells my old belongings on eBay. He's still making money off me. And I continue to find out thirty years later about deals where he stole from me. I'll meet an industry exec who'll reminisce about "paying me well" for a film. I'll respond by saying "I was paid okay." Then the real numbers come out. Ken would tell me the pay and I'd say, "No problem." But I found out decades later, I got a third of what the fee actually was and he'd put the rest in his pocket.

On a lighter note, I also met Seymore Butts at AVN and he's a very nice fellow. He's always a very busy boy who was surrounded by photographers since he had a Showtime reality show at the time. We did some kind of ribbon-cutting ceremony together—what it was for, I have no idea. But the publicity was good anyway. Seymore (Adam Glasser) introduced me to his Cousin Stevie, who was also on their reality show. He's a little older than I am and he's the funniest, nicest, sweetest person. His wife is just wonderful also and she thinks his career as a porn director/producer is a hoot. She's very supportive considering there are naked young women having sex in their living room. Hey, it pays the bills.

In the booth where I was signing, there were four new young hot-bodied babes also doing promotion. I was extremely worried; they were so young and gorgeous I feared this old porn queen would be sitting there twiddling my thumbs. It was astonishing, though, that I had a steady line all day long for all three days. And these little girls didn't know who I was! One of them said, "I've never seen anything like this. I've never had lines like this for me." One of my customers overheard her and said, "And you never will.... There's only one Seka!" They don't have a clue about who came before them or that we made it easier for them to do what they're doing now. They were very naïve to the business and it concerned me they would be eaten alive by it.

Amber Lynn, Nina Hartley, and Candida Royalle were all there. Candida's one of the best directors out today with her couples' films. We always have nice conversations because we don't see each other that often. One of the reasons we all lose touch is I've lived in Chicago and Missouri, and most industry people are in California or New York. I'd done layouts for *Club* with Amber Lynn, and a movie with Nina, but never really worked with Candida. We talked about each other's lives, not so much the business.

Not too long ago I did the AVN Awards for Video-X-Pix, who picked up *Careful, He May Be Watching* for distribution. What was interesting about that show was there were so many people I had not seen in years. It was like a class reunion. Herschel Savage, Randy West, John Leslie, Serena, Kelly Nichols, Ginger Lynn, Amber Lynn, Veronica Hart, director Roy Karch, and Bill Margold were all there. I'd worked with and for all of them except Kelly Nichols. It was a lot of fun. We gabbed like old hens. Amber is working on getting her domain name back. She's doing real estate and has returned to making movies. Ginger's still doing films as well as radio. Veronica is producing and directing horror and sci-fi flicks.

John Leslie was directing tons of adult films in Europe. Things were better between us. We sort of patched things up shortly before he died. His death was, though, rather untimely—a stroke—so it wasn't like he was consciously making deathbed amends. Maybe the soul simply knows more than the conscious mind does.

Randy West does some adult industry work, but not a lot. He lives in Vegas, where the lifestyle certainly suits him. Serena is somewhere in Northern California but I have no idea what she's up to. Kelly's a makeup artist. Nina's still active making movies, too. The MILF thing is very popular now. I could lose a few pounds—or maybe even not—and get back into it if I wanted, and could probably command a pretty penny, but the thought of it just doesn't do it for me. Been there, done that. Time for new chapters of my life to be written.

I got a lot of their contact information and ultimately it served me well because I got together a group of them for another signing in Seattle. That event wasn't all fun, though. One nicely dressed, normal-looking fan wanted a picture taken with me. But as I posed with him I felt his hands sliding down my back. One of the things I do with fans when they put their hand around my waist is I get a firm grip on their thumb. If they try something, all you have to do is pull straight back on their thumb and they'll go straight down to their knees.

So I feel his hand sliding down my back to my butt. I pull slightly and he says, "That hurt."

"I know." But he did the same thing again. So I pulled harder and said, "You see those two guys over there?" I pointed to my two rather large male friends who weren't bodyguards but could have passed for them.

He said, "Yeah."

"Well, if I so much as nod towards them, they'll come over and pulverize you." He behaved very nicely after that.

I tried to get more events together for "The Golden Boys and Girls of Classic Porn," but it became an exercise in frustration I soon gave up on. I would get a call for an appearance and I'd ask, "Will it just be me?" If so, I would consider the venue and wonder if I'd have to sit around all day in an empty store or something, so I'd ask if they'd go for a whole bunch of us. Usually, they'd jump for joy, and with all our names on the ads, people would flock to the events. Since we'd all sell photos, autographs, and swag, we'd all make out.

Since it worked so well, I figured there would be reciprocation. What a cool set-up we could all have!

Nope.

The business had ruined us all when it came to money. Everyone thinks porn messes up your mind as far as sex and love goes. No, at least not for me. For me, and for most of the others, the mind-fuck was money. We'd been stars in a multi-billion dollar industry—bigger by some accounts than regular Hollywood. But the actors, the stars up on the screen? We made pennies, if that. Crumbs from the table.

We should have had a union. We should have had something. I know a bunch of people got together during the AIDS era—Sharon Mitchell and Bill Margold come to mind—to organize us for better health services, but as far as salary goes, we were still treated like children working in Third World sweat shops.

What it did to most people's heads is make them paranoid and greedy—greedy over pennies. It was every man and woman for himself or herself. We all could have helped each other more economically but instead, if someone got a gig or a lead of some sort, they kept it to themselves, even if it was for just a couple hundred dollars. Together, we could have been a power—we could have *had* power. But once a person has been burned over and over again, they get that way—like squirrels hiding their nuts.

When I see people like Ron Jeremy and Nina Hartley, people who are still making movies, and I watch some of their older stuff, I don't see what other people see. Others notice the difference between age and youth. Me,

I see the faces of people who've been ripped off so many times it's changed who they once were. The contrast between the youthful faces of people happy to be making $200 a day, to the faces of people who now realize a lot of people became multimillionaires off their labors. Money that's gone and will never be theirs.

I am no better than any of them. My wanting us to all band together was less altruistic than realistic—it was a way to make more money, or at least I thought so. I've gotten so paranoid from being burned so many times I call a lawyer when someone asks me to sign a voter registration card!

Events like the AVNs are just the tip of the iceberg. We porn people get invited to all sorts of functions. My first horror/sci-fi/comics show was New Jersey's Chiller Convention in April 2005. I thought, "This is going to be interesting," because I had no idea how I would do at a show of this nature. I was a little frightened. One of the things I can't stand to do is bomb. But I ended up doing very well. I hadn't been out doing appearances for a while and figured they wouldn't remember me, but they were so nice and polite. It was also good for my ego to get the response and kinds of comments I got.

"I wondered where you were."

"I can't believe you're here."

"When are you coming back?"

"Why don't you do more appearances?"

I didn't understand the connection between sci-fi, horror, and porn, but somehow it's there. You know it's weird when guys dressed as *Star Wars* storm troopers come up to the porn queen asking for an autograph, but it happens. These things often blend in classic TV and movies in general, as well as professional wrestling and regular pro sports, so when I attend I never know who I'll run into. There's no connective tissue at all, just famous and semi-famous people of all sorts, all congregated under one roof. Quite the autograph orgy.

The fans are just awesome. When you spend part of your life in a field a hell of a lot of people look down upon, it's overwhelming when you get a positive and warm response.

It's fun for me to meet some of the celebrities. Peter Tork from The Monkees is very sweet. Donnie Most and Anson Williams from *Happy Days* were so supportive. They gave me a hug and kiss and said, "Why don't you send some of the people in your line down our way?" There was real camaraderie and respect for each other, much more respect than at adult industry shows. These are professionals who enjoy seeing each other do well. A pleasant environment makes the day go by and there's no place for jealousy and pettiness. They're generally nice, funny, interesting people who have more going on in their lives than just living off a show or movie they did decades ago. I think that makes a difference, too.

I met WWE Hall of Famer "Luscious" Johnny Valiant, who sat right next to me. Johnny sold out Madison Square Garden four times as half of the colorful Valiant Brothers circa 1974–75. Johnny's an actor/comedian now and had a recurring bit part on *The Sopranos*. He's a very funny and warm guy with a one-man show.

Sitting next to Johnny was one of my old co-stars, Richard Bolla. Nobody recognized him at first because he has not aged particularly well. Also known as R. Bolla and with a dozen or so other names on his filmography, he is best known for the notorious *Debbie Does Dallas* with reluctant adult star Bambi Woods, who soon after left the industry and basically disappeared off the face of the earth. Bolla was also a leading man in low-budget European films and was signing the DVD release of the infamous *Cannibal Holocaust*, which actually had the actors killing live animals on screen.

Lovely.

Bolla spent much of the weekend reminiscing about the days when he was paid $500 to fly around the world and have sex with beautiful women. Nice work if you can get it, I guess.

Frank Vincent from *The Sopranos* was sitting behind me. He's a gorgeous man, and one of his daughters was helping him out. She's a pretty girl in her twenties and was flirting with my boyfriend in a friendly sort of way. Turnabout's fair play, and at one point she turned to me and said, "Are you flirting with my dad?"

I responded jokingly, "I sure am."

It was that kind of weekend.

I also met Lou Ferrigno and I absolutely adore him. I've always loved him and thought he was a really incredible person. I also think he has a better body than "The Ah-nold." I knew you had to stand directly in front of him so he can read your lips, so I did just that and told him, "I've always admired you and would like a picture with you." He was very nice and polite. But my boyfriend went over and talked to him, not realizing Lou is deaf. There wasn't a helluva lot of conversation and he came back to the table assuming Lou was rude. When I explained the situation they started chatting again and now we're all fast friends.

Speaking of behemoths, I love working shows with the pro wrestlers. At the 2005 Hollywood Collectors Show in Burbank I sat near Greg "The Hammer" Valentine, Nikolai Volkoff, Lanny "The Genius" Poffo, and The Iron Sheik. They're all very sweet considering they could probably kill you with their bare hands.

There's nobody on the planet like "Sheiky." He's the real deal—his on-screen persona is basically the same as in real life. He's a lovely guy, but also quite volatile. An interviewer really set him off with one question. Before we knew it, his eyes were blazing fire and his voice was booming every politically incorrect comment imaginable.

"Fuck you! I'll fuck that Hulk Hogan in the ass and humble him!" Luckily, with his thick Iranian accent I don't think the audience had any idea what the heck he was saying. Strangely enough, it was me and not "Sheiky" who almost didn't get booked for the event. The stigma of my porn past frightened the lovely host, Ray Court, who puts on a classy event. It took a lot of recommendations from other guests, who vouched for my behavior as "ladylike," to finally change his mind.

If anyone sees me at these events, I try to look glamorous, but I'm dressed conservatively compared to what you see at the AVN events. On the other hand, I had to be careful at the Hollywood Collectors Show in just how risqué my merchandise display could be.

After the show, we all went out to dinner along with talent agent Tony Pellicone. Tony is a colorfully loud and boisterous, short, fat, and shaved bald ex-sailor. He's one of the characters you meet in the business. Tony makes and spends money like water. "Are you making money?" someone would ask Tony. "I don't know, I just want to keep my boys on the road," referring to his beloved wrestlers.

I guess I was one of the boys now, too.

Tony also brought me into New York for a rather expensive party for the late Captain Lou Albano. We had a blast over at Ashford and Simpson's swanky club, The Sugar Bar, with Handsome Jimmy Valiant, Superfly Jimmy Snuka, King Kong Bundy, tons of other wrestlers, and a killer big band—New York City Swing—playing behind host Johnny Valiant. It was wonderful. The only thing was, Tony had neglected to charge a cover. With free food, entertainment, and a host of celebs to pay, there was little chance for ol' Tony to recoup his money, not that he seemed to care at the time.

Whisked away into a limo with a sleepy Sheik, we all did interviews on a late night live TV talk show, ending a great evening.

Tony later disappeared, allegedly owing some people money. Hey, he treated me great the few times he booked me. To the penny in fact. So who am I to judge?

Sometimes events don't do well, which make for awfully long days. I was booked at a convention in Baltimore with the still handsome blaxploitation star Fred Williamson, other name actors, and a ton of wrestlers including the Wild Samoans and The Rock's dad, Rocky Johnson. There was literally a room full of wrestlers who had sold out huge arenas around the world, but I don't think a hundred fans came in the entire day. I guess some promoters know what they're doing and some are just in over their heads—simple as that. I got paid in full up front, but it still didn't make for the greatest experience.

I also met Sybil Danning and her husband Horst at the Hollywood Collector's Show. A very striking and handsome woman, we have several friends in common. She's just a really cool lady who always has different projects and movies going on. Sybil's so gracious and elegant to everyone who comes up to her table; she's not standoffish at all.

Another favorite of mine is Larry Thomas, "The Soup Nazi" from Seinfeld. He's a distinguished character actor. I saw this person, slight and shy, standing at one convention after-party dressed in a checkered shirt and jeans. When I would look at him he'd stare down at the floor like I had caught him peeking at me or something. So I walked over to get a beer and as I passed him I said, "Hello, how are you?"

He said, "My God, I always wanted to meet you!"

Then it hit me. "The Soup Nazi?!"

He grinned and we hit it off immediately.

I met Erik Estrada at the Hollywood Collector's Show. A funny little bastard with a million watt smile, he's totally energetic. I was over at Erik's table looking at some of his stuff because I needed a couple of autographs for friends. I said, "Just tell me how much they are."

"Are you crazy? I'm not charging you."

Katey Sagal from *Married with Children* was sitting there, too, and she had this mug on her like she was pissed off at the world. I thought, "Maybe she doesn't feel well today or something."

Erik glanced at her, then he jokingly said about me, "Everything I know, I learned from this woman."

"Well," Ms. Sagal responded, "I really don't need to hear this."

I said, "What's your problem?"

She responded venomously, "It's just disgusting!"

"Oh, really?"

I thought it was humorous. She had no idea about my industry or who I was. In fact, she's probably someone who has never seen an X-rated film and never even talked to someone in the business. It's hard to get pissed off over stupidity and ignorance. She just turned and walked away.

Erik looked at me sheepishly and said, "Oh, don't take it seriously. Some people are just like that." Don't I know it.

Another "wonderful" experience was at Chiller when I met Val Kilmer. I had looked at the Chiller website and was excited to meet him because I thought he was a good actor. Plus, he had done the John Holmes movie, *Wonderland*. I had probably worked with John more than anyone. I asked one of the security guards if I could meet Val. He was sitting next to someone who I believe was his manager. When I mentioned who I was and about my close relationship with John, the manager was kind of a cold fish. He hit me up for thirty dollars for a photo.

Kilmer turned around and looked at me for a second. When I told Val the same thing I had said to his manager, he coldly responded, "I heard you already. So did everyone else in the line."

He wouldn't even stand up to talk to me so I leaned over and said, "It's a good thing John Holmes didn't have your fucking attitude, because he wouldn't have gone anywhere."

Henry Winkler was on the other side of him and I moved out of there so fast I smacked right into him. I said, "I didn't mean to mow you down like that."

Henry said, "Someone should have told Kilmer that earlier." Afterwards, fan after fan was telling me how rude he was. He sat there playing with his iPod, never even took his sunglasses off, and wouldn't pose for pictures. I also heard he wasn't on time the whole weekend. He just didn't seem to be a nice person. There's absolutely no need for that, especially when you were Batman and have kids for fans.

In spite of exceptions like Kilmer, I'd still say that 99% of the celebrities are nice to their fans. Larry Hagman and Barbara Eden have also been quite friendly whenever our paths cross at these events. And I love Dawn Wells from *Gilligan's Island*.

At one Chiller Con, Paul Reubens was there. I loved him on *Murphy Brown* and of course as Pee Wee Herman. I always thought he'd gotten a bum rap in that porn theater bust that derailed his career for a while.

We both had packed lines. It was just crazy. At the end of the day, I knew a short cut through the kitchen because there's an elevator in there.

All the staff was saying, "Hi, Seka. How are you?" I guess I make friends easily. Then here comes Pee Wee Herman yelling, "Hold the door!"

When I saw him I shrieked, "Oh my God!"

Then he goes, "Oh My God!"

I told him, "I always wanted to meet you!"

So he repeated, "I always wanted to meet YOU!" It was just comical. We started taking pictures of each other on the elevator. We've been great friends ever since. Unfortunately, because of the controversy, we have to kind of play it cool when the general public is around. I guess you could say Pee Wee Herman is my secret lover. Ha!

Erin Moran from *Happy Days* was trying to find a table at one Chiller after a Nor'easter had created some chaos in the big tent we were in. I grabbed one for her and we hit it off. She has so much energy it's ridiculous. And she's just plain funny as hell. I invited her to dinner with a group of celebs who we usually go out with the last night of the show. We started drinking, with Erin downing martinis. In the middle of it all, this one actor next to me keeps looking down my shirt. I finally said, "Do you want to see them?" and pulled them out right there in the restaurant. Then my girlfriend Stevie did the same. Then all the women at the table started taking off their blouses and were down to their bras, including Erin. Of course, we kept our backs to everyone so as not to offend.

It was a memorable evening. As are most of my experiences on the road.

At the Hollywood Collector's Show in Chicago with Playboy Playmate of the Month, August 1982, Cathy St. George. It was her birthday.

With Big Ken Norton, former heavyweight champ.

Making a Soup Nazi sandwich (Larry Thomas) with Marilyn Chambers.

Me and my 'rasslers: The Iron Sheik and Capt. Lou Albano.

No, really, this is what a fan fest looks like. Me and two ghostbusters.

The greatest lover I ever had: Pee Wee Herman (Paul Reubens)"

A real gentleman, Henry Winkler.

50

Orphaned Again

I CAN'T SAY I HAD ANY GREAT LOVE FOR MY MOM.

Mom was always jealous of me. I was daddy's little girl. I later learned that when she was pregnant with me she did everything she could to have a miscarriage. I don't know what the medication was called at the time, but I was told she was taking it.

Hey, it's great to be wanted.

In spite of it all, I came out stronger, bigger, and tougher than my brother and sister. Yet as fate would have it, I looked exactly like my mother. The problem was, she didn't want anyone around who was younger and prettier.

Throughout my life, if I saw her once a year it was a lot. But when I did it was usually a doozy. I'll never forget the time she visited my first husband and I walked into the kitchen and she turned around, gave me an odd look, and wrapped her arms around Frank. "He doesn't want you—he wants me. Why don't you go away so we can finish what we're doing?"

Pretty sick shit. It was just another way to make me feel less of a person, like I wasn't good enough.

Frank just looked at me uncomfortably and said, "I haven't done anything."

"I know," I responded with disgust in my voice.

She was beautiful and used to being the center of attention, but clearly when I started developing it was competition she could not stand. I just looked at her and shook my head. Nothing had changed. It was sad.

The fact I didn't see her all that much was probably a good thing. I guess I was trying to be a good kid because in spite of it all, I bought her a home in Florida. She was taking care of my grandparents and didn't have any money, so I didn't want her to worry about paying a mortgage or rent.

Plus, I didn't need her coming to me all the time for cash. With the house, all she'd have were her normal monthly bills. But I held the title in my name, because I figured she'd do something crazy—she always did.

One day she called out of the blue and said, "Could you send me some autographed pictures?"

"Sure, Mom. Who do you want me to make them out to?"

"Just sign them."

I didn't think much of it until she called a while later. "I just want you to know, I told the carpet guy that Seka was my daughter and he put all new carpeting in my house for the pictures."

Oddly, I think it was the one time she was proud of me.

When AIDS was all over the news, I got a call from a reporter, saying he'd heard from a "good source" that I was HIV positive. "Who's the source?"

"Your mother."

With mothers like that, who needs a knife in the back? I called her. "What's your problem? I don't have AIDS! Are you trying to destroy my career?"

"I dreamed it, so I figured it must be true."

"I'm not even going into how crazy that is, but why the hell did you call the press about it?"

There was no good answer and we both knew it. She did it for the attention. Just calling a reporter and saying she was Seka's mother might not have gotten her much play. But saying her daughter Seka had AIDS? Well, that was newsworthy—if it were true. Thank God I don't think anyone in the media ran with it, but they could have. Thanks, Mom.

My mother would sometimes say to me, "I know you'll take care of me when I get real old. I can come live with you."

"Oh no, old woman. You will not be living in my home and I will not be taking care of you. You need to take care of that part of your life. And I will not take care of your funeral arrangements, either."

"You won't feel the same when you look down at my dying face," she said many times, trying to make me feel guilty.

One day my sister called to tell me Mom was sick. But everyone in the family was well aware of her lifetime of crying wolf. Even at this stage we didn't know whether to believe her or not. She had, however, been on oxygen because she was having a hard time breathing. The doctors told her she couldn't smoke when she was on oxygen, but she did it anyway. The woman basically microwaved her lungs.

Once we realized Mom was, in fact, very ill, my sister stayed with her the whole time. She kept telling me I needed to come to Florida. But I didn't feel guilty about not being there. It was her own damn fault with the cigarettes. Besides, when I was lying in quarantine with spinal meningitis as a kid and told I could die, I don't remember her being there—my dad was. I loved her because she was my mother, but I don't think she would have done the same for me. It was a love built on obligation. Everyone's supposed to love their mother, right? But that was as deep as it went.

I finally told my sister straight out, "I'm not coming to Florida." Mom was going to die and that's all there was to it. Now it was a waiting game.

I did speak to her when she was in the hospital. I think she knew she was dying because out of nowhere she shocked me by saying, "I love you, Dottie."

I'm convinced it was her guilt speaking. I never felt she loved me at all and this was just her way of saying sorry to me.

She died in Florida. I didn't cry a single tear then and haven't since.

Mom wanted to be cremated and my sister said, "I don't know how I'm going to pay for this." I told her to look through Mom's papers. Shockingly, she had actually taken care of it. I think it was one of the few times she ever listened to me, because she knew I meant what I was saying about not doing it all for her.

Since much of the family was still in Virginia, they brought her ashes there and we sort of had a family reunion/ picnic/funeral. My brother decorated little boxes with my mother's ashes in them. He put her initials on the outside of them. This was a nice gesture since he clearly put a lot of effort into it. At an outdoor pavilion, everybody brought a dish for lunch, and there were pictures of my mother by the boxes of ashes.

The little boxes were distributed among us, while some of her ashes were spread along the river. She certainly caused enough turmoil during her life, but on this day my mother, Peggy, was divided up amicably.

I brought my box home, where it sat on a bookshelf in my office for the longest time. Working on the computer one evening, I heard a noise. I had an eerie feeling. One of Mom's initials on the box had fallen off. I picked up the letter, threw it in the box, and said, "Damn, woman, you're bothering me from the grave."

I put her in the closet, where she remains with a bunch of my old movies. It's kind of ironic. She's safe and secure anyway. May she rest in peace.

51

Sibling Rivalries

MOST FAMILIES HAVE SOME DEGREE OF SIBLING RIVALRY. Mine, however, are more like lifelong wars.

I'd never been close with my brother and sister. As the youngest child, you kind of look up to your older siblings and feel they'll protect you. Yet, I was devastated when the entire family deserted me and never really got over it. Should I have? Of course. But no one ever apologized! How do you forgive someone who doesn't ask for forgiveness? It can be done, but it sure ain't easy. Granted, they were just kids at the time, but they could have at least mentioned me when my mom came to school to take them the day they all left. Where did they think I was? Couldn't either of them count to three and say, "Someone's missing"?

I never felt the same way about them since.

But it goes beyond that. If we were not family, I would not choose them as friends.

When I was grown, I'd start getting collection notices on credit cards and at first had no idea what was what. When I investigated, I found my mother and sister, Deborah, had run them to the limit on their little spending sprees and expected me to pay them off.

Very nice.

I may have made an unusual career choice that many people frown upon, but at least I make a living for myself. I don't try to live off someone else. And I certainly make every attempt to honor all my debts.

I wouldn't talk to my sister for four or five years after the credit card incident. But I cared about her two sons very much so when she finally called me, I let it go. She acted like nothing had happened. But this little voice in the back of my head was saying, "What does she *really* want? There has to be an ulterior motive."

And of course, there was.

After my mom passed away she started calling, telling me she hired lawyers to sue a company where my mother worked when I was a kid. But she wouldn't give me all the details. It had something to do with my mother's illness. She wanted to sue the company for asbestos-related disease, even though I doubt there was evidence she actually had that. She also knew what brand of cigarette Mom had smoked and had a lawsuit against that corporation as well. The whole thing smelled of scam to me.

"What are the lawyer's fees? How will any money from the lawsuit be distributed? Is this being done on a contingency?" I got no answers. All I knew was my sister would be in charge of everything. It seemed pretty obsessive on her end, and while going through these lawsuits she had a stroke. Her memory and speech were pretty bad for a while. She lost use of her one side, although it's come back since.

It was like my mother's body died but her spirit went into my sister. I finally found out there were legal fees and I'd be expected to pay one third if they lost. When I refused, the lawyers eventually dropped out of the case. Deborah called and was absolutely furious with me.

"I don't want you to ever darken my door again. I do not want to ever hear your voice again."

"No problem." And I meant that. I haven't spoken to her since.

It wasn't like it was that big a deal to me anyway. She had never really been part of my life. She'd never been there for me when I needed an older sister. There was no real connection. I've always managed to live my life to the best of my abilities without her or my brother.

One day, my brother Ray called me out of the blue because he wanted a truck. Of course, he didn't have the means to pay for it so I not only loaned him money for it, but traveled all the way to Texas to help him fill out the loan application papers because he couldn't manage it on his own. We went to the dealership together, where he told them for whatever reason that he wanted to modify the truck. When they informed him straight out it wouldn't work properly, he nonetheless insisted.

It didn't take long for him to realize the dealership had been absolutely right. He tried to return the truck and they wouldn't take it back. Meanwhile, he never tried to repay me. Then I got a call from him a year or so later. He told me he had a court case regarding this truck. I knew he never should have messed with the truck in the first place, so I just didn't see the point.

"You have to come down here," he demanded.

His lawyer called to tell me the very same thing. I told the lawyer, "I'm not going to lie and perjure myself for my brother. And if you insist on me being in Texas, then he's going to pay for my airfare and hotel, because I am not going to incur these costs on his behalf."

My brother has not spoken to me since. He also believes I betrayed him. Guess I'm two for two in the betrayal department.

Intelligent, capable people should channel their energy into positive avenues. I didn't believe in either of their legal cases, nor did I want any part of them. The whole thing was white trashy bullshit; using the legal system to get something for nothing.

My brother, after many failed marriages, has finally met "the right woman." His current wife is the closest thing you'll ever find to angel on this planet. And they've raised lovely children. I'm sad they don't have Aunt Dottie in their lives, but in spite of our differences, I'm happy Ray has started to put some of the pieces of his own life together. Hey, he is my sibling after all.

For whatever that's worth.

52

Cream Pies

ALL LOT OF MEN AND WOMEN LIKE CREAM PIES—all sorts of cream pies. And I learned a long time ago there's no pie in the sky. But what I didn't know is you can make a good payday getting pie in your eye.

Yes, Seka does fetish films.

I knew there was a whole world of fetish, from grown men in diapers, to girls joyfully popping balloons, to people tied up and hanging from ceilings, and an endless array of other kinks. To each his own, but none of this really did anything for me, and I never had any desire to pursue these markets as far as film work. But I was doing the Glamour Con show in Chicago a few years ago and this nice fellow approached me at my table about doing "pie videos."

"What do you mean?"

"Well, there's some nudity but no sex involved. You get pies thrown at you. We pay $200 a day."

I just laughed. "You've got to be kidding."

They wanted a big name porn star for one of their movies. But $200 doesn't get you Seka. Especially to get butter cream pies thrown in my face. And in several scenes no less.

Several years went by and I had pretty much forgotten about it. Out of nowhere the owner of the company called to tell me they were starting up again and wanted me. I hadn't done anything on film in years. But there was no sex involved. Just out of curiosity I said, "How much are you paying?"

And the pay had risen dramatically.

Hell, Soupy Sales, The Three Stooges, and every silent film comedian I had ever seen had taken a pie or two to the face.

So Seka was about to get "pied."

They took care of all my expenses to come down to Florida and put me up in a lovely hotel not far from the shoot. I brought a hairdresser friend of mine; God knows I was going to need her.

The set was a nice big house where all the other models were staying. There were palm trees and even fruit trees, so it was a relaxing and classy setting. Everywhere I looked there were nude and semi-nude young women running around getting ready to shoot their scenes. I was used to nudity from my years in adult films. But what I found odd was seeing hundreds upon hundreds of pies stacked up around the house. Who ever knew pies were a fetish?

While I was there, I watched their other films being shot. There were huge gallon cans with chocolate and vanilla pudding. The fetish is called "being slimed." They also had a giant tank filled with pudding and the girls would get dunked in these tanks and come out covered from head to toe. It was like they were human desserts.

There was one guy on set who had a thing for washing girls' hair to get the pudding out. He'd do it with a garden hose. He was famous for getting an erection when he washed women's hair. He was harmless enough I guess, so I joked with him, "If you get a boner, I'm going to knock you out."

Another set of films they were shooting involved underwater masturbation scenes. People are into everything I suppose. Again, whatever floats your boat—or floats to the top of your pool.

We used the outdoor area by the pool to do the movie. There was a huge tarp to help contain the mess. Each fifteen-minute scene was pretty much the same. Girls would be talking to each other and suddenly start throwing pies. That was it, basically.

This company has a huge fan base. The fans themselves write and pay for the scenes, including my own. It's their personal fantasies, filmed for a price.

I quickly learned the "rules" specific to this genre in which I was ironically a virgin. You are not allowed to wipe the pie off your face. And you're supposed to stay composed while being hit.

During my first scene, I didn't even have to take my clothes off. I wore a black turtleneck and a tight skirt. I was supposed to play a Russian comedian and have an accent. Seka was suddenly Olga the Russian Comic.

"Vat do you get when you cross a pair of panties and an ocean liner?"

"A panty liner."

Rim shot, please.

It was all pretty goofy. And every time I did a punch line, they'd throw a cream pie in my face. I lost it I was laughing so hard. I'd say the next joke and they'd hit me in the face again. Then one boob. Then the other one. Next came my butt. All in all there were about thirty pies per scene thrown at me and I was scheduled to do several scenes that day. Funny thing was, I had the best time. It all seemed like fun, like kids playing. Even when I started taking off clothes in other scenes, it didn't seem sexual to me.

After I finished one scene, I had around ninety minutes to shower, clean up, and redo make-up and hair before the next. I ended up hit with well over one hundred pies that day.

The filmmakers were wonderful. It was a joy to work for them as they were some of the nicest, most interesting people I've ever met. Lenny, the owner, is one of the kindest people. He'd take us to beautiful restaurants and give us nice gifts for a job well done. I was thinking, "Who is this person and where did he come from?" You never meet anyone like this in my business.

The aftermath was I found my skin was the softest it's ever been, although I smelled like cream pie for a week. And I wasn't exactly running down to the bakery as often as I used to.

Although fetish films are something I'd never thought of doing, this wasn't a bad gig. In fact, it was probably the oddest, but easiest job I've ever done in my career. Now when I hear people getting all horny talking about cream pies (the other kind), all I do is laugh.

53

Along Came Carl

TOWARD THE END OF MY RELATIONSHIP with my boyfriend, Jim, we went to Florida. We settled in the first day. But, as expected, he was gone first thing the next morning. Ditto the following. I didn't know where he went every day and I didn't want to know what he was doing. All I cared was that I was in Florida in a swanky hotel and could do what I wanted. I loved the sun and lay by the pool all the time. The pool boy fixed my lounge chair and brought me mimosas.

I like being a princess.

I was there just under a week when I saw the most stunning man I'd ever seen. I loved the way he carried himself, commanding the space he was in. He owned it; you knew he was there. I could see his crisp green eyes across the pool. Obviously Italian, he had dark hair combed straight back. He was oiled up and tanned as could be. He glistened in the sun; it was like it bounced off him.

About five foot ten, he had broad shoulders. Although not extremely muscular, in his yellow swimming trunks with his slender legs and glowing tan, the whole package made one amazing man. I had to check that my tongue wasn't hanging out of my mouth because I didn't want to look like an idiot.

It was August and in Florida it gets hot very quickly. I walked down to the shallow end of the pool and it wasn't just the sun that was making me warm.

By happenstance, at the end of the pool there stood the object of my fantasy. He took a few steps toward me and just stared before finally blurting out, "Hi, my name is Carl." He kept looking at me for what felt like the longest time. "You know, you remind me of someone."

"That's okay," I responded.

"You remind me of Seka."

I just smiled at him and said, "Hello, nice to meet you."

Turns out I met him before at the radio station in Chicago because the company he worked for had done a lot of advertising. The station was always having cigar parties and different events and would invite all the advertisers to their functions. They had a show with Tom Jones at Grant Park. It turns out I was backstage and Carl was with one of his ex-wives when he came up to me and wanted a picture together. He tells me we had spoken for a good forty minutes. Oddly enough, I didn't recall it at all. Nor did I remember several other functions where he claimed we had chatted. But when I saw him at the pool this time, he was etched in my memory forever.

Carl was with a couple guys at a local trade show where he'd do his job in the morning and then come out to the pool. Each and every day we'd talk. And boy could we talk. It went on for hours. But nothing romantic happened. We shared cocktails, lunch, and conversation and that was it. Plus, I doubted my being sixty pounds overweight would turn him on. Nonetheless, I couldn't wait to see this wonderful man each day.

When he told me his marriage wasn't going to last, I wished we were both available. But he didn't even ask for my number. Nor did I ask for his. I was just thankful for the short amount of time we had together.

When he left a day earlier than I did, I had this empty feeling like vacation was over and someone I had truly connected with had just walked out of my life. When I got home I was still thinking about him.

It was about six months later when I got an e-mail from Carl through my website. A rush of excitement shot through me. I immediately e-mailed him back, "You old dog, you. Here's my number. Call me." And when he did I was simply thrilled.

He had just left his wife and by this point I had left Jim as well. With another trade show for him to hit not that far from me, I invited Carl to sleep on my sofa. But he opted for renting a room instead.

I went over to the Marriott to pick him up and he was sitting at the bar. I had lost those pesky sixty pounds. When I tapped him on the shoulder he looked at me and just went, "Oh, shit."

He kind of expected it would be a very expensive evening and that I was—as Billy Joel put it—an "uptown girl," demanding champagne and caviar. Instead, I took him to this little Italian restaurant that was great and reasonable. I said, "Why don't we split an entree?" That shocked him.

We had a great time. The conversation flowed effortlessly from where we had left half a year earlier. We talked about anything and everything. I said, "Do you want to go somewhere else?"

I took him to a little pizza place where a bunch of my friends were hanging out. They all liked him a lot. Except for my best friend, Agnes, because he was competition for her, I suppose.

I didn't want the night to end. I asked if he wanted to hear a little music and he said, "Sure, why not?" I took him to a place where a friend of mine, Nan Mason, was singing. It was a beautiful mansion and she was a torch singer. She's a great lady with tremendous talent who should have made it bigger than she has. We had some delectable desserts while listening to her perform and it couldn't have been any more romantic. Plus, we were pretty well tanked.

We got in a cab and I couldn't stand it anymore. I kissed him. It was electric. I said, "Do you want to go back to the hotel or my place?" We ended up back at mine. He never saw that hotel room at night the rest of the trip. And so the great romance of my life began.

54

Sweet Home Chicago

CARL AND I DATED FOR THREE YEARS. It was wonderful. He didn't have children; I didn't have children. We liked the same things like lying out in the sun, drinking wine, and going window shopping. He was the right age—not some young punk. Even better, he was employed.

When he explained to me why his marriages didn't work out, I accepted his answers. Frankly, it was refreshing to know he'd *had* marriages and wasn't still married to someone who might be calling me in the middle of the night. But Carl, like many men I'd known, would say things like, "I'm no John Holmes."

To which I'd reply, "I certainly hope not. I want a normal person." A cock like John's could kill a woman if she wasn't careful.

I was still in Chicago, he was out in the suburbs, and it was about an hour each way. He'd stay with me on weekends and I'd go out to see him as well. But it was a pain in the butt. Inevitably, one of us would forget something like toiletries. Yet I never thought of moving out of Chicago. And since he'd already had two wives in his home, I didn't want to be number three and not feel like it was my own place.

As in love as I was with this man, I had some real concerns. He had been married several times and was used to living with someone. Me, I didn't know how to play well with others. For example, I never liked when my kitchen utensils were out of place. Little things like that would make me crazy if someone moved them.

As things got more and more serious, I wondered if this would work. But I loved the guy to death.

One day, I just decided we should be living together. With both of us being burned so many times, I actually had us draw up a kind of prenuptial agreement where if it didn't work out, we'd both leave the relationship with what we brought in. We also drew up living wills at the same time. I was included in his and he was included in mine. It encompassed things like his pension going to me if he passed away. He didn't have much family. I had things of value like a website, which could bring in a decent dollar if something happened to me. I also had jewelry, art, and a condo.

I only had 1,200 square feet of space. We couldn't fall down and hit the floor because it was so packed. He needed office space as did I, so we eliminated the dining room and turned it into a work space.

It was a little trying, to say the least.

So we started looking around for a home. I loved the idea of being in a house as opposed to a condo because there was more space. I loved to garden. One day, he invited me on a business trip to Kansas City. He had lived there before and was interested in us moving there. It was cheaper, and a peaceful place to live.

I also figured the best way for our relationship to stand a chance was to not be in Chicago. There, it would be too easy to just say, "Screw it; I don't want to deal with this anymore," if we ever had a fight. In Kansas City, I'd have to work on this relationship. I knew I really needed a change anyway. It was time to take a large step in my life. A leap of faith if you will. So I said OK to KC.

A real estate agent showed us thirteen different houses that day. I guess thirteen isn't unlucky because I found one I really liked. It wasn't a palace, but it was spacious enough and at the same time, "homey." We decided right then and there we wanted it.

My friends decided to throw me a combination fifty-first birthday and going-away party. It was exciting and kind of sad at the same time because I knew I was leaving my very best friends. I had been in Chicago literally a quarter century and these people had been there for me through thick and thin.

I called everybody I knew. Ron Rapoport is a sports writer for the *Chicago Sun-Times*. I had been friends with him for years. He's an absolutely delightful person to be around. Then there were all my buddies I had gone boating with out on Lake Michigan, like "Boat Bob," and "The Two Ricks—No Waiting." One was a fireman and the other a cop and both are gorgeous. We used to joke that if you couldn't have one you could have the other, although in reality it was all just platonic. There were plenty of firemen and police there like Dave and yet another Rick. Frank Rita and the whole Topo Gigio restaurant clan showed up. I had worked for Cheryl at the Crazy Horse gentleman's club and she was just a great person. A tiny little Jewish girl, she was with her husband Mickey, who towered over her. I was happy my friend Debbie Ippolito was there. Although I only knew her a decade or so, she had changed my life by pushing me hard to start my website. My close friends Steve and Harriet and the whole pool crowd from our Sandburg Village condo were there, as well as Jack and Charlotte Brandenburg and Jerry and Julie Ranalli, both wonderful couples. And then there was the ever-colorful Ronnie Webber. He's a gay man who always lights up a room. He's very well built and handsome. I've never seen him wear a shirt where you couldn't see his ripped muscles. The life of the party. Interestingly enough, he's always with a beautiful girl. He's a hairdresser who just plain likes pretty women.

The party was at a lovely Italian restaurant named Tutto Orsi, where I was bartending at the time. Our party was at the jam-packed bar where we were squeezed in like sardines. There had to be fifty or sixty people in attendance.

And then there was Agnes, my best friend.

In spite of any differences we may have had, leaving her was almost like losing someone to death or illness. We wouldn't see each other as much and even though we could talk on the phone, it wouldn't be the same as seeing her all the time. We were both very sad.

At one point the owner of the restaurant, Louie, came over and said that Ronnie and his girl had to calm down. Although he was gay, they were dancing so seductively it was scandalous. She was exposing her breasts and he was having fun with the whole thing and had his hand up her skirt and would bend her over the bar like he was humping her. But that was just Ronnie.

Bobby Salone was playing piano and different people would go to the mike and either sing a song or make a toast in my honor. One by one they told me they didn't want to see me go, but that they were happy I found someone to share my life with and that we were moving forward. There was toast after toast, all heartfelt. These were my true friends and it was overwhelming hearing them tell me how much love and respect they had. We were always there for one another.

I would go to Topo Gigio for dinner or drinks and if someone needed an autographed picture or some piece of memorabilia, I'd never take money for it. Or if there was a charity event, I'd always volunteer my services as a celebrity bartender. If there was ever an emergency, they could call me at 3 a.m. and I'd be there or vice-versa. There was never a question on either side about the other party's devotion.

I was so very sad leaving these wonderful people, yet I knew I hadn't lost them. And I was excited about starting this new chapter in my life. Nonetheless, I was crying like a baby throughout the evening.

Most people in the world can count their true friends on less than one hand. I felt very blessed and fortunate because I was like that Indian goddess with all those hands. That's how many I'd need to count my friends.

A few days later it was really time to go. My apartment was empty and a moving company had everything ready. My maintenance men Steve and Reggie, who I'd become good friends with living in that building for twenty-five years, were sitting with Carl and I, and everyone was crying. I felt like I was leaving my family.

Getting in the car, they were literally following it as we pulled out of the driveway, waving and crying. I looked back at them and I was crying so hard I was having trouble driving. Turning the comer, I could no longer see them. Suddenly, it felt like there was this void. An emptiness.

But I was about to go on a whole new adventure. I wasn't going to allow myself to be scared. As the old blues song goes, "Kansas City, Kansas City, here I come..."

55

Dorothy Lands in Kansas (City)

IT WAS NO SURPRISE THAT KANSAS CITY was dull compared to Chicago. Hell, I couldn't even find good pizza there. And it was difficult because I didn't have any friends and missed the ones I had in Chicago. Meanwhile, my friends back home were making bets on how long it would be until I'd come back.

I was concerned the new neighbors would not accept me because of my adult film career. We were in the middle of the Baptist belt. Some of the busy bodies in the neighborhood, who had no idea who I was, gossiped about a gay couple in the neighborhood. If that was shocking to them, imagine what they would have thought of me.

Using my own skewed logic, I sought out the gay couple, Joe and Dan, and they became my first Kansas City pals. Incredibly, they told me they don't get involved in Halloween because they fear if anything happens to a kid they'll be blamed. Sick.

Eventually, I told them about my past and my own fears about the neighbors. But it's all managed to work out. Carl and I became fast friends with the elderly couple next door to us. They're downright amused to be living next to an old porn queen who spends much of her day gardening. In fact, it's great having neighbors you actually know rather than just pass in a high-rise hallway like back in Chicago.

About a year after settling in, Carl asked me to lunch one day. He dumped a lot of money into my website to help it grow and said to me, "I need to talk to you about something." I assumed it was business related and was very apprehensive. We went to a little Italian restaurant off the beaten path. He suddenly grabbed my hand and said, "I have a little business proposition I want to talk to you about." The way he said it made me even more nervous. I had never seen him like this.

311

"Okay, let's get on with it," I said nervously.

Carl looked at me oddly for what felt like the longest time. When he started to open his mouth, I wondered what bombshell he was going to hit me with. And then he said it.

"Do you want to go get married?"

I went numb. It was the last thing I expected. I hadn't even noticed there was a waiter standing there with a grin on his face from ear to ear. I turned to him and said, "Bring me a double vodka on the rocks with a lime."

Carl said, "Make that two."

As soon as the waiter walked away, I looked at the love of my life and said, "Absolutely. I would love to."

The numbness started to fade and I realized what just happened.

I felt elated, like I was in the middle of the most delightful dream. I had wanted to marry him for the longest time. To finally meet someone who was faithful and honest and felt as strongly about me as I did him was the greatest feeling in the world. It was like a high no drug had ever given me.

As we sat there, he immediately started making plans. "First, we have to get rings, and then we're going to get married on August 23rd," he announced. "Do you want to go to the Grand Caymans? We can get married on the beach," he continued excitedly. Evidently he had been thinking about this for a long time. It gave me a warm, fuzzy feeling because he was that into it. It was even better than him being on bended knee.

We had our lunch and several cocktails. I think I had more than him, which was unusual and he found it very amusing. "You're in shock," he said.

"You're probably right," I laughed.

When we got home he was like a little kid as he busted out all the wedding materials. I thought, "Wow, the man sure has a romantic side."

Then the process started. I couldn't find my birth certificate and we had to wait on the state of Virginia. I also had to dig up my last divorce papers from 1982.

There was a jewelry show in Kansas City. We looked and looked for half a day and came upon this one booth where the gentleman had made some incredibly gorgeous wedding bands. The one I loved most did not have a center stone in it, so he pulled out loose diamonds. I picked one and Carl said, "That's not big enough." He chose a gorgeous center stone and it turned into one big honkin' ring. Then I picked out a band for him.

When the jeweler put a gadget on my finger to get my ring size, I realized I would be wearing this ring forever. I got very hot, started sweating, and needed a drink of water. The numbness and shock were starting to fade and reality was setting in. This wasn't a dress rehearsal; this was for real.

56

Get Me To the Beach On Time

SEVEN MILE BEACH IN THE GRAND CAYMAN ISLANDS is beautiful, pristine, and romantic, but very, very hot. We were going to hold the ceremony at noon, but moved it to 11 a.m. to beat the worst of the heat, if only slightly.

I wrote something especially for the ceremony. I had actually first found it on a card, but it was just so perfect I borrowed it for my wedding and had the words printed underneath his favorite picture of me. It was rolled up sort of like a scroll with a really pretty ribbon to be put around it. Reading it over and over, I figured it would be easy to recite at the actual ceremony. Oddly, I wasn't worried at all. I figured it would all go off without a hitch. But at the last minute I couldn't find my ribbon and was going crazy. Frantic, I had the concierge search for a ribbon, which he finally dug up close to the start of our ceremony.

We were in the lobby of the most gorgeous hotel I had ever seen in my life. It had twenty-foot ceilings with the most elegant island decor. There were hundreds of fresh tropical flowers. And the service was exquisite. I felt like a queen.

All of our guests gathered in the lobby and were drinking mimosas and waiting for us to arrive. My friend Agnes and I went upstairs to meet everyone. Our closest friends were all there and everyone looked so damn happy.

I wasn't nervous yet, although I kept anticipating I would become shaky. What woman wouldn't be nervous at her wedding? It wasn't like I had done it a hundred times. Well, a few, but none as ornately or as meaningful as this. It was strange in that way. This was my third marriage, yet it felt like my first and only. The other two were unplanned afterthoughts to men I never dreamed of spending the rest of my life with. My non-marriages in between, to people like Ken and Jim, may have lasted longer, but were unhealthy and lacking in true, romantic love from the start and throughout. Sometimes we spend time with a partner simply because it beats being alone. But here I was, over fifty, and for the first time in my life, it was the real thing.

Downing a glass of champagne, I asked Agnes to grab me a couple bottles of water to take with. The company hired to marry us picked us up to bring us to the beach location. We got into this little van. It wasn't a fabulous limousine or grandiose in any way, but none of that mattered. This wasn't for show; it was for life.

When we got there and stepped out it was already really hot and muggy. I started to sweat profusely, and it wasn't because of the heat. It all finally hit me. I was shaking.

The sand was sugary white and the smell of fresh ocean water was overwhelming. I took my shoes off and Carl did the same. We stood on the beach and there was pretty music playing softly in the background on a little boom box. We had a video guy there and while everyone was comfortably dressed and casual in shorts with tropical colors, it still felt very romantic. I had on a cream-colored long ankle-length silky skirt and a gold faux turtleneck short-sleeve little tank top with gold pearls. Not exactly a traditional outfit. Then again, nothing I have ever done is traditional.

I don't think I've ever seen Carl look more handsome than that day. He had a great tan and white linen pants with a short sleeve Cuban-style shirt. Instead of having flowers, we both had a Hawaiian lei. The minister was from the Grand Caymans and had long trousers and a really colorful Hawaiian shirt. But as casual as everyone was dressed, it still felt very serious to me. I had no doubts about Carl. But I still had the sweaty jitters.

They sprinkled lavender and dark pink orchids all over for us to stand. I guess that was supposed to be the altar. In the backdrop was the most aqua pristine ocean I had ever seen.

Carl grabbed my hand and it felt like he was holding on for dear life. I started to read what I'd written to Carl and was crying the entire time. I literally couldn't get through it. It was just so hard to read. Nobody could even hear me because I was talking so quietly.

"It's amazing what merely being near you does to me. It's something that goes beyond my control or understanding. Just your physical closeness triggers something primitive deep inside of me. It makes me want—

no, need—to touch you, breath you in, become a part of your warmth. I think I can live forever in the shelter of your arms, finding sustenance in your embrace, happiness in smoldering kisses that impress more than words ever could. It's such a miracle that out of the whole universe you and I found each other. You are the lover I never believed could exist. The one person who could make my fantasies come true. The one person I could love forever."

When it was all over Carl and I took a walk down the beach. He said, "You were having a really hard time with it. Can you believe we're actually married?" I was even shaking when I signed the marriage license.

After all the cake and champagne we went back to the Ritz Carlton swimming pool for what I'd loosely call a reception. We basically decided to just go back to the pool and get hammered. We were all hanging out, eating, and splashing around in the water.

Our guests decided they'd take us out for our wedding dinner. Two brought two more of their friends and they joined us for the evening festivities. But one of these strange women began hitting on Carl the whole time. He started to look uncomfortable. I mentioned it to him and he said, "I don't know what to do. I don't want to be rude. I'm not doing anything."

"I know you're not," I said. And this was the day I got married no less.

I inched over and sat down next to her. I had a smile on my face the whole time so nobody else would know what was going on. "I just married this man today and I love him dearly, and if you don't leave him alone I'm going to put your head through a wall." She didn't have much to say to that. She left with her friend shortly thereafter. You can take the girl off the basketball court, but you can't take the basketball out of the girl.

We went back to our room for the big wedding night and I was starting to feel the effects of the whole thing. My stomach was sick from everything. When the smoke cleared, we didn't consummate our marriage on our wedding night. Two out of three wedding nights, chaste. Ah, another irony for the porn queen!

But waking in Carl's arms, it was clear why I'd been so nervous all day. I looked and searched so long and hard to find someone who loved me for me. Not because I was Seka, but someone who wanted to be with me, Dottie. I looked at him and realized everything I'd ever wanted was right here.

Some shots Carl took of me in the late 1990's. (left and below)

Bobbie Joe, my "Kansas City husband" when my real husband was out of town. Strictly platonic. Also one of my only straight hairdressers. He told me he'd die a happy man if he got to meet me. He did, and then he did. I miss him terribly.

With Jasper of Jasper's restaurant in Kansas City.

I'll do anything for a laugh. That's me at "Jewelry by Morgan" in Kansas City, dressed as Mae West.

I even work on my honeymoon! 2006 Grand Caymans photo shoot.

2011 Christmas card photo with the love of my life, Carl.

57

Reflections

IF I COULD LIVE MY WHOLE LIFE OVER AGAIN, I wouldn't do anything differently, because if I did, I wouldn't be the person I am today. And I happen to like the person I am today.

I'm certainly aware there's still a stigma attached to having made adult films, and even in what I do today with my website. Hell, I could have become a nun over the past twenty-five years and never erased my "scarlet letter." But I honestly have no regrets.

As far as the people who lied, cheated, and stole from me, I can't say I'm strong enough to forgive them. I believe people who do bad things with a malicious heart don't deserve to be forgiven. Greed is extremely ugly and karma is a bitch. I could look back at my life and say, "Woe is me." But if you're perpetually angry and hurt, it's hard to move forward.

I live a comfortable lifestyle. I'm pleased with it. I have a three-bedroom, two-bath house in a quiet suburban neighborhood with nice neighbors. Nobody would mistake it for a palace, and we'll never end up on one of these shows where celebs take you into their home to show off how rich they are. But since I was a little kid I've always wanted a house with a yard and garden. Carl and I have a place that reflects our personalities and there's a certain mood to each room. I love my gardening and just lying in bed and watching TV. Sure, I could have been more frugal and built a much larger nest egg, but I wanted to travel—to see and experience the world. However, like most others, you get older and calm down a bit. And that's the way I like it.

There was only one person at my husband's job aware of my being Seka the Porn Star. It's not that I'm ashamed of anything, but people pre-judge me and Carl because of my career. Folks are so ignorant and think they know you before they actually get to know you. I tell people I'm "just a housewife." I don't want anything to interrupt our golden years. There's always the possibility of him being released from a job because of my past. We're in the heart of the Bible Belt and sometimes Carl will say "hell" or "damn" at work and they'll actually say, "We don't appreciate that kind of language here." Imagine what they would say if they knew I was the former Platinum Princess of Porn. To me it's ignorance, but it's also reality.

The ironic thing is my movies, comparatively speaking, are actually campy, almost funny. We didn't do the type of "wham, bam, thank you ma'am" brutal gonzo-type porn films that are so prevalent today. We had that canned "wah-wah" ridiculous porno music. Now the music is gone and replaced with "Fuck me, fuck me, fuck me, fuck me," over and over again, screamed at the top of one's lungs. Most of our acting fell under the "so bad it's good" category. We had fun with what little script there was. Some people look upon our work fondly, like it's quaint and even deserving of artistic preservation and analysis, although that makes me laugh, too. I don't take myself too seriously. When comedian Dave Attell asked me to appear on his TV show to laugh at our flicks, I had a blast. I'd do that again in a minute. It's the same when I do radio or other TV shows. I'm less of a sex symbol now and more of bawdy comedian. Every comic talks about sex, but how many actually did porn for a living?

Sometimes I watch the films and think how poorly we were dressed and how ridiculous our hairstyles were. At the time, I was thinking, "Boy, I look hot!" But then again, didn't we all?

The movies will also be a barometer of where this country was sexually in the 1970s and early eighties. When I was doing adult films there was no war and people were open to trying new things. They were a lot looser. But in today's violent world where there are wars everywhere, porn is far more violent. There's a connection, and a lot of what's out in the market today is just ugly to me.

It's also no surprise that politicians who try to be the morality police and shut down the adult industry are the ones who always end up with their hands in the cookie jar in some kind of sex scandal. They should all just realize something—we serve a societal purpose and we've been around forever. I'm no archeologist, but I'll bet a large percentage of cave drawings are of people having sex. If it weren't for sex and our desire for it, none of us would be alive.

Why did I end up in the adult film industry? I'm sure a psychologist could come up with all kinds of reasons. I didn't exactly have your typical childhood. But when all is said and done, sex never seemed weird or bad to me. It was a different era and I was at a different place in my life. It seemed intriguing, fun, and I actually liked what I was doing. If I didn't like someone, I didn't work with them. Ditto if I wasn't attracted to them. And if there was a sex act I wasn't comfortable with, I wouldn't do that either.

As strange as it may sound to some, I'm proud of what I've done. I did a really good job, or at least the best I was capable of. I was paid decently for it—at least compared to others in the same industry. I think I've paved the way for other women in the business. I opened the doors a little wider for other women to make bigger and better inroads into what was once a male-dominated business. I didn't take shit from any man in the industry, and I encouraged the other girls to do the same. When you put yourself in a mindset that you can take it or leave it, the worst that people can hang over your head has been taken away from them. You gain the upper hand.

I was also always honest with my family about what I did for a living. I never made up excuses or placed the blame on anyone but myself. I chose what I did, I did it for money, I liked it, and if they couldn't handle it, that was their problem. They didn't have to hear it from the neighbors, or see me on TV and be shocked by it.

I remember when my grandmother was still alive in the eighties and I had one of my calendars with me. She said, "Honey, what is that?"

I said, "Grandma, it's a calendar of me and most of the pictures are of me nude."

She said, "I'm sure it's very nice, but that's not something I need to see." If only the rest of the world were so accepting.

As miniscule as we are as human beings, I feel we should slow down enough to actually know someone before judging them, and to be kinder to one another. Being happy, loving, and non-judgmental relieves a lot of stress from your life.

Would I recommend the adult industry for everyone? Absolutely not. I can live to one hundred and the stigma will never go away. As proud as I am of myself as a person, it still sucks to be treated shabbily by ignorant haters. I have feelings, too. If you think you can do a few movies, make some quick cash, and get out, you're wrong. It'll never go away. And that's something most people don't think about before they jump in.

I wrote this book to clear up some things about my life: who I was and was not married to. Ken is number one in that field, but I'm shocked to see how many others I've been linked to. The Internet amazes me. So much information, so much of it wrong. There're other things in my life that were misconstrued and far from the truth. I also thought it would be interesting, for a change, to present an adult star who wasn't a teen runaway, wasn't sexually abused as a child, isn't desperate for mainstream crossover success, and doesn't straight out lie and whitewash what she did.

Adult film stars don't have horns. We're not going to come and corrupt you. I'm a normal, everyday person who happens to have chosen a different path. But no matter what I do with my life, I will always be Seka. That won't go away. And while I like my quiet life in the 'burbs, I still enjoy meeting fans and hanging out with colorful and creative people. At my husband's recent sixtieth birthday party, I had industry people like Cousin Stevie mixed with schoolteachers, writers, retirees, and friends and neighbors from every walk of life. I enjoy that. I don't want to be bored.

As far as dollars and cents, like anyone else I'd like to be comfortable. I don't need to be rich. I'll keep improving my site, and one day hopefully find a nice little beach cottage and live out the rest of my life with my husband.

I've had plenty of tragedy, but others have had worse. Just because I had some bad things happen in my life doesn't mean I need to keep it with me at all times. I've tried to let it mold me and make me a better and stronger human being because of it.

In my life, I have had many people judge me because I had sex for money on screen. But I am who I am. And I know who I am. I did what I did willfully and with forethought. Regardless of what you think of me, when you see me walking down that street I will always have my head held high.

When I want to look my best, I use makeup artist Alexis Vogel, as does Pam Anderson and many other major stars.

Seka today.

Seka today.

With my co-author Kerry Zukus and comedian Dave Attell (*Dave's Old Porn*).

My newest hobby: my virtual world at Utherverse.

Afterword
by Bobby Slayton

WOW! When Seka called and asked me to write something for her book the first thing that came to mind was not how many others she asked before she settled on me. No, the first thing that came to mind was, "Seka is calling ME!" There's nothing that affirms your standing as a man, nothing that gives a boost to your masculinity and your testosterone, than having your wife call out from the next room, "Bobby, telephone. It's Seka."

So I didn't really care if I was the first person she asked or the hundredth—Seka was calling. And I'd better say some extremely nice things about her since I'm also writing a book and might need her help. Wonder if she gets all excited when her husband yells out from the next room, "Honey, that idiot Slayton on line two." I'm thinking no.

Seka and I go way back. Long before I knew her as a close friend, I knew her from the very first porn tape I ever bought, back when Betamax video machines first came out (God, I'm so old. But there was a time when Betamax was the new Blu-Ray). The only erotica I'd seen up to that point was in some dimly lit, sticky little booth near Times Square, furiously feeding my hard-earned newspaper route quarters into a battered slot, which sounds like a perfect metaphor for the entire porn industry. But buying the tape meant I could now be home in my bed with not just Seka but dozens of new girlfriends. But Seka was the first. A boy's first porno is right up there with losing his cherry—it's something you never forget.

And I've never forgotten meeting Seka for the first time. In my early standup days I had a joke about my new "Seka (not Seiko) watch—and you should see her at a quarter to three!" (It's all in the telling. Believe me, LIVE that joke used to kill.) I'm working a club in San Francisco and my friend, Paul Rosenberg, shows up with a hot blonde on his arm. And she looks like Seka. And I'd comp him thinking it just might be Seka. I'd play

SF every few months and Paul would always have a new hot blonde and he'd always get comped 'cause he'd always say he was there with Seka. It became a running gag between us because except for that first one, NONE of them actually looked like Seka, although they were always smokin'! Anyway, one overbooked Saturday night at a tiny, misshapen club (The Gollum of nightclubs) the guy at the door comes into my dressing room to tell me, "They don't have tickets but Paul Rosenberg is here with Seka." This is a sold-out show, he hadn't called first, and now he wants a freebie and a table near the stage. The owner was already worried about a visit from the fire marshal so I told the doorman to tell Paul I couldn't get him in. He's back a few minutes later with, "Your friend doesn't think you understand. He's with Seka." Now I was pissed. For months Paul had been getting in free; tonight I just couldn't do it so I go through the crowd as they were entering to tell Rosenberg to stop fucking showing up at the last minute expecting to get in. And he's there at the front door—WITH SEKA! In the flesh! That motherfucker!!

I can still hear Seka's first words to me as I escorted them into the club like visiting royalty: "It doesn't look like there's anywhere for me to sit." (A great straight line if I ever heard one but I didn't take the bait but please, insert your own joke, and just a joke, here.) Turns out there were two seats up front being held for friends who never showed (and if they did it didn't matter cause neither of them was Seka!) so we were good to go. The goddess who'd only existed on Betamax was now at my show, laughing and loving it. Showbiz heaven for me is not on a cloud with Elvis and Bogie and Sinatra. Seka in the front row enjoying my set like she was family; that's my showbiz heaven. She gave me her number after the show and told me to call whenever I played Chicago. And I did.

I played Chicago at least once a year and I'd always call Seka (not the 900 number!) and she'd come to my show and we'd have drinks after. I always wanted to go see any comic friend of mine who might've been in town doing a late show, show up at the door, and have the doorman relay the message, "Bobby Slayton's outside. And he's with Seka." But no such luck.

One night after a show Seka mentions that an old friend is playing a great after-hours blues club. It was already late and the small club—not much bigger than that Times Square photo booth where I'd first met the virtual Seka—was packed.

There was a table upfront waiting for us. I assumed they always put the only white people in the place there but Seka assured me it was because of her clout. The music was awesome and Seka was nudging me to stick my head under the table (Get your minds outta the gutter!) and do a blast of coke off her fingernail. Now it might've been a blues club and I might've been a stand-up comic BUT THAT WAS FUCKING ROCK AND ROLL!!!

When I told my wife about it (AND I TOLD EVERYBODY!) she didn't quite share my enthusiasm. She somehow didn't care that I'd been hanging out late, late, late at night doing blow and drinking with the country's most famous porn star. Funny thing, when they finally met my wife embraced Seka like they were old friends. The feminists are right: sisterhood is powerful. Of course the cartoon bubble over my head had the one word "THREESOME" in bold caps, but that's not my wife's thing and the pressure on me to perform, and I mean really perform, would've been too great… but a boy can dream, can't he? (Although to be honest, my wife would not have been in that dream. Or that threesome. Debbie Harry maybe. Seka, Debbie and me. Now that's a dream.)

And a dream is not what Seka's life has been. Which is why her book should be required reading for anyone who thinks that broken relationships, a crappy childhood, and dirty business dealings are things that happen to other people. Because Seka endured all of those things and more and came out the other side stronger and more committed to life than ever. She continues to look forward and not backward, and I can honestly say I learned about life from Seka in three different media: on Betamax, in real life and now, especially, in the pages of her true-life story.

One last thing: This book is so real and honest it makes sense for me to call her by her real name, Dottie. But I can't. She was my first. She'll always be Seka.

– Bobby Slayton,
comedian/actor

Bobby Slayton

About the Authors

SEKA is an Adult Video News (AVN) Hall of Fame performer and former talk show host on Chicago's The Loop 98.9 FM. She has appeared on *Saturday Night Live, Larry King Live, The Oprah Winfrey Show, Howard Stern, The Today Show, Sally Jesse Raphael, Thicke of the Night, Montel Williams*, and *Donahue*. She appeared on stage in the play *Vampire Lesbians of Sodom*. She has been profiled or interviewed by numerous magazines and newspapers, including *Playboy, Esquire, Vanity Fair, The Wall Street Journal, USA Today* and *The Village Voice*. She also wrote a column exclusively for *Club Magazine*, a job she continued for almost ten years.

Seka supports such charities as battered women's shelters, the Make-A-Wish Foundation, and Rainbow House. Seka is an avid Chicago Cubs fan, amateur photographer, gourmet chef, art collector, pet lover, and webmistress on www.seka.com. She describes herself as a jack-of-all-trades, master of none.

KERRY ZUKUS'S debut novel, *The Fourth House* (Madison Park Press), was a Featured Selection of the Book of the Month Club, the Doubleday Book Club, and The Literary Guild, as well as a finalist for the James Jones First Novel Fellowship. An alumnus of the Berklee College of Music in Boston, he has ghostwritten or collaboratively written forty-three books and counting. Born amidst the coal mines of eastern Pennsylvania, today he lives at the wonderful Jersey shore.

Index

Lightning Source UK Ltd.
Milton Keynes UK
UKHW040409060119
335017UK00010BA/547/P

9 781593 932725